UNCEDED

GEORGE M. ABBOTT

UNCEDED

Understanding British Columbia's Colonial Past and Why It Matters Now

Printed in Canada on FSC-certified ancient-forest-free paper (100% post-consumer recycled) that is processed chlorine- and acid-free.

UBC Press is a Benetech Global Certified Accessible™ publisher. The epub version of this book meets stringent accessibility standards, ensuring it is available to people with diverse needs.

Library and Archives Canada Cataloguing in Publication

Title: Unceded : understanding British Columbia's colonial past and why it matters now / George M. Abbott.

Names: Abbott, George M., author.

Description: Includes index.

Identifiers: Canadiana (print) 20250187779 | Canadiana (ebook) 20250187825 | ISBN 9780774881159 (softcover) | ISBN 9780774881166 (PDF) | ISBN 9780774881173 (EPUB)

Subjects: LCSH: Indigenous peoples – British Columbia – Government relations – History. | CSH: First Nations – British Columbia – Claims – History.

Classification: LCC E78.B9 A23 2025 | DDC 971.1004/97 – dc23

UBC Press gratefully acknowledges the financial support for our publishing program of the Government of Canada and the British Columbia Arts Council.

UBC Press is situated on the traditional, ancestral, and unceded territory of the xʷməθkʷəy̓əm (Musqueam) people. This land has always been a place of learning for the xʷməθkʷəy̓əm, who have passed on their culture, history, and traditions for millennia, from one generation to the next.

Purich Books, an imprint of UBC Press
The University of British Columbia
www.purichbooks.ca

To my awesome grandchildren,
Raiden, Alissa, Serena, Owen, Alison, Joseph, and Lillian.

Sorry about the wicked social and environmental problems my generation has left your generation to solve.

Don't hesitate to call Grandpa if you think I can help!

Contents

Foreword

THE HONOURABLE STEVEN POINT,
GRAND CHIEF OF THE STÓL:Ō AND BRITISH COLUMBIA'S
FIRST INDIGENOUS LIEUTENANT-GOVERNOR

I am pleased to write this short foreword to this very important account of British Columbia's colonial history written by George Abbott. Whereas history does not define modern times, it does illuminate for us today why we are in the current political and legal position with regard to Indigenous land rights in British Columbia.

The simple truth is that when Europeans arrived in the so-called New World, they did not find an empty land but rather a land with millions of Indigenous people who already owned and occupied their homelands.

The colonial government and then the federal government set about buying the land from the "Indians" so the land could be made available to European settlers. This is the treaty process.

In much of British Columbia, this process is still happening. Where land agreements have not been settled, the lands – provincial lands – are still under the cloud of Aboriginal title. According to the *St. Catharines Milling* case (an Indigenous rights case decided by the Privy Council of Great Britain), the province cannot use the forests as a source of tax revenue until Aboriginal title to the land is extinguished. This case essentially stands for the proposition that Aboriginal title to the land includes a beneficial interest in the forests.

For some unknown reason, Governor James Douglas in 1855 stopped the treaty process on Vancouver Island after signing fourteen agreements with the Indigenous groups located between Victoria and Nanaimo and one on the northern tip of the island. Aboriginal title to the land in British Columbia is a legal reality and must be dealt with in our time, if we can.

Indians have been marginalized socially, economically, and physically from the dominant European society. We were placed on Indian reserves that were carved out of our lands. We were forced to remain on these reserves unless we had a letter from the Indian agent allowing us to leave the reserve. We were not allowed to attend public school until after the Second World War. We were not given the right to vote in British Columbia until the 1949 election. Our languages were not permitted in Indian residential schools, and our cultural practices were made illegal in the late 1880s by amendments to the Indian Act.

We live in one of the wealthiest countries in the world, yet most of our Indigenous people still live in third-world conditions on federal reserves.

If we are to reach our collective objective of reconciliation, we must confront the historic wrongs done to Indigenous people and seek ways to redress these wrongs if we can.

We have to conclude respectful treaties that will allow First Nations real benefits from their own homelands. A share in the resources being extracted would allow First Nations to finance their own healing from our oppressive colonial past.

I wish to thank George Abbott for his book about our colonial past. It is only with a better understanding of our history that we can have a better chance of creating a brighter future for First Nations in British Columbia.

Chronology

1846	The Treaty of Oregon asserts British sovereignty over what is now British Columbia.
1849	The British colony of Vancouver Island is established with the Hudson's Bay Company (HBC) as an agent of the Crown to promote settlement.
1851	James Douglas is appointed governor of Vancouver Island while retaining his senior leadership role in the HBC.
1850–54	Douglas completes treaties with several First Nations on Vancouver Island while exercising leadership as both governor and chief factor of the HBC, but under the auspices of the latter.
1858	Douglas is appointed governor of the new Colony of British Columbia (on the Mainland) in addition to continuing as governor on Vancouver Island. The 1858 gold rush brings thousands of miners to the Fraser Canyon region, leading to violent conflict between miners and Indigenous warriors.
1862–63	A smallpox epidemic devastates Indigenous communities in many parts of Vancouver Island and mainland British Columbia.
1864	Douglas retires from gubernatorial duties on Vancouver Island and mainland British Columbia.

Douglas is replaced by Frederick Seymour on the Mainland and by Arthur Kennedy on Vancouver Island.

Joseph Trutch is appointed chief commissioner of land and works for British Columbia.

Indigenous resistance to incursions by road builders and settlers leads to armed conflict between Tŝilhqot'in warriors and colonial authorities alternatively called the "Chilcotin Uprising" or the "Chilcotin War."

1865 Trutch and Seymour initiate efforts to reduce the size of Kamloops and Shuswap Reserves in anticipation of demands related to the Columbia River Gold Rush.

1866 The colonies of Vancouver Island and British Columbia are merged under Governor Seymour.

1867 The Legislative Council of the United Colonies unanimously endorses a resolution demanding that Lower Mainland Indigenous reserves be cut back and "thrown open for settlement."

1869 Anthony Musgrave becomes British Columbia's new governor following the death of Frederick Seymour.

1870 Members of British Columbia's Legislative Council debate union with Canada.

Joseph Trutch leads the BC delegation in Confederation negotiations in Ottawa.

1871 Joseph Trutch is appointed British Columbia's first lieutenant-governor on July 5 in anticipation of the official shift from colony to province on July 20.

1871–77 Canada negotiates and ratifies Numbered Treaties with First Nations in advance of settlement of the Canadian northwest with land allocations of 160 to 640 acres per family.

1872 Prime Minister Sir John A. Macdonald appoints Dr. Israel Powell as Canada's superintendent of Indian affairs for British Columbia.

Macdonald proposes the creation of an Indian Board, with Trutch as chief commissioner and Powell and a Roman Catholic as subordinates.

1873 Canada proposes in April that Aboriginal title settlements could be achieved in British Columbia if each Indigenous family were assigned "80 acres of land of average quality."

In July, British Columbia rejects Canada's proposal, recommending that reserves "should not exceed a quantity of twenty acres of land for each head of a family of five persons."

1874 Fifty-five Chiefs draw up a petition, presented to Indian Commissioner Powell, demanding reserves based on eighty acres per family.

Powell advises the provincial secretary, John Ash, that Canada has reluctantly accepted British Columbia's suggestion to allocate reserve lands based on the standard of twenty acres for each family of five.

In late July, Powell advises the chief commissioner of lands and works, Robert Beaven, that survey teams are standing by to add acreage to the Musqueam and Tsawwassen Reserves, consistent with the twenty-acre-per-family standard.

BC officials claim the twenty-acre standard applied only to new reserves, not expanding existing ones.

1875 Premier George Walkem prepares, and cabinet approves, the "Report of the Government of British Columbia on the Subject of Indian Reserves."

1876 Governor General Lord Dufferin delivers a speech at Government House in Victoria on the necessity of extinguishing Aboriginal title through treaty negotiations.

Canada's minister of the interior, David Laird, reports that British Columbia and Canada have agreed to appoint a Joint Indian Reserve Commission (JIRC).

Canada introduces the Indian Act.

1877 As it undertakes its work in the southern Interior, the JIRC reports that there is a severe danger of Indigenous insurrection. It negotiates reserve expansions to stem a potential revolt.

1878 After persistent complaints from British Columbia, primarily about costs, the JIRC is reduced to a sole commissioner, Gilbert Sproat.

1880 After persistent criticism from provincial officials, Sproat resigns and is replaced by Peter O'Reilly, former colonial official and politician (and Trutch's brother-in-law).

1887 A Nisga̱'a and Ts'msyen delegation travels to Victoria to press land issues but is dismissed with derision by Premier William Smithe.

1898 Indigenous resistance at Fort St. John to the influx of Klondike-bound miners encourages Canada to move forward with Treaty 8 in northeastern British Columbia.

1906 Chiefs travel to London, England, to petition Edward VII for recognition of Aboriginal title.

1909 Lawyers working on behalf of BC First Nations draft the Cowichan Petition for the Privy Council in London arguing that British Columbia has broken the law by not respecting Aboriginal title.

1910 Interior Chiefs present their case for fair treatment to Prime Minister Sir Wilfrid Laurier during his visit to Kamloops.

1912–16 The Royal Commission on Indian Affairs in British Columbia (commonly known as the McKenna-McBride Commission) is formed and tours British Columbia, generating recommendations on reserve creation and adjustments in its wake.

1927 In response to petitions from the Allied Tribes of British Columbia, a Joint Committee of the Senate and House of Commons holds hearings in Ottawa, then subsequently denies the existence of Aboriginal title. Committee recommendations also trigger amendments to the Indian Act, making it an offence for First Nations to engage legal counsel in pursuit of Aboriginal title or for legal counsel to provide advice on Aboriginal title.

1930 Contrary to the McKenna-McBride Commission's mandate, and over the objections of First Nations in the province, British Columbia and Canada agree to cut over thirty-six thousand acres from Indigenous reserves.

1938 After decades of opposition, British Columbia officially relinquishes its claims to minerals and timber on reserves. Approximately one thousand reserves created through the Indian Reserve Commission are officially conveyed from the province to the Dominion.

1941 Premier Duff Pattullo urges the Aluminum Company of Canada to consider investment in British Columbia.

1947 E.T. Kenney, British Columbia's minister of lands and forests, renews the quest for aluminum production in the province.

1951 Indian Commissioner W.S. Arneil notifies the Indian Affairs Branch of Alcan's advice that should Fisheries' issues be resolved, two Cheslatta Carrier Nation reserves would "likely be flooded."

1952 Fisheries and Alcan reach an agreement on a remedy for the anticipated impact on migrating salmon of the Nechako Canyon dam, a reservoir to be created by inundating Murray and Cheslatta Lakes. All Cheslatta reserves would be flooded or lost under the plan.

1961 Premier W.A.C. Bennett expropriates BC Electric and expresses his hope "that BC Electric directors will call tenders right away for a pilot tunnel and reservoir clearing" for what was subsequently known as the W.A.C. Bennett Dam and the Williston Reservoir.

1962 A conditional water licence is issued to BC Electric facilitating the construction of the W.A.C. Bennett Dam and creation of the Williston Reservoir.

1969 A protracted dispute between Ottawa and Victoria over replacement reserves for the Tsay Keh Dene (Ingenika) First Nation is not resolved until January 1969, when the Department of Indian Affairs accepts new reserve sites "under protest."

1971 Dissatisfaction with new reserves prompts most Tsay Keh Dene to settle at Ingenika Point, where, in the absence of reserve status, they are deemed "squatters on Crown lands."

1973 The Supreme Court of Canada hands down the *Calder v Attorney-General of British Columbia* decision.

1978 Bill Bennett's Social Credit government prepares *Response of the Government of British Columbia to the Position Paper of the Nishga Tribal Council,* rejecting the notion of British Columbia's participation in title discussions.

1982 Indigenous rights are enshrined in section 35(1) of the Constitution Act, 1982, which recognizes and affirms Aboriginal and treaty rights.

1987 The Native Affairs Secretariat, created within British Columbia's Ministry of Intergovernmental Relations, is taken over by the Ingenika issue.

1989 After difficult and protracted negotiations, a tripartite agreement is signed providing the Tsay Keh Dene with land, financial compensation, and additional benefits.

1991 The Throne Speech (authored by the Bill Vander Zalm's Social Credit government) promises "the first land claims framework agreement in the province's history, with the Nisga'a Tribal Council" and a tripartite task force (with the First Nations Summit and Canada) "to determine how best to proceed with other pending aboriginal claims."

1992 The Throne Speech (authored by the Mike Harcourt's NDP government) recognizes Aboriginal title and the inherent right of Indigenous peoples to self-government. It also promises to establish a new treaty commission.

1996 Intense negotiations among Nisga'a leaders, British Columbia, and Canada conclude with an historic treaty agreement in principle.

The *Report of the Royal Commission on Aboriginal Peoples* is released. The commission was appointed to examine the relationship between Aboriginal peoples and non-Indigenous governments.

2000 Final ratification and royal assent for the Nisga'a Treaty is completed.

2005 Gordon Campbell announces "The New Relationship" document after clandestine negotiations with First Nations organizations.

2006 Indigenous leaders, Canada, the provinces, and territories meet in Kelowna to produce the Transformative Change Accord, commonly known as the Kelowna Accord.

2007 The Tsawwassen Treaty is ratified amid much controversy.

The United Nations adopts the Declaration on the Rights of Indigenous Peoples (UNDRIP). Canada is one of four nations that oppose its adoption.

2008 The Musqueam Reconciliation, Settlement and Benefits Agreement Implementation Act is approved by the Musqueam First Nation and the BC legislature.

2008–15 The Truth and Reconciliation Commission gathers testimony across Canada from residential school Survivors and others and then issues a highly critical report.

2009 The Campbell government notes in the Throne Speech that it "is working with First Nations to develop a *Recognition and Reconciliation Act* that will establish a new statutory framework to further the implementation of the *New Relationship*."

2011 The Maa-nulth First Nations Treaty comes into effect on April 1, 2011. It breaks new ground as the first multi–First Nation treaty in British Columbia and the first modern treaty on Vancouver Island.

2014 The Supreme Court of Canada breaks new ground in its *Tsilhqot'in* decision by upholding the claim to Aboriginal title.

2019 The BC legislature unanimously adopts the Declaration on the Rights of Indigenous Peoples Act.

2021 Canada adopts and gives royal assent to UNDRIP and commits to making its laws consistent with the spirit of the declaration.

2024 The BC government and the Council of the Haida Nation jointly announce an agreement on the Haida Nation Recognition Act, which recognizes Aboriginal title on Haida Gwaii.

Notes on Terminology

I strive in *Unceded* to present materials in a manner that is respectful as well as informative. As readers are likely aware, the acceptability of using certain words and phrases has changed across time and will likely continue to evolve. For this reason, wherever possible, I use the terms "First Nations" or "Indigenous" rather than "Aboriginal" or "Native" (both of which were commonly used in the late twentieth century), or "Indian" (which was commonly used before that time). All of these words are still employed in certain instances (for example, in the current organizational titles of the Union of British Columbia Indian Chiefs or the BC Association of Aboriginal Friendship Centres, or in legal terms such as "Aboriginal title").

Readers will find that the language used in some historical quotations is insensitive, offensive, or racist. Unfortunately, my account of colonial policies and prejudices in British Columbia and Canada would be incomplete without such references. For example, Joseph Trutch's insatiable hunger, as a colonial chief commissioner of lands and works, to "cut back and free up" Indigenous lands for white settlement is best understood within the context of his overt contempt for Indigenous people. His reflexive dismissal of Indigenous rights was rooted in the persistent racism that often characterized settler colonialism.

I have also attempted to accurately convey both historical and contemporary names of First Nations. Some primary sources, such as the transcripts of the McKenna-McBride Commission (1912 to 1916), are frequently inaccurate in that regard. I regret any instances where I have failed to identify and correct such inaccuracies.

UNCEDED

Prologue
Ghosts from the Colonial Past

In 1887, Nisga'a Chiefs launched a fifteen-metre cedar canoe into the Nass River in northwest British Columbia and paddled south toward Victoria, determined to secure a treaty recognizing their land rights. Weeks later, they completed their epic journey of over 500 nautical miles (900 kilometres) to Victoria's Inner Harbour, only to be barred from the legislature by the premier, William Smithe. He reluctantly agreed to meet the delegation, but only outside the legislative precinct and dismissed their land aspirations with condescension and contempt:

> The land all belongs to the Queen ... A reserve is given to each tribe, and they are not required to pay for it. It is the Queen's land just the same, but the Queen gives it to her Indian children because they do not know so well how to make their own living the same as a white man, and special indulgence is extended to them, and special care shown. Thus, instead of being treated as a white man, the Indian is treated better. But it is the hope of everybody that in a little while the Indians will be so far advanced as to be the same as a white man in every respect. Do you understand what I say?[1]

Over a century later, in 1998, Chief Joseph Gosnell, president of the Nisga'a Tribal Council, likewise arrived in Victoria to discuss the Nisga'a Treaty. In stark contrast to the reception accorded his ancestors, Gosnell addressed the Legislative Assembly at the unanimous invitation of its members.

The *Vancouver Sun* reported, "The doors of the legislative chamber were thrown back and Gosnell stood at the gold bar of the house ... a red and black button blanket draped over a dark business suit."[2]

In his address, Gosnell described the Nisga'a Treaty as "a turning point in the history of British Columbia," rightly so given the province's long and often fierce resistance to treaty negotiation. Treaty ratification would see the Nisga'a "collectively own approximately 2,000 square kilometres of land," Gosnell explained, a far cry from "the postage-stamp reserve set aside for us by colonial governments," which his ancestors had protested without success in 1887. As Gosnell noted, Premier Smithe had "rejected all our aspirations to settle the land question" and launched an insult that would never be forgotten: "When the white man first came among you, you were little better than wild beasts of the field."

Gosnell's retrospective rejoinder was compelling and evocative: "Wild beasts of the field. Little wonder, then, that this brutal racism was translated into narrow policies which plunged British Columbia into a century of darkness for the Nisga'a and other Aboriginal people."[3]

The "century of darkness" Gosnell described was rooted in the politics, policies, and prejudices of British Columbia's colonial era. Colonial leaders, with very few exceptions, were just as disdainful of First Nations as William Smithe. To give one prominent example, Joseph Trutch, colonial chief commissioner of lands and works and British Columbia's first lieutenant-governor in 1871, dismissed Indigenous peoples as "utter savages" who "have really no right to the lands they claim."[4]

Trutch's reputation has not been enhanced by the passage of time. In 2003, British Columbia's twenty-seventh lieutenant-governor, Iona Campagnolo, delivered a scathing rebuke of her first and "least illustrious" predecessor. Trutch, she argued, had "cemented a negative attitude" against Indigenous rights and title that "continued to haunt" British Columbia "for at least the next 120 years." In a rare departure from her office's customary diplomatic language, Campagnolo blamed him for the "prejudices and injustices that stain our provincial history."[5]

Trutch's disrepute persists. In 2022, the City of Richmond, on British Columbia's Lower Mainland, held a ceremony to celebrate renaming Trutch Avenue to Point Avenue, in honour of Steven Point, Campagnolo's immediate successor and the province's first Indigenous lieutenant-governor (serving from 2007 to 2012). At the ceremony, Point noted that Trutch was "certainly a racist" and added: "We shouldn't bury our history just because we find it distasteful ... When we turn back and look at the steps we've taken, we should acknowledge that's where we were and this is the distance we have come, so that our children can understand we have changed for the better."

Learning from history, Point argued, means never "painting over the bad spots."[6]

Sadly, the history of British Columbia's treatment of Indigenous people offers all too many "bad spots" to identify and assess. Trutch and Smithe were not exceptional in their "brutal racism." They were surrounded and supported by politicians and officials firmly convinced of white biological and moral superiority and, as Iona Campagnolo suggested, colonial ghosts haunt the politics and policies of the province to this day.

How This Book Came to Be

I met more than a few colonial ghosts while serving as British Columbia's minister of Aboriginal services from 2001 to 2004 and minister of Aboriginal relations and reconciliation from 2009 to 2010. In fact, the genesis of *Unceded* lies in a 2010 visit I made to Tsay Keh Dene Village, about 350 kilometres by air north of Prince George. The village is located at the north end of Williston Reservoir, one of the world's largest human-made waterbodies, created by the construction of the W.A.C. Bennett Dam. On reaching full capacity in 1968, the reservoir flooded 1,761 square kilometres of land, inundating much of the Traditional Territories of the Tsay Keh Dene Nation (then known as the Ingenika).

More than forty years after that dam's rising waters brought the dispossession and dislocation of the Tsay Keh Dene Nation, the province – along with BC Hydro – finally acknowledged responsibility for those harms. I felt no reluctance in offering an apology on behalf of British Columbia. I was shocked by what I'd learned from ministerial briefings. How could such injustices have occurred only a few decades earlier? The Tsay Keh Dene had been uprooted by my predecessors in government, rendered "refugees on their own lands," then capriciously neglected and disregarded in the years that followed. Sadly, the Tsay Keh Dene were not alone in the callous treatment they suffered at the hands of the government.

Indigenous issues also emerged during my other ministerial assignments. As the minister of sustainable resource management from 2004 to 2005, I participated in broad-based regional-planning discussions (including the Central Coast Plan and the Great Bear Rainforest) with First Nations. I was also responsible for the Agricultural Land Commission and played a key role in defending Bill 27 (2004), which introduced new provisions that allowed the Tsawwassen Nation – and future treaty nations – to request the removal of treaty lands from the Agricultural Land Reserve without needing prior approval from local government.

As minister of health from 2005 to 2009, I was involved in the extensive discussion and negotiation that led to the First Nations Health Plan of 2006 and the subsequent creation of the First Nations Health Authority (FNHA), a "first" among Canadian provinces.[7] The FNHA offered important lessons on partnership and reconciliation to the government, including the Ministry of Education, where I served from 2010 to 2012. British Columbia has enjoyed some success in narrowing the unacceptable gap in educational outcomes between Indigenous and non-Indigenous students, but that vital goal is far from complete. Like other colonial policies discussed in this book, the haunting legacy of Indian residential schools is not easily overcome.

After leaving elected office in 2013, I further explored British Columbia's history of Indigenous relations during doctoral studies in political science at the University of Victoria. I enjoy archival research, and what I learned from documents in the Royal BC Museum and Archives, Library and Archives Canada, and elsewhere underscored the persistence of colonial policies and prejudice throughout our history. My archival research led to the publication of an article in 2017 in the journal *BC Studies*, which now stands as a vital foundation for *Unceded*.[8]

To my surprise, just a few weeks after I had submitted my final draft of *Unceded* to my publisher in early 2025, I received a phone call from BC's minister of Indigenous relations and reconciliation, Christine Boyle, asking if I would be interested in serving as the province's representative on the BC Treaty Commission. After recovering my jaw from the floor, I advised Minister Boyle that I would be deeply honoured and grateful to serve in that capacity. If I'm truly fortunate in my term as a treaty commissioner, I'll have the opportunity to bring at least a few lessons and learnings from *Unceded* to treaty tables.

In the pages ahead, I aim to better acquaint British Columbians and Canadians, particularly my fellow settlers, with how and why our province's history of Indigenous relations unfolded as it did. *Unceded* examines the persistence of colonial policies and prejudices from the 1850s until today, and it focuses on two key features of that history. The first is British Columbia's insistence, both as a colony and later as a province, on the creation of very small Indigenous reserves in comparison to those established by Canada east of the Rocky

Mountains. "Postage stamp" was the apt phrase used by Chief Gosnell to characterize British Columbia's reserves.

The second key feature, closely linked to British Columbia's small and scattered reserves, is the near absence of treaties, or even treaty discussions, during the latter years of colonial governance and the first 120 years of provincehood. Consequently, much of British Columbia remains – as is often recognized during land acknowledgments – unceded territory, land never formally exchanged between First Nations and the Crown as part of treaty negotiations.

It did not have to be this way. A more constructive path was followed during the early colonial years under Governor James Douglas, but his approach crashed up against settler resistance, ushering in the brutal racism of Joseph Trutch and William Smithe and innumerable injustices in the century of darkness that followed.

Roots and Branches

During my years in government, meetings with Indigenous communities and organizations often began with a personal introduction involving geographic roots, family, and life experience – a valuable way to set in context the discussion that would follow.

A similar introduction may be appropriate here. I'm a descendant of Anglo-Irish settlers who came to Upper Canada in the early 1800s and the grandson of Canadians who moved to British Columbia from the Prairies amid the economic and social dislocation of the 1930s. I'm also the son of parents who, after the Second World War, took on a Veterans' Land Act loan to pursue their farming dreams in the BC Interior.

I grew up in the small town of Sicamous, on the eastern end of Shuswap Lake. Our farm was on Old Town Road, only a kilometre or two from the "old town" of Eagle Pass Landing, the terminus for steamers bearing gold miners bound for the Columbia goldfields in the late 1860s. Before the arrival of the miners, the Splatsin people had long occupied the prime fishing and hunting areas around the mouth of what is today known as the Eagle River. During the gold rush, the Splatsin were forced from their lands, not for the last time. Following recommendations from the McKenna-McBride Commission in 1914, the Splatsin reserves were dramatically cut back.[9] Like many non-Indigenous people in British Columbia, I grew up knowing little about the painful history of Indigenous dispossession. I never questioned how or why our family farm (and thousands like it) had benefited from that dispossession.

I'm also now a grandfather who hopes to better understand some of the more painful aspects of my province's history so that I can answer difficult questions from my grandchildren. If lands were never acquired by the Crown through treaties or other agreements, why were Indigenous claims to those lands ignored by BC governments for over a century? Why are so many of British Columbia's Indigenous reserves small and scattered, often amid a vast expanse of mountains and lakes?

As I've learned, these small reserves have long been a source of frustration and despair for First Nations, as reflected in Nisg̲a'a Chief John Naas's address to the McKenna-McBride Commission during its 1915 visit to the Nass Agency:

> We are here as it were men in prison ... If it had not been for the reserves we would have been able to get out as the white men do and take up pieces of land occupied by our great grandfathers and work there and improve it. We want this to be taken away from us – the term "RESERVE" – and we want you to give us in place of it the land we now ask for.[10]

The colonial objective of "throwing open" prime agricultural and resource lands to white settlers – while simultaneously denying the Nisg̲a'a the opportunity to negotiate a treaty – had robbed Chief Naas and his people not only of large swaths of their Traditional Territory but also of the opportunity to maintain seasonal rounds: to fish, hunt, and harvest across extensive and varied landscapes, as they had for thousands of years.

Alan Hanna, a scholar of Blackfoot, French, and Scottish ancestry, explains how Western and Indigenous world views differ: "Western civilization's concept of progress is based on the steady, linear trajectory from the undeveloped to the developed (e.g., resources, land, societies). In contrast, many Indigenous understandings of being in and movement through the world consist of cyclical patterns (seasonal rounds, renewable harvests, reciprocal relationships)."[11] The disruption of seasonal rounds – and the interruption of long-standing economic and social relationships – was deliberate, aimed at "civilizing" Indigenous peoples.

The BC government argued in 1875 that small reserves would lead to off-reserve employment and interactions with settlers that would wean Indigenous people "by degrees from savage life," leading them "by example and precept to adopt habits of peace, honesty, and industry."[12] But as William Smithe would demonstrate a decade later, such assertions about the benign nature of small reserves were typically backstopped by less-than-subtle presumptions about white superiority and the long-term goal of assimilating First Nations.

Can Understanding Our Past Help Us Identify Paths Forward?

The Nuu-chah-nulth people of western Vancouver Island embrace the expression *hishuk'ish tsawalk*, "Everything is one, and all is interconnected."[13] British Columbia's history of Indigenous-settler relations offers many threads to connect and consider. Political ideas – both good and bad – live on and evolve. For example, a vital thread runs from colonial governor James Douglas's aim (set out in 1859) to make "the Indians independent and the settlements self-supporting" to the goals of the BC Treaty Commission (established in 1992), which included "greater self-reliance for First Nations communities to close social and economic gaps" and "authority to manage their own affairs."[14]

The Huu-ay-aht First Nations are members of the Nuu-chah-nulth Tribal Council and signatories to the Maa-nulth First Nations Final Agreement of April 2011, the first modern treaty concluded on Vancouver Island. The final agreement was, in the words of Indigenous author and BC treaty commissioner Angela Wesley, "the culmination of fifteen years of negotiations in the modern-day treaty process, preceded by a generations-long struggle for recognition of our territories and jurisdictions and of our journey back to self-determination and self-reliance." Like other Indigenous peoples, the Huu-ay-aht had been displaced by pre-emptions and provincial forest tenures and then alienated from their traditions and territories by the residential school experience. A new community was established at Pachena Bay in the 1960s amid chronic social and economic challenges. The treaty process offered, in Wesley's words,

> our chance to begin the work of rebuilding our First Nations and reclaiming and reasserting ourselves in our territories. We knew it was time to govern ourselves again. It was time to finish what our ancestors had begun. It was time to rebuild our nation and its governing capacity from the ground up, beginning with the people and creating a government that reflects who we are, where we come from, and what we want to be.[15]

For the Huu-ay-aht, the treaty process offered an opportunity to recover unceded lands and stolen dreams, to rebuild their Nation after a century of destructive and compounding public policy.

Some Indigenous leaders and organizations – most notably the Union of British Columbia Indian Chiefs – reject the treaty process. Recent reforms aim, in the words of a former federal minister, to "allay a lot of fears" and deal "with the cynicism that's rightfully there after 150-plus years of broken promises."[16]

However, when it comes to government relations with First Nations, actions have always proven louder than words. Words alone will not produce a shift in perspective. Governments must find paths to reconciliation beyond treaty making, and they are slowly beginning to do so.

Time has seen profound changes to British Columbia's legislative cast of characters and statutory initiatives. In 1872, British Columbia's first Legislative Assembly – uniformly composed of white male property owners – unanimously approved the *Qualification and Registration of Voters Act*, which formally stripped Indigenous and Chinese British Columbians of their right to vote. In 2019, a Legislative Assembly far more reflective of British Columbia's diverse population adopted, again unanimously, the Declaration on the Rights of Indigenous Peoples Act (DRIPA). The act was developed in collaboration with the First Nations Leadership Council and consistent with the Truth and Reconciliation Commission of Canada's Calls to Action and the United Nations Declaration on the Rights of Indigenous Peoples.[17] The legislation marks a vital milestone on our journey toward reconciliation, which is far from over.

British Columbia recently witnessed the remarkable resurgence of a provincial Conservative party after close to a century in the political wilderness. During the hard-fought 2024 election campaign, Conservative leader John Rustad promised to "address the issue of returning land to First Nations, who do not currently have sufficient property rights needed to secure prosperity." But he also promised to repeal DRIPA, a statute he'd supported in 2019. Three prominent Indigenous organizations – the BC Assembly of First Nations, the First Nations Summit, and the Union of British Columbia Indian Chiefs – denounced Rustad's plans. But Rustad argued that DRIPA had become a barrier to "economic reconciliation and Indigenous autonomy" and promised "new legislation that advances, not stalls," achievement of those goals.[18]

At the time of writing, the scope and content of what this legislation might entail has not been articulated, but Rustad appears to be contemplating a model and pace for change well beyond the BC Treaty Commission's process. Should the Conservatives form a government in the future, Rustad has one promising nontreaty model within his own constituency of Nechako Lakes – the Lake Babine Nation Foundation Agreement of September 2020, which includes substantial commitments of land and cash from the province and Canada.[19] However, given British Columbia's economic and geographic diversity and its tortured history of Indigenous relations, Rustad would be well advised to develop or sustain multiple paths to reconciliation, including the BC Treaty Commission.

The Shared Dilemma of Climate Change

British Columbia's relationship with Indigenous peoples is now unfolding against the backdrop of climate change. Several years ago, at the request of then-premier John Horgan, I had the honour of cochairing, with Chief Maureen Chapman, a review of the 2017 flood and wildfire seasons. We were privileged to visit many central and southern BC communities, including several First Nations that had been threatened or affected by fire or flood. We heard all too frequently that Indigenous ecological knowledge was being ignored in emergency response.[20] Our report emphasized the importance of integrating that knowledge into disaster prevention and response while embracing Indigenous communities as true partners in emergency management.[21]

We deliberately titled our report *Addressing the New Normal,* and our vulnerability to the catastrophic symptoms of climate change was certainly reconfirmed by subsequent events: the destruction of the historic town of Lytton by wildfire in June 2021, an atmospheric river that devastated communities, businesses, and infrastructure along the Fraser River five months later, and the most destructive wildfire season ever recorded in British Columbia and Canada in 2023.

Indigenous legal scholar John Borrows offers sage counsel on our shared dilemma: "Reconciliation between Indigenous peoples and the Crown requires our collective reconciliation with the earth. Practices and partnerships of resurgence and reconciliation must sustain the living earth and our more-than-human relatives for future generations."[22] Resurgence and reconciliation engage competing (but not necessarily conflicting) goals: Indigenous independence and societal interdependence. Finding an effective and workable balance between these goals may be pivotal to sustaining a healthy environment for our grandchildren.

In my early days as the minister of Aboriginal relations and reconciliation, Gary Mason of the *Globe and Mail* asked what I aimed to achieve in my new ministry. I replied: "We're attempting to bridge gaps that have been created by 150 years of history. There is much in that history that is somewhere between unfortunate and shameful, and resolving the distrust that grows out of it is going to be difficult. But it shouldn't stop us from trying."[23]

1

A Bold Vision Meets Resistance

In July 1854, Victoria was rife with rumours of pending hostilities with Russia, a threat that Governor James Douglas took seriously, proposing "to call out and arm all the men of the Colony capable of bearing arms, and to levy and arm an auxiliary body of native Indians." But the small body of appointed advisers who constituted Vancouver Island's Legislative Council said it would be "dangerous to arm and drill the natives, who might then become more formidable to the Colony than a foreign enemy."[1] This difference of opinion reflected the gulf between the settler community and Douglas, who thought expansively about the place of Indigenous people and anticipated their participation in colonial society.[2]

Douglas's views were shaped by his life experiences. He was born in Demerara (Guyana) in 1803, the son of a prominent Scottish trader and his Creole (mixed-race) wife. He received much of his formal education in Scotland but as a young man entered the fur trade with the North West Company at Fort William (Thunder Bay). After its merger with the Hudson's Bay Company (HBC) in 1821, Douglas was transferred to Athabasca Lake and then to the Pacific Northwest's Columbia District. In 1828, he married Amelia Connolly, daughter of HBC chief factor William Connolly and his wife, Suzanne, daughter of a Cree Chief. Douglas rose rapidly in the HBC's ranks – first to chief trader (1835) and then to chief factor (1839) – at a time when the company was still regarded (at least by Great Britain) as the de facto governing authority in the territories now known as British Columbia.

Rising tensions between Great Britain and the United States in 1849 prompted the creation of the Colony of Vancouver Island. Richard Blanshard was selected to serve as the colony's first governor, despite the HBC's endorsement of Douglas. Blanshard's tenure proved brief and disappointing, as most of the settlers were employees of the HBC.[3] Blanshard was replaced by Douglas in 1851, an appropriate shift given the latter's understanding of the physical and social dimensions of the Pacific Northwest, including the Oregon Territory (Washington and Oregon). As Douglas assumed his new role, he brought with him vivid memories of how Indigenous peoples had been displaced by the influx of American homesteaders along the Oregon Trail.[4] These experiences fuelled Douglas's resentment toward American frontiersmen, their policies regarding Indigenous peoples, and their legal and political systems, reinforcing his determination to build a more just society.[5]

Douglas's life experience gave him more balanced views on race and indigeneity than those held by many of his colonial colleagues, who believed in white superiority and Indigenous inferiority, a belief common across the British Empire. His policies were anchored in a genuine belief that Indigenous people "should in all respects be treated as rational beings, capable of acting and thinking for themselves."[6] He was not, as geographer Cole Harris argues, "a biological racist." He did not think that Native people were inherently inferior, but he did believe they could be "civilized." To Douglas, civilization meant adopting British education, religion, and values, leading – over time – to assimilation.

Douglas's views were progressive for the time but not by twenty-first-century standards. He was open to employing an iron fist to sustain law and order, for instance, by having a warship anchor offshore and "its crew ostentatiously prepare the guns."[7] Legal historian Hamar Foster offers this balanced and pithy assessment: "Douglas was an autocrat, but he seems to have wanted equality between whites and Indians, buffered by transitional protections and extensive reserves."[8]

Douglas's unique character and vision re-emerged when a gold-mining boom on the Fraser River brought an influx of twenty-five thousand miners to British Columbia in 1858 and extended his gubernatorial authority to the Mainland. In his first visit to the new colony in late May, Douglas attempted to address the bitter and sometimes violent conflict between incoming white miners and the Indigenous people they too often disrespected. He met with miners and declared, in "great plainness of speech," that "the Laws would protect the rights of the Indians no less than those of the white man." Later on his visit, Douglas resolved an Indigenous "claim to a particular part of the river, which they wished to be reserved for their own purposes." The request, he noted, "was immediately granted, the space staked off, and the miners who had taken claims there were immediately removed and public notice was given that the place was reserved for the Indians, and that no one could be allowed to occupy it without their consent."[9]

Despite Douglas's efforts, the conflict escalated in July and August, as "a flood of human greed and desire swept up the Fraser Canyon with the miners, invading the hitherto quiet, isolated river terrace homes of the Nlaka'pamux," and targeting women and girls.[10] The Nlaka'pamux fought back. Following the rape of a Nlaka'pamux woman, they killed two French miners. In turn, white miners sought revenge, triggering a back-and-forth battle that led to dozens of deaths among the miners and the Nlaka'pamux. By late August, cooler heads prevailed, and a tentative truce was achieved, just before Douglas returned to the Fraser with a small military contingent in early September.[11] He spent close to a month on the Mainland firming up the fragile peace, an experience that would shape his policies in the years ahead.

Early in 1859, Douglas laid out his ideas and plans for Indigenous relations in correspondence with Sir Edward Bulwer Lytton, British secretary of state for the colonies. Douglas believed British Columbia and Vancouver Island could avoid the "numberless evils" that had followed colonization in America and elsewhere, flowing from "the aggression of immigrants." Such evils, he believed, "naturally follow in the train of every course of national injustice" and led to "the native Indian tribes arrayed in vindictive warfare against the white settlements." Armed conflict, and the "wretchedness and physical suffering" that arose from it, posed the gravest threat to the "growth and material development" of the newly formed colonies of Vancouver Island and British Columbia. Douglas twice emphasized the vital importance of Indigenous peoples being independent and their settlements self-supporting. Reserves should "in all cases include their cultivated fields and village sites, for which from habit and association they invariably conceive a strong attachment."[12]

Douglas's goals were not rooted in a distant, shadowy dream. The Indigenous peoples he met across decades as a Hudson's Bay Company official were independent and self-supporting, just as their ancestors had been for thousands of years. Douglas believed such qualities could be sustained, despite the pressures of colonization. Lytton appeared supportive of that vision, but with a caveat: Douglas should make "ample provision" for "the future sustenance and improvement of native tribes," but should also "bear in mind the importance of exercising due care in laying out and defining the several reserves, so as to avoid checking at a future day the progress of the white colonists."[13]

Treaties were a vital component of Douglas's plan. He "made it a practice up to the year 1859, to purchase the native rights to the land, in every case, prior to the settlement of any district."[14] He made these purchases and agreements, commonly known as the Douglas Treaties, as the senior HBC official on Vancouver Island, not as governor.[15] He concluded fourteen treaties with Vancouver Island First Nations that were full of ambiguities and rudimentary in comparison to modern treaties but recognized prior Indigenous occupation and use of Traditional Territories.[16]

With the creation of the Colony of British Columbia in 1858, which reduced the HBC's role, Douglas looked elsewhere for treaty funding with little success. In a letter to the secretary of state for the colonies in 1861, Douglas appealed "for the aid of Her Majesty's Government in extinguishing the Indian title to the public lands in this Colony."[17] Douglas had reason to believe his request might be favourably received. Senior British officials had claimed to support Douglas's vision for Indigenous treaties. Lord Carnarvon (on behalf of Secretary Lytton) stated that when the "advancing requirements of colonization" affected Indigenous lands, "measures of liberality and justice may be adopted for compensating them for the surrender of the territory which they have been taught to regard as their own."[18] But would Britain's generosity extend to future treaty funding? The House of Assembly of Vancouver Island, a hybrid body of appointed and elected members created in 1856, certainly hoped that it would.[19]

In a petition, members of the assembly stated that many prospective settlers were being deterred from buying land "as they could not rely on having peaceful possession; seeing that the Indian Title was still unextinguished to several of the most eligible agricultural districts on the Island."[20] The assembly's petition reflected settler sentiment. As historian John Lutz notes: "Far from opposing treaties, settlers in the newly opened regions of Cowichan and Chemainus put steady pressure on the government to make treaties."[21] However, in the assembly's view, responsibility resided in London, not Victoria, making "extinction of the aboriginal title ... obligatory on the Imperial Government.[22]

Given the assembly's position, Douglas hoped diplomatic persuasion might win over the Colonial Office. In his subsequent letter to Secretary Lytton, Douglas reluctantly brought up the assembly's opinion on the imperial government's liability "for all expenses connected with the purchase of the claims of the aborigines to the public land." Douglas suggested the cost of the agreements would be modest and recovered through the sale of public lands. He promised to "carefully attend to the repayment of the sum advanced, in full," thus promoting Indigenous reconciliation "without putting the Mother Country to a serious expense."[23]

Lord Newcastle, Britain's new secretary of state for the colonies, dismissed Douglas's suggestion. Britain, he argued, had "recognized aboriginal possession and therefore the extinguishment of Indian land title" prior to settlement, as exemplified by Douglas's Vancouver Island treaties. But bearing the cost for such treaties was another question entirely: "I am fully sensible of the great importance of purchasing without loss of time the native title ... But the acquisition of the title is a purely colonial interest, and the Legislature must not entertain any expectation that the British taxpayer will be burthened to supply the funds." Governmental authorities were agreed on "the evils that may result from a neglect of this precaution,"[24] but parsimony trumped precaution.

As governor of the fledgling colonies of Vancouver Island and British Columbia, Douglas had to deal with a host of competing demands for new roads, bridges, ports, and assorted amenities. He suffered "the utmost difficulty in raising money enough to defray the most indispensable wants of Government" and was obliged "for want of funds" to discontinue treaty making.[25] By the mid-1860s, treaties had dropped off his agenda altogether.[26] As white settlement proceeded, treaty making was not among the tools Douglas could employ to resolve the inevitable land disputes. Short-term "want of funds" seeded long-term challenges.

Douglas's Vision for Indigenous Lands in the Absence of Treaties

James Douglas was a practical, principled man. Treaties were beyond his constrained public purse, but he still maintained a vision of independent, self-supporting First Nations. Douglas's alternative approach engaged two key elements: generous reserve allocations (particularly compared with those of his successors) and the Indigenous right to pre-emption of public lands (over and above designated reserve lands). In British Columbia, pre-emption provided prospective farmers, depending on their location east or west of the Cascade Mountains, with 160 or 320 acres at minimal cost.

Douglas believed Indigenous people would work hard and prosper on reserve lands, devoting "their earnings to the purchase of property apart from the reserve, which would be left entirely at their own disposal and control."[27]

He envisaged Indigenous people freely buying and selling land, except for land held collectively as reserves. Douglas fleshed out his reserve policies in a note written a decade after his retirement as governor. In 1874, with Victoria and Ottawa at loggerheads over the expansion of existing reserves, Canada's superintendent of Indian affairs, Israel Powell, wrote the former governor to ask "if there was any particular basis of acreage used in setting apart Indian Reserves?" Douglas replied:

> The principle followed in all cases was to leave the extent and selection of the land entirely optional with the Indians who were immediately interested in the Reserve. The surveying officers having instructions to meet their wishes in every particular, and to include in each Reserve, the permanent village sites, the fisheries, the burial grounds, cultivated land ... in short to keep every piece of ground, to which they had acquired an equitable title through continuous occupation, tillage, or investment of their labour.[28]

Powell undoubtedly hoped Douglas's words would support Canada's interpretation of Article 13 in the Terms of Union, an interpretation that emphasized the generosity of the phrase "as liberal as that hitherto pursued" in colonial Indigenous policy. Further confirmation of Douglas's approach is contained in *Papers Connected to the Indian Land Question, 1850–1875,* the official historical record.

The creation of the Colony of British Columbia in 1858 had raised questions about the anticipated size of new First Nations reserves. Colonel Richard Moody (chief commissioner of lands and works, surveyor general, and senior officer of the Royal Engineers) replied to many of those questions after conferring with the governor. In 1859, Douglas directed Moody to map out reserves covering "several hundred acres around each [First Nations] village."[29] Two years later, Douglas signalled at least a modest shift in direction, instructing his officials to define the "extent of the Indian reserves ... as they may be severally pointed out by the Natives themselves."[30] In turn, when asked by Captain R.M. Parsons of the Royal Engineers about land allocation for reserves, Moody stated: "What the Tyhee [Chief] of the village points out – (within reason). If anything extreme is asked for postpone decision until further communication with me."

Parsons dutifully passed this direction down the ranks to Corporal Turner: "Colonel Moody desires that the Indians *shall put down the stakes themselves* and that you look at them and report to him the position and quantity of land claimed."[31] Douglas was not always satisfied with the product subsequently rendered. He bluntly reminded officials that "the wishes of the Natives themselves, with respect to boundaries, should in all cases be complied with." Despite his instructions, he'd heard "general complaints of the smallness of the areas set apart for their use" and demanded "instant measures to inquire into such complaints" and enlarge the reserves.[32]

Douglas's colonial officials appeared to understand and accept his instructions, if sometimes reluctantly. In February 1861, William Cox, a freshly appointed gold commissioner and justice of the peace, wrote Moody for advice on resolving disputes over reserve boundaries in the North Okanagan. "Mines have lately been discovered there," Cox noted, "hence the altercations ... that have arisen between the natives and white men." In his response, Moody passed along Douglas's direction to define reserve boundaries as "severally pointed out by the Indians themselves." But he added, "Be particular in scrutinizing the claims of the Indians, as I have every reason to believe that others (white persons) have, in some instances, influenced the natives in asserting claims they would not otherwise have made."[33]

Moody's quiet resistance to Douglas was reflected elsewhere. Challenged by the governor to expand the Coquitlam (Kwikwetlem First Nation) Reserve, Moody protested that the "reserve in question was most carefully laid out, the Indians being present, and after they had *themselves* marked according to their own wishes the bounds, the area was further enlarged. I resisted the appeal of the neighbouring settler, and acceded to the amplest request of the Indians."[34] In short, Moody claimed the Coquitlam Reserve boundaries were already generous, even to the extent of reducing a settler pre-emption.

Douglas was unpersuaded by Moody's concerns. The Coquitlam Reserve, he said, was "so small, not exceeding 50 acres of land, as to be altogether insufficient to raise vegetables enough for their own use." He advised Moody in the bluntest terms that earlier instructions "be carried out to the letter, and in all cases where the land pointed out by the Indians appears to the officer employed on the service to be inadequate for their support, a larger area is at once to be set apart."[35]

Douglas's instructions on reserve boundaries were clear and emphatic but rendered much less so as they moved down the chain of command. For example, Captain Parsons in New Westminster directed sapper James Turnbull (also of the Royal Engineers) to "take an early opportunity of staking and marking out ... all Indian villages, burial places, reserves, etc., as they may be pointed out to you by the Indians themselves, subject, however, to the decision of the District Magistrate as to the extent of the land so claimed by them."

Parsons further qualified Douglas's instructions by warning: "Be very careful to satisfy the Indians so long as their claims are reasonable, and do not mark out any disputed lands between whites and Indians before the matter is settled by the Magistrate."[36] In such cases, Douglas's aim of making Indigenous communities entirely self-supporting was easily overshadowed by the colonial prejudices that dominated settler society.

The second key element in Douglas's vision for Indigenous independence was their right to pre-emption of public lands. In theory, this allowed for land allocations similar to treaties east of the Rockies but without conflicts over Aboriginal title or treaty funding. During Douglas's tenure, no formal distinctions were made between natural-born British subjects, "Indians," or "aliens" born outside the British Empire.[37] Douglas was unique and radical in supporting the right of Indigenous people to pre-empt public land just like all British subjects. He "displayed a spirit of tolerance, compassion, and humane understanding" at a time when public sentiment held scant sympathy for Indigenous people.[38]

Douglas's position on the Indigenous right to pre-emption was well understood among senior officials. Judge Matthew Begbie, for example, declared that "Indians have perfectly the right of pre-emption, like all other British subjects."[39] However, Douglas's position also prompted quiet resistance among his officials, including Chief Commissioner Moody. "I understand Indians are pre-empting in 'extended order' along the [Fraser] River and elsewhere to considerable extent," Moody wrote in 1863, "and that such extent is likely to increase very considerably and very rapidly." That situation, he said, raised the question of "Indians pre-empting lands precisely as a white man could."[40]

Moody's alarm was notable. The prospect of white settlers pre-empting in "extended order" along the Fraser River would have been welcomed, not discouraged (indeed, that was the very goal of pre-emption). The core of his concern was conveyed in a letter to Douglas a few months later: "The Roman Catholic priests have moved the Indians to pre-empt as freely as any other persons ... It is a growing question that will have to be met."[41]

Moody aired his concerns at a time when the Indigenous population was at least four times larger than that of the white settlers. In this context, he perceived generous Indigenous land policies as a threat to white settlement. Moody's attitude may also have reflected his personal interests and experience: he owned 3,750 acres on the Lower Mainland, chiefly on the North Road and around Burnaby Lake.[42] Where Douglas saw the legitimate aspirations of Indigenous people, Moody saw nefarious schemes to facilitate "double dipping" in land. In Moody's mind, reserves were ample recognition of past

Indigenous occupation. In contrast, there was no "either-or" in Douglas's thinking: reserve boundaries were not designed to justify limitations on Indigenous people's right to pre-emption.

Parsimony Seeds Future Challenges

The end of treaty making in colonial British Columbia was made worse by a lack of money to properly survey reserve boundaries. In June 1862, Moody wrote the colonial secretary, William Young, requesting modest funding for "marking out and surveying the spots occupied by Indians with their villages and isolated 'provision grounds.'" Moody promised that the "cost [would] not exceed thirty-five Pounds per month."[43] Young responded after what was a difficult conversation with Douglas:

> He [Douglas] was under the impression that the work of marking out (*not surveying*) the Indian Reserves had been long ago carried out ... His Excellency is not aware what necessity may exist for the present survey of these Indian Reserves, but unless the reasons are very weighty, His Excellency would not, under the existing heavy pressure on the resources of the Colony, feel justified in authorizing an outlay to the extent you mention.

Douglas believed that "for all present purposes, the marking of such Reserves by conspicuous posts driven into the ground would be sufficient, and that the survey thereof could be postponed until the Colony can better afford the expense."[44]

Douglas's understandable but unfortunate parsimony undermined his best intentions around reserve construction. Posts could be moved, and without a definitive survey, interested parties could claim that the reserve boundaries had been covertly shifted. For example, a review of the Kamloops and Shuswap Reserves in 1866 suggested that "the extent of at least one of these reserves ... has been largely added to by the changing of the position of the boundary stakes by Indian claimants." In another example, from the Lower Mainland in 1867, Katzie Chief Michel successfully argued that settler John McIvor had moved stakes to expand his pre-emption.[45]

The decision to postpone formal surveys led to disputes that remain unresolved more than 160 years later. The lack of formal surveys would provide Douglas's critics with one more weapon in their relentless battle against his "unnecessarily large" reserves. The personalized and informal character of Douglas's approach to reserve creation proved to be its undoing.

Douglas's principled and steadfast direction on reserve creation is difficult to reconcile with his address to the Legislative Council of mainland British Columbia on the eve of his departure from office in 1864. The colony's reserves, he said, "in no case exceed the proportion of ten acres for each family concerned."[46] Douglas was well aware that the council contained critics of his land policies. Did he aim to pre-emptively refute claims that his reserves were overly generous and should be cut back? Although the council's record of proceedings appears to provide a verbatim account of Douglas's remarks, both the content and tone of the address are dramatically at odds with his 1874 letter to the superintendent of Indian affairs, Israel Powell:

> Before my retirement from office several of the Reserves, chiefly in the lower district of Frasers River and Vancouvers Island, were regularly surveyed and marked out with the sanction and approval of the several communities concerned, and it was found on a comparison of acreages with population that the land reserved, in none of the cases, exceeded the proportion of 10 acres per family ... It was however never intended that they should be restricted or limited to the possession of 10 acres of land, on the contrary, we were prepared, if such had been their wish to have made for their use much more extensive grants.

He then noted the much larger reserves in the Interior, designed "to allow sufficient space and range for their cattle at all seasons."[47]

Douglas's 1864 address to the council is more understandable in the context of the words that immediately followed: reserves were "not intended to interfere with [the] same rights of acquiring and possessing land, in their individual capacity, either by purchase or by occupation under the Pre-emption law, as other classes of Her Majesty's subjects."[48] Douglas believed that reserve size was important, but equally important was ensuring that Indigenous people had the same rights as settlers to pre-empt or buy land. The council was not persuaded. Neither the principle of reserves "as severally pointed out by the Natives themselves" nor the Indigenous right to pre-emption survived for long after Douglas's retirement.

Members of the Mainland's Legislative Council were, indeed, inclined to question Douglas's reserve policies and did so fewer than two weeks after his retirement when the council unanimously resolved:

> that whereas certain reservations in the valley of Chilwayhock [Chilliwack] and elsewhere throughout the Colony are being made for the benefit of the

> Indians, and whereas such reservations are considered to be unnecessarily large (10 acres to each family), and in several instances including lands already pre-empted by actual settlers, thereby seriously interfering with the development of the agricultural resources of the Colony; be it resolved that His Excellency [incoming Governor Frederick Seymour] be respectfully requested to give the matter his consideration at as early a date as convenient, in order to avoid difficulties between the Settlers and the Indians.[49]

Notably, the council accepted at face value Douglas's assertion of "ten acres to each family" but dismissed reservations as "unnecessarily large."

The council would never have criticized pre-emptions by "actual settlers" (160 to 320 acres, depending on location) as unnecessarily large. Its members presumed that only white settlers would make good use of land. Further, in a breathtaking example of revisionist history, Indigenous people also stood accused of retroactively stripping away lands "already pre-empted by actual settlers." In the council's conception of a budding settler society, farmers and ranchers were vital pillars of prosperous, growing communities, and they were there to stay. That conception did not include First Nations.

Unfortunately, Douglas's failure to formalize his reserve policies and his reference to ten acres per family opened the door for others – such as the incoming chief commissioner of lands and works, Joseph Trutch – to reduce reserves while restricting access to pre-emption.[50] Douglas's aim to make First Nations independent and self-supporting was quickly undermined by colonial demands for Indigenous dispossession.

2

Joseph Trutch and the Road to Dispossession

Joseph Trutch was a powerful figure in the early history of British Columbia. As colonial chief commissioner of lands and works, he drove public policy on the size and configuration of reserves in the latter 1860s. He was also a highly influential member of the Legislative Council. As British Columbia considered confederation with Canada in 1870, it was Trutch who led the delegation that negotiated the terms of union. Another member of that delegation, John Helmcken, described Trutch as "the front and general of the whole affair ... from the word go, we were not on an equal footing, and soon discovered this at Ottawa. Trutch was everything and everybody."[1] After Confederation in 1871, Trutch was appointed British Columbia's first lieutenant-governor by Sir John A. Macdonald's Conservative government. He retained influence long after leaving his vice-regal role, acting as Macdonald's "confidential agent" on Indigenous relations in British Columbia until Macdonald's death in 1891.

Trutch was typical of the emerging settler society around him, thoroughly grounded in his belief in white superiority. He was born in England in 1826 and apprenticed as an engineer and surveyor. In 1849, he was attracted to North America by the California Gold Rush but settled in the Oregon Territory, where his professional skills were in demand. His experiences there influenced his disdain for Indigenous peoples. In a letter to his mother, Charlotte, in 1850, he described the Indigenous people of the Oregon Territory as "the ugliest and laziest creatures I ever saw."[2] The vile and racist views he brought to British Columbia in 1859 were not limited to Indigenous peoples. Anglican Bishop

George Hills was perturbed by Trutch's declaration that "he had objection to sit near some black people, not that he felt any unkind sentiment, but because of the peculiar odour."[3]

Trutch had been drawn north by the Fraser River Gold Rush and perhaps by his brother John's presence in Victoria.[4] He soon gained prominence in road and bridge construction. His success in that field made him a strong candidate for chief commissioner of lands and works, the position he secured in 1864. Trutch's prejudices frequently rose to the surface in his public offices. Soon after his appointment, he declared himself "satisfied from my own observation that the claims of Indians over tracts of land, on which they assume to exercise ownership, but of which they make no real use, operate very materially to prevent settlement and cultivation."[5] Indigenous people, Trutch contended, "have really no right to the lands they claim."[6] Indigenous land – even in the form of small and scattered reserves – was wasted land, he believed, and worked doggedly "to allow part of the lands now uselessly shut up in these Reserves to be thrown open to pre-emption."[7]

Trutch's beliefs were far from unique. He was aided and abetted in his mission by prominent colonial and post-Confederation BC politicians such as Amor De Cosmos, John Robson, and Frank Barnard, whose message was remarkably consistent: settler interests must prevail.

Neither time nor experience moderated Trutch's overtly racist ideas. Ensconced as the province's first lieutenant-governor in 1871, he dismissed Indigenous people as "utter savages" in his correspondence with Macdonald.[8] In other startling comments directed at Joseph Howe, Canada's secretary of state for the provinces, Trutch boldly declared: "I state it most regretfully, in my twenty years' experience among the Aborigines of this Coast, I have not yet met with a single Indian of pure blood whom I consider to have attained to even the most glimmering perception of the Christian creed." Trutch presumed the secretary a kindred spirit, adding: "In fact the idiosyncrasy of the Indians of this country appears to incapacitate them from appreciating any abstract idea, nor do their languages contain words by which such a conception could be expressed." He concluded that "the policy which has prevailed in British Columbia since its settlement by Europeans, has been essentially benevolent towards the Indians; that the degree of civilization which we have introduced into their country has in fact conferred infinite benefits upon them."[9]

To Trutch, the notion of "civilizing" Indigenous peoples served as a convenient excuse for seizing their lands – even reserve lands formally recognized by Governor James Douglas. By Trutch's reckoning, Indigenous "advancement" would flow from their labours off small reserves, not from labour on large reserves. He cast his racist and miserly land policies as sagacious generosity aimed at "promoting the well-being of our Indian population."[10] He proved tenacious and devious in stripping First Nations of lands that had long sustained them.

Trutch's views were rooted at the far end of settler racism.[11] He used the power of his political offices – along with lies and intimidation, when needed – to undermine Douglas's vision for Indigenous relations.

Encouraged by Kindred Spirits

Unlike his predecessor as chief commissioner, Richard Moody, Trutch did not have to deal with a governor who possessed deep experience and pronounced views on Indigenous relations. Douglas's successors typically deferred to Trutch on these matters. In the case of Governor Frederick Seymour (governor of the Colony of British Columbia from 1864 to 1866 and the United Colony of British Columbia from 1866 to 1869), Trutch found a ready ally. Seymour's appointment coincided with what he called the "Chilcotin Insurrection" (described elsewhere as the Chilcotin Uprising or the Chilcotin War) in his Throne Speech to the Legislative Council. In a tragic series of events in 1864, over a dozen road builders and settlers were killed by Tŝilhqot'in warriors intent on defending their lands from what they regarded as a European invasion. After colonial officials deviously invited them to "peace talks," six Tŝilhqot'in Chiefs were captured and hanged.

Seymour's account of these events in his Throne Speech was suffused with inaccuracies.[12] He lay all responsibility on the Tŝilhqot'in warriors, who, he claimed, attacked and killed with "no provocation." He offered the "utmost praise" to "the men who came forward ... to engage in a conflict formidable from the nature and extent of the Country over which it raged," reducing insurgents "to the sole alternatives of suicide or surrender."[13] The Tŝilhqot'in insurgency undoubtedly hardened Seymour's attitudes toward Indigenous peoples, creating a favourable context for Trutch's revision of Douglas's Indigenous policies.

Like Trutch, British Columbia's new governor believed that the reserves laid out during his predecessor's tenure were far too generous and "should be reduced as soon as is practicable. The Indians have no right to any land beyond what may be necessary for their actual requirements, and all beyond this should be excluded from the boundaries of the reserve." Seymour even shared Trutch's remarkable capacity to find virtue in miserly reserve allocations:

The amount of ground reserved should be amply sufficient for all the actual wants and requirements of the tribe ... But in no case should it be of such extent as to engender the feeling in the mind of the Indian that the land is of no use to him, and that it will be to his benefit to part with it.[14]

With Douglas's retirement in early 1864, officials could comfortably assert claims that good agricultural land was "uselessly shut up" in reserves, posing a barrier to the advancement of white settlement. Among them was Philip Nind, gold commissioner at Lytton and an appointed member of the mainland Legislative Council, who complained that "Indians do nothing more with their land than cultivate a few small patches of potatoes here and there; they are a vagrant people who live by fishing, hunting, and bartering skins; and the cultivation of their ground contributes no more to their livelihood than a few days of digging wild roots." He added that Indigenous people were "jealous of their possessory rights," which had put a "stop to settlement in these parts." He suggested that the government "extinguish the Indian claims, paying them what is proper for so doing, and giving them certain reservations for their sole use."[15] From Nind's perspective, the true value of colonial lands would only be realized only after they were placed in the hands of "actual" settlers.

Nind's suggestions found immediate favour with Trutch: "In reference to Mr. Nind's letter ... I have the honor to state that the settlement of the boundaries of Indian reserves is, in my opinion, a question of very material and prospective importance, and should engage immediately the attention of all interested."[16] Nind's letter landed in the Mainland's capital of New Westminster at a critical juncture. Gold had been discovered at French Creek, north of Revelstoke, on the Columbia River. Within months, French Creek City grew to over four thousand people.

The gold rush caught the attention of Seymour, who thought "it very desirable that the Shuswap and Kamloops Reserves should be reduced, without further delay, to reasonable limits, as it would perhaps be a matter of greater difficulty to settle the affair should the route by Kamloops become the main thoroughfare to the Columbia River." Seymour correctly anticipated that many miners would go by steamer from Kamloops to Eagle Pass Landing (Sicamous) and then overland to Revelstoke. He directed Trutch to dispatch Walter Moberly, assistant surveyor general, to the southern Interior with a specific goal: to "reduce these reserves if he is of the opinion that it can be effected without much dissatisfaction to the Indians."[17]

Trutch's enthusiasm for reserve reduction was reflected in his instructions to Moberly: "The Indian Reserves at Kamloops and Shuswap, laid out by

Mr. Cox [assistant gold commissioner and justice of the peace], being considered entirely disproportionate to the numbers and requirements of the Indians residing in those Districts," should be reduced and thrown open to pre-emption.[18] Trutch's instructions did not refer to Douglas or his more generous approach to reserve boundaries. In his early years as chief commissioner, Trutch was loath to challenge Douglas's judgment directly. He preferred to challenge the colonial officials who had carried out the former governor's directions, in this case, William Cox.

Moberly met with Tk'emlúps and Secwépemc (Kamloops and Shuswap) Chiefs in late 1865 and "learnt from the Indians that they claim these lands by virtue of certain papers given them by Mr. W.G. Cox acting under instructions received by him from Governor Sir James Douglas, and that such portions of these reserves not cultivated by them would be useful for grazing their cattle upon." For Moberly, "it appeared ... quite out of the question" that Douglas could have given Cox "instructions to make such extensive reservations for a tribe that I should say does not number more than four hundred souls, and have not one hundred acres of land under cultivation." Moberly was setting the table for reserve reductions:

> I told them it was my impression the reserves claimed by them, and as they said defined by Mr. Cox, were not laid out in accordance with the intention of Governor Douglas' instructions to him, and if so, that Mr. Cox's grants to them are worthless, as the Governor of the Colony is the only person who can give them a title to any land, and that Mr. Cox had given them what it was not in his power to grant.

Moberly's strategy was a devious and entirely dishonourable model for reserve reductions: "I think by showing the Indians in the first place that their titles from Mr. Cox are of no value, and by judicious expenditure of a small amount of money, that arrangements can be effected to get the greater portion of the reserves quietly given up."[19]

Shortly after receiving Moberly's report, Trutch contacted William Young, colonial secretary to Seymour, with two critical questions, both aimed at seeding doubts about earlier processes and agreements: "1st. – Whether or not Mr. Cox's agency in the matter is binding on the Government? And secondly – are the boundaries of the reserves now claimed by the Indians those which Mr. Cox really gave them assurance of?" In his report to Seymour, Trutch reconfirmed what his instructions had invited Moberly to conclude: "These reserves are entirely disproportionate to the numbers or requirements of the

Indian Tribes to which they are represented to have been appropriated by Mr. Cox."[20]

The first step in Trutch's mission to liberate lands "now uselessly shut up" in reserves was taken in 1866. The forty-mile stretch along the Thompson River set aside for the Tk'emlúps and Secwépemc was reduced to six thousand and five thousand acres, respectively.[21]

Consistent with his practice in the years ahead, Trutch framed his recommendations as vital to the broader public interest:

> Much of the land in question is of good quality, and it is very desirable, from a public point of view, that it should be placed in possession of white settlers as soon as practicable, so that a supply of fresh provisions may be furnished for consumption in the Columbia River Mines, and for the accommodation of those travelling to and from the District.[22]

Within that sentence, Trutch set out a core theme for British Columbia's Indigenous relations in the decades ahead: Indigenous people were a barrier to – rather than a partner in – the province's current and future economic development.

Further reductions followed elsewhere in the southern Interior. Reserve boundaries across the Okanagan Valley were reviewed and reduced by James Turnbull, of the Lands and Works Department, under the direction of John C. Haynes, magistrate and member of the mainland Legislative Council. Haynes was also a rancher who would eventually own 22,000 acres in the southern Okanagan.[23] He was hardly a dispassionate adjudicator. Turnbull cast William Cox as the villain of the piece: "Mr. Cox, several years ago, reserved nearly all the agricultural lands situated about the head of the lake, as well as that on the south end ... The results of this reservation were that many men have been prevented from settling on what may be considered the only real agricultural and grazing land in the country."[24] With new reserve boundaries in hand, Trutch immediately recommended that "the lands around Okanagan Lake heretofore held as Indian Reserves should be declared open to pre-emption."[25]

Trutch drew a vital lesson from the reduction of the southern Interior's reserves: Douglas's generous but informal reserve boundaries could be key to the undoing of them. Henceforth, the Lands and Works Department would "ascertain as exactly as practicable what lands are claimed by Indians, what lands have been authoritatively assured to the various tribes, and to what extent such reserves can be modified with the concurrence of the Indians interested in them – either with or without money or other equivalent."[26] Under Trutch's leadership, the department would use whatever means it had at its disposal – lies, bullying, subterfuge, or cash – to undermine and reverse what Douglas had promised only a few years before.

Reserve Reduction Takes on a Broader Scope

Joseph Trutch's "success" in reducing the southern Interior reserves did not escape the attention of his colleagues in the Legislative Council. (After 1866, the council represented the united colonies of Vancouver Island and the Mainland and, like its predecessors, was a hybrid body of elected and appointed members.) Amor De Cosmos, an elected member for the Victoria District (and future premier), asked the colonial secretary whether "it is the intention of the Government to throw open the whole or any portion of the Indian Reserves at Cowichan for settlement?"[27]

His question appeared to inspire a broader resolution at the next sitting of the council from elected members John Robson (New Westminster, and another future premier) and Frank Barnard (Yale): "That an address be presented to His Excellency the governor, urging the desirability of having the Indian Reserves of the Colony reduced to what is necessary for the actual use of the Natives, and to have such Reserves properly defined, the remainder to be thrown open for settlement." The resolution was quickly amended from "of the Colony" to "on the lower Fraser," then passed unanimously.[28]

Trutch immediately turned his attention to the Fraser Valley reserves, now with the explicit support of the council. His report, delivered to the governor in August 1867, offered rare overt criticism of Douglas: "The subject of reserving lands for the use of the Indian tribes does not appear to have been dealt with on any established system during Sir James Douglas' administration." In a purposeful misconstruction of Douglas's policies, Trutch claimed that the "rights of Indians to hold lands were totally undefined, and the whole matter seems to have been kept in abeyance." In another critical passage, Trutch falsely asserted that "those [Lower Fraser River] Indian Reserves that were informally made seem to be so reserved in furtherance of verbal instructions only from the Governor [Douglas], as there are no written directions on this subject in the correspondence on record in this office."[29] As detailed earlier, Douglas had provided explicit written direction on multiple occasions, directly and through his colonial secretary. Douglas's reserves were not undefined; rather, they were defined "as severally pointed out by the Natives themselves," a prescription utterly repugnant to Trutch.

Trutch's dissembling extended to misinterpreting a straightforward note from surveyor William McColl. "In addition to the written instructions [from the office of the surveyor general]," McColl wrote in 1864, "I had further verbal orders given to me by Sir James Douglas, to the effect that all lands claimed by the Indians were to be included in the reserve; the Indians were to have as much land as they wished, and in no case to lay off a reserve under 100 acres. The reserves have been laid off accordingly."[30]

As he had with William Cox and the southern Interior reserves, Trutch shot the messenger: "Acting on this latter indefinite authority [meaning Douglas's explicit instructions, which no sensible public servant was apt to ignore] ... McColl marked out reserves of most unreasonable extent, amounting, as estimated by himself, to 50, 60, 69, 109, and even as much in one case as 200 acres for each grown man in the tribe." Trutch concluded that the Lower Fraser reserves were "out of all proportion to the numbers or requirements of the tribes to which they were assigned."

Trutch's report to Governor Seymour reiterated some now-familiar themes, again cloaked in claims of protecting the broader public interest: "The Indians have really no right to the lands they claim, nor are they of any actual value or utility to them; and I cannot see why they should either retain these lands to the prejudice of the general interests of the Colony, or be allowed to make a market of them either to Government *or to individuals.*" Trutch recognized the bountiful agricultural potential of the Lower Fraser Valley; the land, he wrote, "much of which is either rich pasture or available for cultivation and greatly desired for immediate settlement, remains in an unproductive condition – is of no real value to the Indians and utterly unprofitable to the public interests." Trutch believed it "both just and politic" that reserves should be reduced to "lands only as are sufficient for their probable requirements for purposes of cultivation and pasturage, and that the remainder of the land now shut up in these reserves should be thrown open to pre-emption."[31]

Trutch's claim that farmland held "no real value to the Indians" was premised on entirely disproportionate expectations of land utilization by Indigenous and white farmers. By one estimate, only 250 acres (of a total of 27,997 acres taken up by pre-emption) in the New Westminster district were under cultivation by white settlers in 1868. An early settler on the south side of the Fraser complained that "not a week passes without one or two parties visiting this side of the river looking for land to pre-empt, and when they find out that all this wilderness around me is taken up and secured by gentlemen of ease and position, their curses are loud and long."[32] Despite many "gentlemen" landowners not actually farming the desirable lands they had pre-empted, Trutch and his council colleagues presumed that white landowners would be ambitious and successful and that Indigenous farmers would be indolent and unsuccessful.

Governor Seymour nursed such views and welcomed Trutch's suggestions for undoing McColl's work. "There is good reason to believe," Seymour wrote, "that Mr. McColl very greatly misunderstood the instructions conveyed to him in respect to marking out these reserves in the first instance, and he has in consequence created reserves of land far beyond the wants or expectations of the Indians." Like Trutch, Seymour blamed McColl for the perceived failings of Douglas's reserve policies: "As for the verbal instructions which Mr. McColl *is said to have received* from Governor Douglas – that the Indians were to have as much land as they wished – it is apprehended that Mr. McColl entirely misinterpreted Governor Douglas' wishes." McColl was in many ways the perfect scapegoat. He had died in June 1865 and would not be authoring any conflicting narratives. Seymour fully agreed on how to remedy McColl's supposed failings: reduce reserves to the "actual requirements" of each First Nation.[33]

When First Nations pushed back, Seymour resorted to deception and duplicity. Seventy Chiefs signed and submitted an 1867 petition asking that their "reserves not be interfered with." In response, Seymour assured them that his "heart was as good to the Indians as to the White man," a claim starkly at odds with his actions.[34]

With Seymour's blessing, Trutch visited the Lower Fraser reserves and applied the same strategy he'd employed in the southern Interior. He pressed First Nations to accept reserve reductions. At each village, he warned "that McColl had [had] no authority for laying off the excessive amounts of land included by him in these reserves, and that his action in this respect was entirely disavowed." The governor, Trutch said, "would direct that such amounts of land should be secured to the use of each tribe as he should determine to be proportionate to their numbers and requirements." Ever anxious to secure a formal, linear, and tight-fisted expression of colonial policy for reserve creation, Trutch declared that reserve lands "will amount in the aggregate to ten acres of tillable land to each adult male in the tribe, together with a moderate amount of grazing land for those tribes which possess cattle and horses."[35]

Trutch was extremely resourceful in justifying the resurveying and redefinition of nearly every existing reserve.[36] His manipulative tactics led to a drastic 92 percent reduction in the reserves originally mapped by McColl under Douglas's guidance.[37] In October 1868, the surveyor general, H.M. Ball, proudly reported that all Fraser River reserves but one had been reduced to ten acres per adult male, yielding valuable farmland "which has hitherto been locked up and unused by white settlers."[38]

Trutch's systematic reserve reductions were enabled by a comfortable consensus among the governor, the chief commissioner of lands and works, and the Legislative Council. None would have challenged the following claim, expressed in an 1869 editorial in the *British Columbian:* "According to the strict rule of international law, territory occupied by a barbarous or wholly uncivilized people may be rightfully appropriated by a civilized or Christian nation."[39]

Seymour's address to the council on May 1, 1868, reflected that colonialist belief. The address provided his official response to a settler petition regarding the Bonaparte First Nation Reserves near Hat Creek. He noted that "some misapprehension exists as to the size" of the reserves and added: "Their extent is but one-half of that stated in the petition presented to you. I will see if they can be still further reduced, but I apprize you that the land which could be reclaimed from the Indians would barely pay for the expense of the survey."[40] In short, land values and survey costs were relevant factors in addressing the size of the Bonaparte Reserves. Indigenous rights and title were not.

In due course, Trutch directed Peter O'Reilly, a prominent colonial official and his brother-in-law, to visit the Bonaparte reserves. If O'Reilly found that the reserves were "as has been represented" in the petition, he was to reduce them:

> The extent of land to be included in each of these reservations must be determined by you on the spot, with due regard to the numbers and industrial habits of the Indians living on the land ... As a general rule it is considered that an allotment of about ten acres of good land should be made to each family in the tribe.[41]

O'Reilly concluded that "the extent of land claimed by them was out of all proportion to their requirements." Their principal reserve, "nearly 7 miles in length along the valley of the Bonaparte," was reduced to one square mile. As Trutch's ten-acre formula was implemented, the assistant surveyor general, B.W. Pearse, boasted that reserve reduction would "throw open about 40,000 acres for settlement by white men."[42] James Douglas's informal but generous policy of reserves "as severally pointed out by the Natives themselves" was thus supplanted by Trutch's miserly ten-acre edict.

Reserve creation continued even as British Columbia transitioned from colony to province. In his 1870 diary, O'Reilly noted that three reserves were "laid out" in the Upper Fraser Valley in just one day and that others followed in quick succession.[43] His new reserves had one common characteristic: they were small, so small that anthropologist James Teit noted in 1906 that they were "hardly sufficient in many places to grow enough potatoes and other vegetables for their own use."[44] O'Reilly and his surveyor (and brother-in-law), John Trutch, had few contacts with Indigenous peoples and knew little about the "worlds they were rearranging."[45] Indigenous people's wishes were of no consequence in a lands and works department directed by Joseph Trutch.

Trutch dismissed Douglas's other Indigenous land policies. On January 29, 1870, he discounted the notion of Aboriginal title:

> The title of the Indians in the fee of the public lands, or of any portion thereof, has never been acknowledged by Government, but, on the contrary is distinctly denied. In no case has any special agreement been made with any of the tribes of the Mainland for the extinction of their claims of possession; but these claims have been held to have been fully satisfied by securing to each tribe, as the progress of the country seemed to require, the use of sufficient tracts of land for their wants for agricultural and pastoral purposes.[46]

Similarly, Trutch dismissed the Douglas Treaties on Vancouver Island as mere payments "for the purpose of securing friendly relations between those Indians and the settlement of Victoria, then in its infancy, and certainly not in acknowledgment of any general title of the Indians to the land they occupy."[47] Trutch dismissed the notion of Aboriginal title out of hand, as most of his successors would for the next 125 years.

One of the first acts of the united colonies of British Columbia in 1866 was to undermine another key element in Douglas's land framework. It passed an ordinance that severely restricted Indigenous rights to pre-emption by requiring the special permission of the governor, a provision confirmed in the Land Ordinance Act of 1870.[48] The destructive combination of small reserves and severely constrained Indigenous access to pre-emption ensured that only white settlers would have even the chance to succeed. Sadly, Trutch's approach to Indigenous relations prevailed as the Colony of British Columbia contemplated union with Canada.

Political Eyes Turn to the East

The Legislative Council's 1870 sessions were largely devoted to developing and articulating British Columbia's conditions for union with Canada. Following the death of Governor Seymour on June 10, 1869, the colony was enjoying new leadership. His successor, Anthony Musgrave, arrived in Victoria two months later with a clear understanding of his marching orders. "Between ourselves, mind, Doctor," he confided to John Helmcken, physician and speaker of the Legislative Council, "HM [Her Majesty's] Govt wish BC to come into the Confederation." He also advised that "the Canadian Government want BC to join – [they] are afraid that BC may, if left alone, choose to join the U.S. and the annexation cry makes them anxious."[49]

On February 15, 1870, Musgrave provided an optimistic assessment of Confederation to the full Legislative Council: "I am convinced that on certain terms which I believe would not be difficult to arrange, this Colony may derive substantial benefit from such a union. But the only manner in which it can be ascertained whether Canada will agree to such arrangements as will suit us, is to propose such as we would be ready to accept."[50]

Musgrave and his executive prepared draft terms of union and presented them for consideration by the Legislative Council.[51] No reference to First Nations was contained within the terms, deliberately so. In a letter dated February 20, 1870, Musgrave noted that Lord Granville, Britain's secretary of state for the colonies, had advised him that "the condition of the Indian Tribes [was] among some questions upon which the Constitution of British Columbia will oblige the Governor [Musgrave] to enter personally. I have, purposely, omitted any reference to this subject in the terms proposed to the Legislative Council." Musgrave added that "any arrangement which may be regarded as proper by Her Majesty's Government, can, I think best be settled by the Secretary of State, or by me, under his direction with the Government of Canada."[52]

British Columbia's Confederation debates were underway on March 9, 1870, and concluded with the endorsement of a "Confederation Resolution" just over two weeks later. The debate, at least in Helmcken's opinion, altered the draft terms "a little but added nothing material."[53] The council approved a list of sixteen demands ranging from assumption of colonial debt, to roads and railways, to ports and hospitals, to parliamentary representation, but it made no mention of the Indigenous people who would compose over 70 percent of the new province's population.[54]

One council member, Henry Holbrook of New Westminster, called attention to the omission but was firmly rebuked by his colleagues. Holbrook's motion noted that "the Indians number four to one [the] white man, and they ought to be considered. They should receive protection ... the same protection under Confederation as now." Attorney General Henry Crease objected to further discussion: "On a former occasion a very evil impression was introduced in the Indian mind on the occasion of Sir James Douglas' retirement. I ask the

Hon. gentleman to be cautious, for Indians do get information of what is going on."[55] Crease's concern, according to Nicholas Claxton and John Price, was amplifying Indigenous expectations: "On leaving office in 1864, Douglas made a grand gesture – he held a party in New Westminster and invited Stó:lō leaders to attend. He promised to create larger reserves in the lower Fraser region and dispatched a surveyor to do so."[56] For Crease, peace and order were anchored to maintaining low expectations: "I say our policy has been, let the Indians alone."[57]

Some members shared Crease's reluctance to continue the debate. Frank Barnard (Yale) went so far as to ask that Holbrook's resolution be withdrawn and expunged from the record because "we cannot keep back from the Indians anything that happens here, and it will have a bad effect." Edward Alston, registrar general, wanted to expunge the resolution despite his apparent support for it: "I must support the Hon Member for New Westminster. I say there is no Indian policy here, and I am sure that the Canadian policy is good." Dr. Robert Carrall (Cariboo–Soda Creek) echoed this argument: "The Hon. Member for New Westminster has affirmed how good the Canadian system is. The goodness of that system is in itself sufficient to render the resolution needless. I shall, therefore, vote against it." In the end, Holbrook refused to withdraw the resolution, and it was defeated by a vote of twenty to one.[58] Indigenous relations would later be recognized through Article 13 of the Terms of Union Act, but not at the instigation of British Columbia's fathers of Confederation.

Council members Trutch, Helmcken, and Carrall were dispatched to Ottawa as British Columbia's representatives in the negotiations.[59] Helmcken was, for personal reasons, a reluctant participant and proposed Amor De Cosmos in his stead. However, as Helmcken later noted, Trutch was "particularly anxious that I should go with him. He had a great dislike for De Cosmos personally as well as politically."[60] Indeed, Trutch found much to dislike in De Cosmos, describing him as a man whose vanity was ludicrous and whose disposition was cantankerous.[61] Happily for historians, Trutch's wishes prevailed, and Helmcken subsequently provided vital insights into the confidential negotiations that set the terms for British Columbia's union with Canada.

British Columbia's delegation departed Victoria by steamer for San Francisco on May 14, 1870. The next leg of their journey was important from Helmcken's perspective: "The journey from San Francisco by railway opened our eyes not a little, for the railway had been built through a mountainous country quite as bad as that of B. Columbia – if this one could be built so could one through B. Columbia. The balloon grew smaller – the scheme looked now very practicable – but the means?"[62] Helmcken had expressed deep skepticism about the prospects of union with Canada only two months earlier. The rail journey and negotiating "the means" in Ottawa prompted a shift in his thinking.

By all accounts, including Helmcken's, negotiations focused primarily on railway construction, tariffs, grants, and subsidies. One notable exception was a closed-door meeting in late June 1870 during which, he stated, the "clause about Indians was very fully discussed." Helmcken's meeting summary, included in his diary, noted that the federal ministers "thought our system better than theirs in some respects, but what system would be adopted remained for the future to determine."[63] Helmcken's reference to a "system" is intriguing. What in British Columbia's colonial Indigenous relations would Canadian ministers have regarded as "better" – small and scattered reserves, post-settlement reserve creation, or the eschewal of treaties?

Successive Canadian governments had methodically negotiated treaties with Indigenous Nations prior to white settlement, so treaties flowed largely from east to west. The approach was guided by the Royal Proclamation of 1763, which embraced the principle that Indigenous rights in land "could be acquired only by the Crown through formal treaty, cession, or purchase."[64] Reserve allocations within those treaties typically provided 160 to 640 acres per family.[65] British Columbia's reserves varied widely in size but were typically a small fraction of those east of the Rockies. Unlike Canada, reserve creation in British Columbia typically followed – rather than preceded – white settlement, unaided by treaty.

The Dominion cabinet was well aware of treaty making when British Columbia joined the federation. Treaties 1 and 2 had been concluded by Sir John A. Macdonald's Conservative government in August 1871, based on a formula of 160 acres per family of five, just a few days after British Columbia entered Confederation.[66] Did Macdonald's ministers genuinely admire British Columbia's system of Indigenous relations? Post-Confederation discussions and debates between the governments of Canada and British Columbia suggest that Canadian ministers (and Macdonald himself) knew remarkably little about British Columbia's relationship with Indigenous peoples prior to union. Their positive comments were likely hollow platitudes aimed at reassuring the BC delegates that they had nothing to fear from Canada.

Relations with Indigenous Nations were not a paramount concern for either government. From Canada's perspective, British Columbia needed to be brought into the federation as a vital partner to create a transcontinental state.[67] The imperative of nation building pushed questions about Indigenous relations – from reserve size to treaty making – to a later date. Conversely, from British Columbia's perspective, Confederation held out the promise of immediate relief from chronic colonial debt and, more importantly, a transnational railway that would fuel white settlement and economic development. Neither side wanted these goals to be imperilled by debate about conflicting approaches to Indigenous relations.

Article 13 of the Terms of Union proved to be a convenient way for the Dominion and the colony to set aside Indigenous issues and focus on their primary concerns. The terms committed Canada, in its conduct of Indigenous affairs in British Columbia, to "a policy as liberal as that hitherto pursued" by British Columbia's colonial governments (meaning, from British Columbia's 1870 perspective, not very liberal at all). To advance this policy, the agreement included a provincial obligation to transfer public land (also called provincial Crown land) to the Dominion for the creation of reserves. If a dispute arose over the amount of land to be transferred, the matter could be referred for decision to the secretary of state for the colonies.[68] The illusion of collaboration on Indigenous relations would not survive the upheavals of the post-Confederation years.

A Transnational Railway Helps Helmcken See the Light

Helmcken had been a Confederation skeptic when he entered negotiations but, according to Trutch, "changed his view and policy to a wonderful extent during his month's stay in Canada."[69] The transcontinental railway played a pivotal role in shifting his thinking. In a speech reported in the Toronto *Globe* on June 10, 1870, he stated: "I accept it, and the people of British Columbia will accept it, but only on this condition – that through the exertions of the people of the Dominion a railway from the Atlantic to the Pacific is the result."[70] By the end of his visit, he was an enthusiastic advocate of Confederation: "What else could I do seeing that the Canadian Government had granted nearly everything asked for!!"[71]

Trutch was firmly pro-Confederation and embraced a role as adviser and intermediary in the process. In October 1870, he advised Sir George-Étienne Cartier (Macdonald's lieutenant and a powerful leader of the Quebec wing of the governing Conservative party) that British Columbia's ratification would "not be effected without struggle." Certain agitators who favoured union with or annexation by the United States were determined to alter the terms, Trutch noted, but he was confident that Confederation would prevail.[72] He relished the role of confidential agent, a role that would continue post-Confederation, particularly in the realm of Indigenous relations.

According to Trutch, British Columbia's swift entry into Confederation – and the fate of the transcontinental railway – was in jeopardy until the intervention of Cartier, who soothed Conservative legislators gripped by fears of financial collapse: "I assure you that but for the pluck and determination of the 'lightning striker' ... the measure would have been defeated and the Govt. broken up."[73] Cartier reassured nervous colleagues that the benefits of having a nation from sea to sea outweighed the financial costs and political risks of the railway.

W.J. Macdonald, Victoria's mayor and soon-to-be senator, was relieved to report that the "Pacific Railway Bill has passed the Commons with very few amendments although many were proposed ... Many think that BC is rather an expensive toy."[74] In the realm of Indigenous relations, British Columbia quickly proved to be a troublesome and intractable toy. Creating a mutually agreeable Indigenous lands policy would prove even more challenging than constructing a transnational railway.

3

Confederation Brings Conflict

British Columbia officially shifted from being a British colony to a Canadian province on July 20, 1871.[1] Not everyone was thrilled. E.G. Alston, British Columbia's registrar general before and during the transition, declared to a colleague, "We are a conquered country and the Canucks take possession tomorrow."[2] Alston feared the shift to a more democratic form of government. The colonial Legislative Council, a hybrid mix of appointed and elected members, was replaced by an elected Legislative Assembly, which operated on the British parliamentary model. The colonial Executive Council, appointed by the governor, gave way to a provincial cabinet drawn from elected members of the Legislative Assembly. When the transition to provincehood was completed, Alston abandoned British Columbia to assume the role of Queen's advocate in the colony of Sierra Leone.

But much less changed than Alston feared. Some prominent leaders, along with their prejudices, survived the transition. Joseph Trutch was among them. His leadership in the Confederation negotiations had impressed John A. Macdonald, leading to Trutch's appointment as British Columbia's first lieutenant-governor on July 5, 1871. His first exercise of vice-regal power was controversial. Trutch declined to appoint either of the colony's main advocates for Confederation and responsible government as the first premier. Instead of choosing De Cosmos or Robson, he selected John Foster McCreight, a respected, socially prominent lawyer who'd had little involvement in politics. Trutch then underlined his continuing political power by sitting in on McCreight cabinet meetings, "undermining the principle of popular sovereignty."[3] In 1871, British

Columbia was still three decades away from adopting formal party lines, which left considerable discretion in the hands of the lieutenant-governor in the selection of premiers.

Trutch's policies and prejudices also survived the shift to provincehood. In his early correspondence as lieutenant-governor with Joseph Howe, Canada's secretary of state for the provinces, Trutch conferred high praise on the colonial government's (and, of course, his own) conduct of Indigenous relations, referring to "a well-considered system, ably devised by experienced men specially interested in favour of the Indians, to suit the circumstances of this country, and consistently carried out so far as the pecuniary means at command would admit of." Trutch bluntly rejected criticism from the Aborigines' Protection Society, an international human rights organization founded in 1837, and some prominent clergymen that the colonial government had neglected the needs of Indigenous people. "Our Indian population," Trutch claimed, had "partaken on equal, and in some cases more than equal, terms with our white people in all the advantages of civilization which we have brought to them."[4]

British Columbia's provincial legislature quickly dispelled any notions of "equal terms." One of its first acts was to explicitly limit the right to vote along racial lines leaving "a minority of ten thousand white settlers to dominate the estimated forty thousand Indigenous and Chinese people then in the province."[5] Disenfranchisement resulted from the second of two proposed amendments to the Qualification and Registration of Voters Act, 1872. The first, aimed at preventing elected members of the federal Parliament from concurrently holding provincial office, excited vigorous debate and was narrowly defeated. The second was proposed by MLA John Robson, author of the Legislative Council's 1867 demand for reserve reductions along the Lower Fraser River. His motion to insert a new clause into the bill – "Nothing in this Act shall be construed to, or include, or apply to Chinese or Indians" – passed unanimously, with no evidence of debate.[6]

Trutch Maintains a Keen Interest in Indigenous Relations

Macdonald soon sought his new lieutenant-governor's advice on Indigenous relations in British Columbia, and Trutch was eager to comply. In July 1872, Trutch shared his confidential assessment of "Indian troubles." Trutch claimed he felt alarmed by the "feeling of agitation" within Indigenous communities: "But for the vessels of war ... we would be powerless to keep in order the 30 to 40,000 Indians along our Coast, and there is no calculating to what loss of life" might occur. Trutch was often dismissive of potential Indigenous discord, so his alarm might have been a pretext for expanding his vice-regal powers. He reminded Macdonald of the role "you wished me to take until you had appointed some special agent to take charge of Indian matters in this Province." He added, "The charge of our Indians is the most ticklish business ... I am compelled therefore to apply for such authorization to expend Dominion funds" to maintain the peace.[7]

Macdonald soon adopted a more conventional approach to the conduct of Indigenous affairs, then employed a conciliatory tone in breaking the news to Trutch. His note of September 25, 1872, signalled the Dominion's pending direction: "All, or most of the Members [of Parliament] from British Columbia press Dr. [Israel] Powell upon the Government as Indian Agent, and I do not know how we can resist ... If he is at all fit for it, I think we will have to appoint him."[8] Trutch did not fully share the enthusiasm of Dominion MPs; he considered Powell "in very good standing here," but possessing only a limited understanding of Indigenous matters. With his usual self-confidence, Trutch declared (twice within the same letter): "I am of the opinion, and that very strongly, that for some time to come at least the general charge of all Indian affairs in BC should be vested in the Lt. Governor."[9]

Trutch was keen to lead the province's conduct of Indigenous relations and to lay the foundation for future Dominion-provincial discussions. He advised Macdonald that

> the Canadian system as I understand it will hardly work here. We have never bought out any Indian claims to lands, nor do they expect we should, but we reserve for their use and benefit from time to time tracts of sufficient extent to fulfill their reasonable requirements for cultivation and grazing. If you now commence to buy out Indian title to the lands of BC you would go back on all that has been done here for 30 years past and would be equitably bound to compensate the tribes who inhabited the districts now settled farmed [sic] by white people equally with those in the more remote and uncultivated portions. Our Indians are sufficiently satisfied and had better be left alone as far as a new system towards them is concerned.[10]

Trutch's advice to Macdonald is notable for a few reasons. First, he didn't mention James Douglas and his early treaties on Vancouver Island. Second, Trutch discouraged any initiative to "buy out Indian title." He was well aware of Canadian treaty making east of the Rockies, an activity inconsistent with "all that has been done here for 30 years past." Further, First Nations were far from "sufficiently satisfied," a description starkly at odds with his claims of Indigenous agitation and impending conflict set out in his letter to Macdonald only two months earlier. Trutch was always prepared to deceive, distort, or outright lie to achieve his ends.

Macdonald appeared to embrace Trutch's advice on all aspects of Indigenous relations. He did not want Powell's appointment to sully his relationship with Trutch. He wrote that he supposed that Powell would "be a good enough man, but he ought to have known more about the Indians. I would like to still hear more from you confidentially as to the best mode of management generally, with some information as to what system you have hitherto pursued with respect to Indian matters."[11]

Two months later, Macdonald went even further, claiming the "appointment of Dr. Powell as Indian Agent was forced upon the Government by our political friends." He proposed the creation of an Indian Board, with Trutch as chief commissioner, along with "Powell and a Roman Catholic" as subordinate commissioners. Trutch was undoubtedly gratified to hear back from Macdonald that the board would direct general policy and management under the lieutenant-governor's supervision.[12]

Notwithstanding the prime minister's apparent enthusiasm for the board, his Conservative government never defined or formalized roles and responsibilities within it, an omission that gave rise to awkward questions following Macdonald's defeat in 1873. In May 1874, Trutch advised the recently appointed Liberal minister of the interior, David Laird, that he was still waiting for the commission to formalize his leadership role on the board, along with his "subordinate" commissioners, namely, Powell and his assistant superintendent James Lenihan (the Roman Catholic promised by Macdonald).[13]

Laird's reply was polite and perfunctory: the requisite Order in Council had been delayed by other ministerial priorities. Subsequent events prompted Trutch to take a more aggressive tone. He had invited his subordinate commissioners to a meeting of the Indian Board and was dismayed that "Dr. Powell questioned the authority, and in fact the existence of the Board, and has continued to act independently under instructions ... directly from yourself."[14] Twelve days later, Trutch threatened to leave the board until it was "fully empowered to give effect to its conclusions and the status and proper functions of the Lt. Governor as a member of that Board shall have been clearly defined."[15]

Laird had little interest in placating Trutch: "It is evident from your Despatch and from letters received from other Members of the Board [Powell and Lenihan], that the Commissioners are not working together harmoniously, and you are disposed to think that your present status on the Board is hardly consistent with your duties and position." Unlike the Macdonald Conservatives, Laird doubted that his Liberal colleagues "would be prepared to delegate to any person ... the general control and management of Indian Affairs." He suggested that Trutch's role on the board was to "offer suggestions and render general assistance," but "not so much to exercise authority over its individual Members."[16]

When Trutch expressed interest in being reappointed lieutenant-governor in 1876, neither David Laird nor the broader Alexander Mackenzie Liberal government supported him. Trutch was a Macdonald political appointee and held views on Indigenous relations that were repugnant to Mackenzie and Laird. Nothing in British Columbia's early history as a province supported a continuing role for Trutch as Mackenzie's confidential agent in that field.

Canada Assumes Responsibility for Indigenous Relations with British Columbia's Blessing

Primary responsibility for Indigenous relations moved from colony to the Dominion in 1871. The secretary of state for the provinces, Joseph Howe, wrote Trutch on August 19, 1871, requesting "statistics on Indian matters" along with maps of "the various tracts of land held under reserve by Government for the use and benefit of the Indians."[17] The surveyor general, B.W. Pearse, responded on Trutch's behalf: "I have no statistics as to the number of Indians in each tribe, and have no means of obtaining them. It would cost a great deal of time and money, and would involve a visit to each Indian Village throughout the Province." By Pearse's reckoning, Indigenous reserves covered a total of 28,487 acres, but he added: "There are, especially on Vancouver Island, a great many tribes which have no Reserves marked out either on plan or on the ground."[18]

At Confederation, British Columbia had concluded no treaties beyond the Douglas Treaties, nor had reserves been established in large swaths of the colony. Pearse acknowledged that in colonial British Columbia, reserve creation had typically followed rather than preceded settlement:

> It has generally been the practice to lay out on the ground the Indian Reserves synchronously with the settlement of the district by the whites. This system has been found effectual and far less costly than that of surveying the reserves all together, as they are naturally scattered and often at great distances apart.[19]

Such parsimony laid the seeds for future discord. All too often, Indigenous communities saw prime farmland incorporated into pre-emptions based on the colonial assumption that only "actual settlers" would make the best use of it. Decades later, First Nations would repeatedly complain, with good reason, that reserves had been created from the residual "guts and feathers" after settler demands were met. But Pearse proudly claimed that the Executive Council always "exercised a general control and supervision over the Indians and their lands, and has always prevented them from alienating in any way any portion of their reserves."[20] That claim was certainly true. Colonial governments, particularly after Douglas's retirement and Trutch's ascension to chief commissioner of lands and works, did not allow First Nations to sell their lands and instead retained for themselves the opportunity to alienate reserve lands – typically as cut-off lands "freed up" for white settlement. Provincehood prompted no shift in policies on Indigenous lands. Old prejudices simply found expression in new institutions. British Columbia's new provincial cabinet ministers quickly learned to deflect "Indian problems" inherited from the colonial era onto the Dominion government.

The newly appointed Indian superintendent, Israel Powell, was still awaiting "instructions in respect to his active duties" from Ottawa when he received an urgent appeal from Attorney General George Walkem. Walkem wanted advice on steps being taken "at once" to map out Tŝilhqot'in (Chilcotin) reservations and "throw the country open to intending settlers." His concern was prompted by a "quarrel" between Tŝilhqot'in Chiefs and a settler, John Salmon, who had "recently pre-empted land in their midst." Walkem anticipated "collisions of a more serious character" as more settlers came and suggested that Powell should "authorize some person to proceed to the Chilcotin country at once, and lay off, in a rough form, such reserves as may be required until a survey can be made." Walkem concluded, "It is highly undesirable that intending settlers should be longer excluded from the District."[21]

Robert Beaven, chief commissioner of lands and works, now a cabinet position responsible for handling settler demands in the province, pushed Walkem's request further: the provincial government wanted the entire Chilcotin Valley opened up for settlement, excluding portions Powell might wish to retain for "Indian purposes."[22] Powell, well aware of the Tŝilhqot'in insurgency a decade earlier, was not about to be stampeded into such a drastic step: "I consider *the removal of the whole of the present reservation* would prove a fruitful source of Indian difficulty, were no special Reserve provided for the Native tribes, and of danger to the white settler who might be sufficiently courageous to take up land in their country previous to such Reserve being made."[23]

Beaven again wrote Powell, this time prompted by complaints from settlers anxious to pre-empt lands at Alberni on Vancouver Island, two hundred kilometres north of Victoria. "Indians in that locality," said Beaven, "claim the lands as their property, and threaten to molest parties occupying said land." He called Powell's attention "to the imperative necessity of *at once having all Indian land claims settled,* not only at Alberni, but in other parts of the Province." Beaven did not want a new treaty process. Nor did he want provincial Crown lands to be transferred to create or expand reserves under Article 13. He wanted the Dominion government to settle "all Indian land claims" without recourse to provincial lands. Beaven, just like Joseph Trutch before him, thought Indigenous communities had simply become an awkward barrier to the unrestrained settlement of the young province. Many settlers wished to settle in British Columbia, he argued, "but the fact of Indians being located in almost every District where white settlers would wish to locate is preventing many from doing so, and is consequently retarding the settlement of the Province."[24]

The fact that Indigenous peoples had occupied those lands for hundreds or thousands of years was of no consequence to Beaven; he shed all concern for the rights and title of First Nations just as quickly he and his colleagues had dismissed their voting rights.

Provincial cabinet ministers regarded Powell as a persistent nuisance, someone to be bullied, cajoled, and disparaged. When the prospect of an Indigenous insurgency arose in the southern Interior in late 1873, Walkem admonished Powell: "The real cause of discontent is the fact that you have not paid them a visit, and that they feel that they have been neglected by the Indian Department." To his credit, Powell pushed back: "From all I can learn, the fear that they will lose their land and not be sufficiently provided for in this respect, is the real cause of disturbance."[25]

Over his seventeen years as Indian superintendent, Powell would advocate for larger reserves despite sharing the assimilationist views (for example, on residential schools and the Potlatch) common among his contemporaries.[26] Much like James Douglas a decade earlier, Powell "fought for the establishment of reserves so that Indians would have a sound economic base."[27]

The Persistence of Regressive Policies Spawns Discord

Early provincial cabinets largely maintained the policies and practices of the late colonial period. The Indigenous right to pre-emption, severely restricted after Douglas's retirement, was formally abolished after Confederation. Other legislation, including the Land Amendment Act, 1873, was designed to spur the flow of white settlers into the province. Soon after, prominent newspaper advertisements appeared with the headline "Free Grants." The grants were substantial: 160 acres west of the Cascade Mountains, and 240 acres to the east. This generous offer was confirmed with the signatures of Premier Amor De Cosmos, elected in December 1872, and Lieutenant-Governor Joseph Trutch.[28]

First Nations were justifiably angered when white settlers moved in and began fencing off "free grant" lands long considered their own. The collision of aggressive provincial land policies and Indigenous resistance to displacement sparked anger and apprehension. Just two years after British Columbia's union with Canada, the province was fearful and divided. Such fears were reflected in newspaper headlines. The *British Colonist* warned that "Indian War Threatened!!" and claimed that at a meeting of "the Council of Chiefs in that vicinity [Clinton], seven were for war and two opposed ... The Indians were liable to commence hostilities at any moment." A subsequent article confirmed pending hostilities, reporting that "irate Chiefs" around Kamloops were "discussing measures of war" in "a condition of dangerous unrest. They either have a cause of war or think they have." The story noted the existence of "difficulties" in other districts – notably Cowichan, Vancouver Island – "which if not attended to in time, may prove to be the seeds of serious trouble and ripen in blood."[29]

The *Colonist*'s primary competitor, the *Victoria Daily Standard*, was not to be outdone. It reported that "the telegraph office in this city is being anxiously watched ... with regard to the report of the Indians being about to rise against the whites ... The Indians around Yale have been investing in muskets and bayonets, and have stolen a keg of powder from Nelson's store." The report led to "much uneasiness" as "Yale is almost defenceless, there being no arms to speak of." Happily, at least from the *Standard*'s perspective, "proper measures" would be "resorted to at once to repress any Indian raid which might dare be attempted." Three days later, the *Standard* reported that "braves were congregating for the purpose of 'cleaning out the whites,'" but "despite a rumour of their making a raid on the whites, there is no danger at present." The newspaper also reported on discord in Cowichan, where "Indians are in a state of complete insubordination ... rather than give up the land they are now trespassing on." Reflecting settler sentiment of the day, the *Standard* deemed Indigenous people "trespassers" on their own lands.[30]

Incendiary news headlines and accounts undoubtedly gave pause to white settlers, who numbered only 8,576 in 1871, compared with an Indigenous population estimated at 28,500 but likely closer to 35,000.[31] Did headlines exaggerate the danger of insurrection to sell newspapers? Perhaps. But informed observers such as Father Grandidier of Okanagan Mission were deeply concerned "that the Indians were liable to commence hostilities at any moment."[32] The authorities also took the potential for insurrection seriously. Walkem contacted Powell, reiterating that "Indians had assumed a hostile attitude to the whites." He suggested that "an immediate personal visit by you is due to the whites as well as to the Indians, as the threatened danger may thus be averted, without expense or – the still more serious contingency – loss of life."[33]

Fear of an insurrection kindled a bitter debate between Canada and its newest province over reserve sizes. Powell accepted Walkem's challenge, departing for meetings in Kamloops and Cache Creek. He also restated his belief that Indigenous people's discord was rooted in "fear that they will lose their land and not be sufficiently provided for." In Powell's view, the province's confirmation of larger reserves, the object of early discussions with Dominion officials, would quell "the most fruitful source of anxiety or fear of injustice on their part."[34]

British Columbia was ever loath to contemplate more generous reserves but never reluctant to blame the Dominion for fuelling Indigenous people's discontent. In his letter to Powell on February 26, 1874, Walkem mentioned the disturbance at Cowichan: "Indians emboldened by the failure of your negotiations have assumed an attitude of aggression ... Loss of lives of white settlers, as you are aware, is not at all an impossible contingency." Powell and his department had unrealistically and needlessly heightened Indigenous people's expectations, he wrote, and immediate steps were needed to settle "these and other Indian difficulties."[35]

Walkem signalled BC's approach to Indigenous land issues for the century ahead: Canada bore constitutional responsibility for the resolution of Indigenous issues, and the federal government should fulfill its responsibility without diminishing British Columbia's public lands. Less than three years after entering Confederation, the BC government had abandoned all pretense of governing in the interests of both Indigenous and non-Indigenous citizens.

Confederation Partners Locked in a Protracted Battle

From the moment of his appointment, Powell regularly received demands from BC cabinet ministers to resolve "difficulties with Indians," but they never suggested how the province might help achieve that goal. Nevertheless, the Dominion government still nursed hopes that British Columbia might be persuaded or cajoled into accepting more extensive reserve lands as the basis for settling Indigenous grievances and claims.

The federal cabinet tested how far their provincial colleagues might go to achieve peace and security for future settlement. A Privy Council report of March 21, 1873, set out the Macdonald government's position on Indigenous demands in British Columbia. Officials correctly anticipated the province's resistance to creating reserves like those negotiated east of the Rocky Mountains. They proposed more modest allocations, suggesting "that each family be assigned a location of 80 acres of land of average quality, which shall remain permanently the property of the family for whose benefit it is allotted." They aimed to "remove any spirit of discontent which in various quarters appears to prevail," a less-than-subtle reference to newspaper headlines. To achieve the eighty-acre objective, the cabinet authorized Powell to confer with the province on extending Indigenous lands and creating new reserves as required for the fulfillment of "the just expectations" of Indigenous people.[36]

Powell tendered the proposal to Chief Commissioner of Lands and Works Beaven, who clearly was more accustomed to dishing out demands than responding to them. Obfuscation was Beaven's first line of defence. He replied with detailed questions he knew Powell could not possibly answer: What were the names and numbers of individuals and families in each Indigenous Nation? What was the name, locality, and acreage of each reserve "claimed by you on behalf of the various tribes?"[37] Ironically, similar questions had been posed to Beaven's predecessor eighteen months earlier by Dominion officials preparing to assume constitutional responsibility for Indigenous relations. Beaven's questions, by contrast, simply aimed to buy time. He knew full well from his department's immediate history that no answers could be rendered. Given his appeal to Powell only three weeks earlier, citing "the imperative necessity of at once having all Indian land claims settled," his questions were, at best, disingenuous.

Powell's response was polite but pointed: "The names of the individual population of Indians in this Province is quite unattainable, except under the most extraordinary circumstances – certainly not now at my command." He estimated the Indigenous population to be 28,500 but acknowledged that no comprehensive census had been undertaken. On the question of the name and location of all Indigenous reserves, Powell noted, perhaps with a wry smile, "I beg to refer you to a schedule (furnished me by your predecessor) and maps at present in the Land Office, a copy of which I have in my possession."[38]

Beaven had no appetite for adopting the Dominion's reserve proposal but was reluctant to reject it outright. His note to Powell of April 30, 1873, reflected both obfuscation and tight-fistedness:

> In regard to the suggestion that "each family will be assigned a location of 80 acres of land," it will be found in the first place necessary to define the number as applied to the term "family," and would suggest that we adopt the rule in use in the North-West Territory, viz:–"six" as applied to that term; but in doing so, consider that 80 acres is far too large an average for each family of six.

Beaven took Powell's estimated Indigenous population of 28,500 and assumed an average family size of six, yielding a sum of 4,750 families. He then took the Lands and Works Department's estimated sum of reserve lands at Confederation (28,487 acres) and divided it by the number of families. His calculation yielded the conclusion that "reservations so far in this Province have averaged about six acres to each family."[39]

Beaven did not refer to Article 13 or the policy of previous colonial governments, but the genesis of British Columbia's long-standing opposition to larger reserves (particularly if drawn from provincial public lands) was contained in his short note to Powell: if the colonial standard was six acres per family, how could the Dominion possibly expect the province to accept a policy of eighty acres per family? Beaven's argument was entirely specious. He conveniently ignored his predecessor's acknowledgment, made only two years earlier, that no census had been conducted and that "a great many tribes" had no reserves at all. Their exchange was merely an opening salvo in a much longer battle over reserve size.

Powell ramped up the pressure a few weeks later after a tour of Indigenous communities on Vancouver Island. In a letter to Lieutenant-Governor Trutch, Powell argued that "in some instances great injustice has been done the Indians in not reserving sufficient land for their use, and in some cases, such as Comox, Chemainus, and others, land actually occupied by Indians ... has been pre-empted by white settlers and certificates granted." Powell asked Trutch to arrange a meeting for him with the provincial cabinet: "Abundant discontent prevails among Indians, both on the Island and Mainland, and I regard it as a matter of urgent and paramount importance, not only to the future peaceful settlement of the Province by whites, but as a matter of justice to the Indians themselves." Reserves should be created where they did not exist, he concluded, and adjusted where they did not meet Indigenous people's needs.[40]

Powell's letter prompted a response from the provincial cabinet on July 25, 1873. The Dominion's eighty-acre-per-family proposal was specifically rejected, as noted in the cabinet minutes: "This quantity is greatly in excess of the grants considered sufficient by the previous Governments of British Columbia, and recommend that throughout the Province Indian Reserves should not exceed a quantity of twenty acres of land for each head of a family of five persons."[41] The twenty-acre figure cited in the minutes appeared to signal a compromise when compared with Trutch's ten-acre rule for reserves. However, the number was advanced as a maximum, not as an average, and certainly not as a minimum. A subsequent note from the provincial secretary, John Ash, to Powell, appeared to offer clarity. Ash reiterated the cabinet's position that "land to be reserved for Indians should not exceed 20 acres of land for each head of a family of five persons" but added that "all future reserves will be adjusted on the basis of twenty acres of land for each head of a family of five persons."[42]

Powell knew that reserves of twenty acres per family would be entirely unacceptable to First Nations in the southern Interior. He wrote Ash, requesting "that the quantity of land to be reserved for Indians east of the Cascades should be forty acres for each Indian family, instead of twenty ... interior Indians are nearly all possessed of horses and cattle, and I am convinced that twenty acres would not be found to be sufficient." The principle of larger Interior reserves, he argued, was implicit in the pre-emption law for white settlers, which allowed for 320 acres to the east and 160 acres to the west of the Cascade Mountains. In his response, Ash noted that larger reserves had already been created east of the Cascades but that cabinet would give Powell's suggestion "mature consideration."[43]

Walkem provided the first indication of mature consideration in late December 1873. He called Powell's attention to the "really in some instances, enormous, and in all cases, sufficient reserves, already laid aside for the Indians residing near Cache Creek, Kamloops, Okanagan, Shuswap, and other places." Walkem was certain that Powell would agree "that many of the reserves must be cut down, being out of all proportion to the strength of the tribes to which they have been respectively granted in days gone by, when land in the vicinity referred to seems to have been considered of little value." As of 1873, "days gone by" reflected less than a dozen years, from the creation of the Douglas reserves in the early 1860s to Trutch's reductions in the late 1860s.

In a lengthy postscript to his letter, Walkem offered an olive branch of sorts to Powell and Ottawa:

> As Mr. De Cosmos stated that there would be no difficulty in granting any extra lands to the Indians if absolutely necessary, and as your views and mine

coincide as to a just treatment of the Indians, I take the responsibility of stating that you may tell the Indians that where the lands occupied by them are only suitable for grazing purposes and are inadequate to meet their wants, that twenty acres more than the twenty now conceded, should be given to each Indian family requiring them for pastoral use, regard, of course, being had in the disposition of the lands to the average acreage per family of all the reserves hitherto granted or hereafter added.[44]

Despite its congenial tone, Walkem was offering the opportunity for additional grazing lands but subject to proportional reductions in Indigenous land allocations elsewhere. This concession was certainly not what Powell and Ottawa had in mind.

First Nations west of the Cascade Mountains were determined to expand their lands. Chief Peter Ayessik of the Hope (Chawathil) First Nation petitioned Powell on behalf of Indigenous Nations at Douglas Portage and the Lower Fraser, who, he wrote, "view, with a great anxiety, the standing question of the quantity of land to be reserved for the use of each Indian family." Chief Ayessik appreciated the more generous reserves created elsewhere in Canada, "and we have been at a loss to understand the views of the Local Government of British Columbia, in curtailing our land so much as to leave, in many instances, but few acres of land per family." He argued that their demands for redress had been ignored: "We have felt like men trampled on, and are commencing to believe that the aim of the white men is to exterminate us as soon as they can, although we have always been quiet, obedient, kind, and friendly to the whites." He concluded that "80 acres per family is absolutely necessary for our support." Anything less would "create ill feelings, irritation amongst our people, and we cannot say what will be the consequence."[45]

Beset by irreconcilable demands, and frustrated by ever-evolving provincial government positions, Ottawa deliberately or inadvertently adopted a generous interpretation of its "agreement" with British Columbia. Canada's position was set out by an Order in Council attached to a letter from Powell to Provincial Secretary Ash on May 15, 1874. Ottawa presumed it would secure reserves containing a minimum of twenty acres per family across the province and larger allocations where warranted, such as grazing lands for Indigenous ranches. First and foremost, the agreement would dramatically increase reserve size west of the Cascade Mountains, including Vancouver Island. But would this apparent agreement prove durable? Powell would soon test the province's willingness to compromise.

Canada Gets a Lesson on Dishonour of the Crown

On July 31, 1874, Powell advised Beaven in separate dispatches that survey crews were on site and ready to proceed at both the Musqueam and Tsawwassen Reserves. In the case of Musqueam, based on a survey of the area and population, an additional 1,197 acres would be drawn from adjacent public lands to meet the twenty-acre benchmark.[46]

When Beaven asked how the actual number of families had been determined, Powell replied, "By counting."[47] His straightforward reply was greeted with more obfuscation. The province, Beaven argued, "should know who supplied the information, whether it was taken under oath or how, and whether any penalty can be imposed for making a false return."[48] British Columbia had been remarkably confident in its population estimates when it came to reducing reserves in the latter colonial years. That confidence evaporated in the wake of its "agreement" to expand them.

In the case of Tsawwassen, Powell noted that "a large portion" of reserve lands were "swampy and useless except for grazing purposes." He reckoned that another hundred acres would need to be set aside to meet the twenty-acre benchmark. Beaven, taken aback, challenged the very existence of the Tsawwassen Reserve, claiming ignorance of any land being returned to the Dominion government as part of the Act of Union, as an Indian reserve, "under that name or in that locality." Powell patiently responded, "I now send you the book of tracings as the only record of any land having been reserved for this band of Indians." The Tsawwassen, he added, were one of several Nations "for whom lands have been reserved by former Governments, but which were omitted in the schedule furnished the Dominion Government at the time of union." Such omissions were, Powell presumed, unintentional but had caused "great dissatisfaction."[49]

The province's commitment to reserve expansion was short-lived. On August 10, 1874, Beaven advised Powell: "I am unable to advise the extension of present reservations, until positively informed that you are authorized to reduce as well as increase such reservations; and that you are prepared on behalf of the Dominion Government to guarantee that the Indians will agree quietly to reduction, if the Provincial Government agree to an increase."[50] In short, for any reserve expansion to proceed consistent with the twenty-acre benchmark, First Nations elsewhere would have to agree (quietly) to potential reserve reductions. Powell could not and would not agree, knowing full well Indigenous people's anger over meagre reserves and range land allotments.

Powell did not give up easily. He wrote Ash to challenge Beaven's letter: "I sincerely trust the interpretation seemingly conveyed in [Beaven's] letter, of confining the grant to new reserves, is not that intended by the Government in lieu of *all* reserves containing 20 acres to every head of a native family." Powell reminded Ash that "many of the present reserves do not contain *five* acres to each head of a family." Failure to extend the reserves would be a grave injustice, he warned. To promote peace, Powell committed "at considerable expense, to survey all reserves, with a view to allotment on the basis agreed upon." In the case of reserves west of the Cascade Mountains, he promised to notify Beaven of excesses that might be surveyed for pre-emptions. Powell was likely confident, having visited many reserves, that few, if any, west of the Cascade Mountains would have survived Trutch's reductions with more than twenty acres per family. For lands east of the Cascades, Powell argued: "It would be too great an undertaking on my part to guarantee quietude on the part of the Indians generally, because throughout the Interior ... where Indians possess many horses and cattle, *and have no grazing lands,* they consider 20 acres to each head altogether insufficient."[51]

Ash was uncharacteristically cautious in his response to Powell. He confirmed that "all future Reserves for Indians will be adjusted on the basis of 20 acres of land for each head of a family of five persons," but in an obvious attempt to buy time, he promised that the potential expansion of existing reserves would be "fully considered" on the return of the lieutenant-governor.[52] Powell responded that he would "anxiously await" receipt of an answer "in view of the trouble which would at once be created among the Indians should it be fully decided by the Provincial Government that the proposed quantity of twenty acres to each family is not to apply to those having claim to present Reserves."[53]

Trutch's 1874 advice to the cabinet, which was embedded in Order in Council 838/74, undoubtedly reinforced the province's resistance to expanding existing reserves: "The lands conveyed [in the expansion of existing reserves] would probably be of the best quality available ... Such lands are in request for the purpose of actual and useful settlement and ... it is contrary to the public welfare for such lands to be left uncultivated in the hands of a nominal and irresponsible proprietary."[54] Trutch's depiction of First Nations as "a nominal and irresponsible proprietary" aimed to reinforce the long-standing belief that only white, actual settlers could make good use of agricultural lands.

Powell's hopes for reserve expansion were officially dashed a few weeks later. Ash explained that the BC cabinet's "interpretation" of the Dominion's

Order in Council on reserve expansion was that it "was not intended to affect or unsettle Reservations already established, but its operation is altogether confined to the cases in which, at the time of Confederation, aboriginal tribes or communities were not provided with lands set apart for their separate and exclusive use."[55] In short, any reserve created (or, more precisely, created then reduced by Joseph Trutch) before Confederation would not be adjusted based on the twenty-acre benchmark. Even reserves averaging a few acres or less per family would continue without the prospect of being expanded.

Powell was bitterly disappointed. He had no choice but to recall his survey parties from Musqueam and Tsawwassen. In a note to Ash, Powell claimed he had "not a doubt of the dissatisfaction of the Indians which will follow delay in adjusting all Reserves upon the basis mutually understood and agreed upon."[56] In stark contrast, provincial ministers exhibited a smug confidence that they had won the day. The larger allocation for post-Confederation reserves was proof, Ash claimed, that the province had "been more liberal than it was called upon to be by the Terms of Union." Ash exploited the words of Article 13 – "policy as liberal as that hitherto pursued" – to defeat Ottawa's hopes for larger reserves.[57]

Article 13 Underpins Conflict in the Decades Ahead

In 1871, the ambiguous and imprecise wording of Article 13 enabled political union between partners with markedly different approaches to Indigenous relations. Just three years later, those words were weaponized in British Columbia's battle against reserve expansion. British Columbia's interpretation of Article 13 was reinforced by its broader constitutional arrangements with Canada. Under section 92(5) of the British North America Act, British Columbia assumed jurisdiction over public lands while the Dominion undertook responsibility for "Indians and lands reserved for Indians" under section 91(24). This division of authority created major challenges for Indigenous relations.

First, it spawned the persistent narrative that responsibility for the management or resolution of "Indian troubles" rested entirely with the Dominion, thereby allowing the province its singular focus on promoting white settlement and economic development. Second, British Columbia's control of public lands made those lands its dominant asset. Any diminution of that asset without a compelling reason (such as building a railway) was stoutly resisted. The creation or expansion of Indigenous reserves – through Article 13 transfers –

was viewed in precisely that light. BC governments were loath to give up "their lands," just to help the Dominion solve its "Indian land question."

In 1871, and for more than a century thereafter, the province saw its prospects as being inextricably linked to public lands. Land was current and future wealth: farmers and ranchers and the settlements that grew up to serve them were the anchors of economic and social life; mountains and waters held a bounty of precious minerals and fish stocks that would enrich the province; and roads and railways were the vital connections that would facilitate discovery and exploitation of that wealth. Passion for resources shifted over time – from agriculture and railways to mines, forests, oil, and liquefied natural gas – but throughout it all, First Nations were perceived as "obstacles to progress" in resource exploitation and only rarely as partners. British Columbia's intransigence would soon breed discord.

4

Intransigence Breeds Discord

Only three years after Confederation, British Columbia and Canada were at loggerheads on the issue of reserve allocation for First Nations. British Columbia's small reserves stood in stark contrast to those east of the Rocky Mountains, and the province resisted Canada's proposals to remedy that disparity. Canada wanted to build a constructive relationship with its newest province, but British Columbia's refusal to consider anything more than modest increases in land allocation for new reserves posed a challenge. From Ottawa's perspective, giving in to British Columbia would foster only more discord. British Columbia's formula of twenty acres per family might increase the bitterness and frustration felt by Indigenous people on adjacent existing reserves. The formula could – and would – be a recipe for ongoing discontent and turmoil.

Ottawa was by no means persuaded by British Columbia's claim of being "more liberal than it was called upon to be by the Terms of Union": from its perspective, British Columbia had abrogated its agreement to expand reserves. David Laird, the minister of the interior, suggested as much in his annual report for 1874. Laird is remembered negatively as the minister responsible for the consolidation of the Indian Act in 1876.[1] But he was also a determined critic of British Columbia's tight-fisted, punitive approach to Indigenous reserves. In his annual report, he recounted Canada's proposal of eighty acres per family and British Columbia's response:

> They were not prepared to go beyond twenty acres to each family of five persons, that being a larger amount [than] has been previously granted to the Indians of that Province, and more, therefore, as they contended, than they were bound under the terms of the union ... This concession on the part of the Local Government of twenty acres to each Indian family of five persons (inadequate as it would have been considered by the Indians) was subsequently declared by them to apply to those cases only where the Indians, at the time of union with Canada, were not provided with reserves, and not to apply to the old reserves, however much these latter might fall below the average of twenty acres to a family.[2]

Laird then offered an angry rebuke: Indigenous people had been promised "the liberal policy heretofore pursued" before union. British Columbia's refusal to embrace more generous reserves was "little short of a mockery" of that promise. Perhaps with Douglas's more generous reserves in mind, Laird hoped a "calm review" by the province would produce "a spirit of equal liberality."[3] He feared that the ongoing disparity in reserve sizes – which he called "most unsatisfactory" – would cause growing discontent among Indigenous peoples and "serious alarm" among white settlers.[4]

Superintendent Israel Powell's contribution to the 1874 annual report was also provocative and seemingly aimed at Lieutenant-Governor Trutch as well as the BC cabinet. Powell quoted from his 1874 correspondence with Douglas, including Douglas's direction to colonial officials "to leave the extent and selection of lands entirely optional with the Indians who were immediately interested in the Reserves." In Powell's reckoning, this

> system was highly satisfactory to the Indians during the Government of Mr. Douglas, but since that time his successors have, from time to time, at the request of White settlers, who in some localities were envious of the fine tracts given to the Indians, cut them down or reserved other lands not so valuable as those originally laid aside for them.[5]

By this time, Powell had abandoned any pretense of working collegially with Trutch, whether as lieutenant-governor or as chief commissioner of Macdonald's nonofficial Indian Board.

Powell's commentary reiterated his minister's concerns. New reserves of twenty acres per family would be inescapably contentious, he argued, as "many of these lands do not contain two acres to each family of the Tribe interested." Consequently, to "make any discrimination between Tribes by restricting those Indians for whom Reserves have already been made to the quantity set aside for them, and granting a larger or different acreage to those at present unprovided for, is to provoke envious and jealous feelings quite foreign to the intention or aim of either Government." Like Laird, Powell had not entirely abandoned hopes for a more generous BC policy: "I greatly trust that this unfortunate interpretation of our agreement will be of temporary duration, and that this vexed question, upon which depends the contentment of more than 30,000 aborigines, and the peace of the whole Province will be finally settled to the satisfaction of all concerned."[6]

Powell and Laird were not the only public figures critical of British Columbia's opposition to reserve expansion. Governor General Lord Dufferin set out his views in a letter of November 26, 1874, to the Earl of Carnarvon, Britain's secretary of state for the colonies:

> That Province appears to be treating its Indian subjects with great harshness. It does not recognize any obligation to extinguish the Indian title, before dealing with the Crown Lands, and when it creates a reserve instead of allowing eighty acres to each family of five persons – as we do – it will not give more than twenty and this only in new reserves. In the old reserves they have not even half that quantity of land, and yet their Indians appear of a rather superior race, and within the last few years have acquired a considerable stock of cattle and horses.[7]

Prominent clergymen voiced comparable concerns in 1874, including Father Joseph Grandidier of Okanagan Mission. In a long letter to the editor of the *Victoria Standard*, he argued:

> Before settlement of this Province the natives were in possession of it. There was no one to restrain them in that possession ... The whites came, took land, fenced it, and little by little hemmed the Indians in their small reservations ... Their reservations have been repeatedly cut off smaller for the benefit of the whites and the best and most useful part of them taken away till some tribes are corralled on a small piece of ground, as at Canoe Creek and elsewhere, or even have not an inch of ground, as at Williams Lake.

Grandidier took direct aim at British Columbia's miserly allocations for Indigenous lands: "If a white man can scarcely eke out a living with his 320 acres how can an Indian do it with 20?"[8]

Similarly, Roman Catholic bishop Louis-Joseph d'Herbomez wrote to the assistant Indian superintendent, James Lenihan, expressing his fear that Indigenous anger "about their land is far from abating. Bad feelings amongst them are increasing so much that I really fear we may soon have serious troubles." Further delays in addressing the question, d'Herbomez warned, "would very probably expose the Province to a disastrous war."[9]

In a letter to the provincial secretary, John Ash, Lenihan quoted both clerical authorities in a renewed attempt to shift the provincial cabinet's thinking: "I believe the Government will agree with me in the opinion that the cause of the Indians is very fully, justly, and ably stated by the Rev. Father Grandidier. I cannot conceive how the Government can hesitate for a moment in conceding to the Indians demands so just and reasonable."[10] British Columbia's cabinet was unmoved by the appeal. "All that it is 'reasonable and just' to demand of the Provincial Government is that the 13th Section of the Terms of Union be faithfully observed," Ash replied: "Should the Dominion Government be of [the] opinion that concessions beyond those provided for in the said section are necessary, it becomes the duty of that Government to make provisions accordingly."[11] In other words, if the Dominion believed there was a problem, the Dominion should fix it – with no cost to the province.

Four years after its union with Canada, much of British Columbia was without Indigenous reserves of any size. Dominion-provincial disagreement over reserve size brought a halt to the creation of new reserves. In his submission to the 1875 annual report, Powell noted: "No Reserves have been made north of Burrard Inlet on the Coast of the Mainland, nor North of the Shuswap Nationality in the Interior. On the Island no land has been reserved for any of the Tribes north of Comox, nor on the West Coast." He rightly surmised that long delays in reserve creation would end in future demands for their construction from the scraps that remained after white settlement.[12]

British Columbia States Its Case on Indigenous Reserves

The provincial cabinet was offended – if not stung – by David Laird's public criticism of British Columbia's reserve policies. His criticism prompted an official rebuttal, titled "Report of the Government of British Columbia on the Subject of Indian Reserves." The report was prepared by George Walkem (British Columbia's third premier) and endorsed by his cabinet on August 17, 1875. Just four years after union, the Walkem cabinet felt obliged to set out a detailed defence of the province's relationship with Indigenous peoples within its borders.

Walkem's report stated its mission bluntly: to defend "the Indian policy of the Crown Colony" (and, by extension, that of post-Confederation BC governments) with a "view of removing the very unjust impressions respecting it which have been created in the public mind by the Minister of the Interior." According to the report, Laird had completely misconstrued British Columbia's benign and wise conduct of Indigenous relations. The report articulated what the Walkem cabinet hoped would be an enduring narrative in the new province: because of its enlightened Indian policy, the colony had, on the day of Confederation, handed over "to the trusteeship of the Dominion, a community of 40,000 Indians – loyal, peaceable, contented, and in many ways honest and industrious."[13]

This "fact," the report continued, "is in itself the best commentary that can be offered upon the policy pursued towards the Indians during the 13 years preceding Confederation." Its author marvelled that, despite British Columbia's vast expanse of 220,000 square miles, "it is doubtful whether any parallel exists of so large a number of savage tribes, a vast majority of whom never saw a white face until 1858, being successfully controlled and governed by, comparatively speaking, a mere handful of people of a European race."

But "since Confederation," the report continued, "the Indians have undoubtedly become discontented." The Dominion had fuelled discontent by the "notorious fact that 80 acres were promised, of course without authority, to each head of an Indian family before the question of Reserves was even laid before the Provincial Government." The "peaceable and contented" were now "uneasy and restless as to their future." Walkem laid the blame squarely on Ottawa: "The real causes of this failure are attributable to the want of proper information on the part of the Dominion Government of the physical structure of this country and the habits of the Indians."

Canada's large reserves east of the Rockies were unsuitable to British Columbia, Walkem argued, because they promoted "a concentration of Indians upon Reserves," a recipe for isolation and poverty. Instead, under British Columbia's reserve policy, "Natives were invited and encouraged to mingle with and live amongst the white population with a view of weaning them by degrees from savage life, and of gradually leading them by example and precept to adopt habits of peace, honesty, and industry."[14]

In short, small reserves were deemed a boon for Indigenous people's social and economic progress because they would help assimilate them into the dominant white culture. The report attributed the Dominion's affection for larger reserves to an ignorance of British Columbia's challenging geography.

Large reserves might be fine in Ontario, "where there is abundance of good agricultural land," but were "fraught with mischief" and "worse than useless" in British Columbia.[15]

In his province, Walkem argued, reserves "rich in soil and situated in the centre of white settlements" were "unproductive to the country, owing partly to Indian indolence and partly to the good wages offered by the white population." He argued that Indigenous people would be welcomed into the workforce "as labour was scarce and in great demand. Every Indian therefore who could and would work – and they were numerous – was employed in almost every branch of industrial and of domestic life, at wages which would appear excessively high in England or in Canada."[16]

Indigenous labour was, indeed, widely employed during the first decades after Confederation in agriculture, mining, domestic service, fishing and canning, and construction. However, the golden age of Indigenous employment described in the report proved to be short-lived. Jobs often went to white people as they arrived in the province, particularly after the completion of the Canadian Pacific Railway in 1885. Indigenous people were, as historian John Lutz wryly notes, "placed in a functional role that Karl Marx referred to as the 'reserve army of the unemployed.' Only in this case, 'reserve' would have a double meaning." British Columbia would soon be a "white man's province" where businesses were chastised for hiring "Indians."[17]

In one of his most specious arguments, Walkem claimed that the "enlargement of past Reserves is in many instances practically impossible, as they are surrounded by white settlements." At Confederation, the province's white population numbered 8,576 people, largely situated around Victoria on southern Vancouver Island and New Westminster on the Lower Mainland. Enlargement of reserves, where they existed, would have been entirely possible. If reserves were "surrounded," they were surrounded by design: hemmed in by white pre-emptions of prime farmland, "cut back and freed up" from the original Douglas reserves at the direction of the former chief commissioner of lands and works, Joseph Trutch.

The report was an aggregation of self-serving prejudices consistent with Trutch's tight-fisted reserve policies. Neither the Dominion nor James Douglas advocated for larger reserves to discourage Indigenous people from participating in economic or social life; rather, they hoped to provide them with the same opportunities for independence and self-sufficiency enjoyed by white settlers. In 1875, Indigenous people far outnumbered whites. From Walkem's perspective, adding to reserves would mean less land for white settlers. In the boosterism of the day, small settlements would soon grow into mighty cities. Why constrain future growth by expanding reserves? Larger reserves in such circumstances would simply be "wasted land" bereft of value.

Victoria and Ottawa Identify a New Path to Resolve Differences

At the conclusion of his report, Walkem cited suggestions made by missionary William Duncan for resolving the Dominion-provincial dispute over reserve size. Duncan enjoyed some acclaim for his work in the Indigenous community of Metlakatla, on BC's northern coast. Based on his experience, Duncan proposed that the practice of a uniform, formula-based acreage for each First Nation should be abandoned. Band population would be determined by the census, but the nature and quantity of reserve acreage should also reflect the "habits and pursuits" of each Nation. With objective information in hand – such as acreage under cultivation, livestock numbers, and the number of fishing boats owned – reserves would "be enlarged or diminished as the case may be."[18]

Such suggestions found favour with the Walkem cabinet and, in the absence of a more promising path forward, with Canada. David Laird was pleased to announce, in a late addition to his 1875 report, that British Columbia and Canada had "at last agreed upon a basis for the settlement of this grave and complicated controversy," the Joint Indian Reserve Commission (JIRC). He hoped that the joint process would "secure for the Red man a fair and liberal proportion of the lands of the province without in any ways unduly interfering with the interests of the white settlers."[19]

In 1875, Ottawa had used its power of disallowance to strike down British Columbia's Crown Land Act based on the absence of provisions for expanding Indigenous lands. A year later, Canada allowed the passage of a virtually unchanged Crown Land Act to secure the province's participation in the JIRC.[20] It proved to be a poor bargain. Laird's renewed hopes that British Columbia might embrace "a spirit of equal liberality" would go unfulfilled.

Why did Canada not use its opportunity under Article 13 to refer its dispute over the Crown Land Act to the secretary of state for the colonies? Canada may well have obtained a favourable decision from the secretary, but what impact would that decision have had on a political union only a few years old? Canada's minister of justice in 1876, Edward Blake, considered "the condition of the question at issue between the two governments very much improved" since the disallowance of 1875.[21] Why risk a serious setback in Dominion-provincial relations if the JIRC process could be shaped in positive and constructive ways?

British Columbia soon demonstrated why Canada's hopes were ill-founded. The province directed its newly appointed commissioner, Archibald McKinlay, in a memorandum of instruction, not to "allow allotments of any unnecessarily large reserves such as would interfere with White Settlement."[22] The province also wanted the JIRC's work restricted to "places where the whites and natives are living in close proximity," or where overt turmoil demanded attention.[23]

The commission's work was then delayed by another familiar issue: provincial tight-fistedness. Canada held constitutional responsibility for the resolution of Indigenous issues, hence Ottawa should bear the full cost for the JIRC![24] On January 8, 1876, the province officially relented and agreed to the Dominion's proposed formula: the per diem and expenses of each commissioner would be "paid by the Government appointing him," while those of the joint commissioner would be borne equally.[25] A new process was underway, albeit burdened by the lingering policies and prejudices of the late colonial era.

As the JIRC undertook its work in the southern Interior during the summer of 1877, it encountered discord caused by lack of progress on reserve expansion. Of particular concern was growing militancy in the form of a Secwépemc (Shuswap) and Syilx (Okanagan) confederacy. On their arrival in Kamloops, commissioners learned there was widespread apprehension of an "Indian war," a threat they took seriously. In a note to Ottawa, Gilbert Sproat, who'd been jointly appointed BC Indian reserve commissioner by Canada and British Columbia, stated that should the "Shuswap tribes – bold well-armed Horse Indians" go to war, "I do not see what force there is in this country to put them down. There would probably be much bloodshed and an expenditure of many millions of dollars, accompanied by discredit to both governments."[26]

Early and informal meetings with magistrates and local officials underlined such concerns, prompting Sproat and Dominion commissioner Alexander Anderson to dispatch a covert appeal by telegram to Ottawa:

> Indian situation very grave from Kamloops to American frontier. General dissatisfaction – outbreak possible. Indians attempting to confederate. American Indian representatives present at the meeting. Some British Columbian Indians reported to have joined the outbreak across the line ... Very prudent action necessary to avoid bloodshed. We think, after deliberation and consultation that at least 100 mounted police should be secretly sent to Kamloops via Tete Jeune Cache at once. People here quite helpless – any action on their part might precipitate crisis.[27]

Canada declined to send troops, instead suggesting that both governments should remove the "causes of irritation" prompting discord.[28]

David Mills, Canada's new minister of the interior and the Liberal successor to David Laird, believed that the primary irritant was the province's policy "that the Indians have no right in the soil to extinguish ... wholly at variance with that which has been hitherto pursued by the Crown in dealing with the aboriginal population of this Continent." He noted that "British Columbia is the only one [of the former colonies] which has undertaken to deal with the Territory without the Indian title having first been extinguished by treaties with the different native tribes."[29]

He was prepared, however, to let principle yield to pragmatism. He said he was reluctant to "raise the question at present but Local Government must instruct Commissioners to make reserves so large as to completely satisfy Indians."[30] To avert a war, Mills suggested that commissioners should meet "every reasonable demand on the part of the Indians, both as to the extent and locality of their Reservations," perhaps deliberately echoing Douglas's directions to colonial officials over a decade earlier. Mills was not swayed by British Columbia's long-standing claim that it possessed too little agricultural land to accommodate larger reserves. In his view, more generous reserve allocations were possible and practical in a province "so extensive, containing so small a white and so large an Indian population that the Indians should not be made dangerous and discontented by being cooped up on small reservations."[31]

On hearing of Mills's opinion, Premier A.C. Elliott, who replaced Walkem in January 1876, launched an aggressive rebuttal:

> If the Hon. The [sic] Minister of the Interior – at a distance of thousands of miles from the scene, and without any knowledge of the merits of the question or of the facts connected therewith – presumes first to charge to the policy of the Provincial Government the discontent of a portion of Indians of British Columbia and also undertakes to place a definite minimum on the amount of land to be apportioned to the native race, it obviously follows that the necessity for the Commission has ceased to exist.

Elliott assumed the worst regarding Ottawa's intentions and bluntly threatened that the province might "reject the labours of the commissioners."[32]

Elliott was no fan of Mills or his views on the necessity of extinguishing Aboriginal title prior to settlement. Elliott had suffered through similar sentiments being expressed by Governor General Lord Dufferin in an 1876 speech at Government House in Victoria: "In Canada, no Government, whether provincial or central, has failed to acknowledge that the original titles to the land existed in the Indian Tribes and the communities that hunted or wandered over them ... Not until [we negotiate treaties] do we consider that we are entitled to deal with a single acre."[33]

For Elliott, reminders of Aboriginal title were no more welcome from Dufferin than from Mills. He dismissed Dufferin as a vice-regal troublemaker: "Before Confederation a discontented Indian could hardly be found in British Columbia; and the Indian title question ... had no existence until raised during the past year by His Excellency the Governor General."[34] Reflecting a long-standing colonialist attitude, he characterized Dufferin and Mills as the problem rather than the injustices they'd highlighted.

British Columbia Demands Changes in the Wake of the JIRC's Success

Ottawa's reluctance to resolve potential discord with a show of force obliged commissioners to adopt a policy of appeasement. They would try to break up the confederation by allotting the Secwépemc and Syilx large reserves.[35] The JIRC travelled across the southern Interior negotiating with Indigenous leaders and adding or expanding reserves where and when agreements were reached. Their strategy proved successful because, in their own words, they had "steadily and quietly kept in view the need of separating the chiefs, if possible."[36] Sadly, as soon as the immediate threat of violent resistance ended, the BC government was far less tolerant of reserve expansion.

Following the 1877 crisis, Premier Elliott demanded that the JIRC move to a sole-commissioner model, reflecting his growing skepticism about the cost and effectiveness of the three-member commission. He bemoaned "the extremely expensive method now in operation of adjusting the difficulties existing between the white and native population of this province" and suggested that "many years will necessarily elapse before the work can be completed; while the costs to both Governments must be excessive, and entirely disproportionate to the results attained." Elliott wanted the commission to confine its labour to "places where the whites and natives are living in close proximity, and to those localities where the Indians are dissatisfied with the area of land of which they now hold possession."[37]

He demanded, in short, a continuation of the colonial practice of laying out "reserves synchronously with the settlement of the district by the whites."

The Dominion initially rejected British Columbia's demand for a sole commissioner but soon reluctantly acceded to it. Ottawa's resolve dissipated in the face of British Columbia's obstructionism, particularly after Sir John A. Macdonald's Conservatives returned to power in the 1878 election. The joint commission was replaced by a single Indian commissioner, Gilbert Sproat, with the proviso that any additions to reserve lands he proposed would require federal and provincial approval. Sproat's tenure would prove to be brief and turbulent. His approach to reserve creation quickly brought him into conflict with politicians still wed to colonial policies and prejudices.

5

Colonial Prejudice Meets Purposeful Ignorance

With Sir John A. Macdonald's Conservatives returned to office in 1878, Joseph Trutch once again became a man of influence. Time and experience had not shifted the colonial prejudices that Trutch had brought to the role of chief commissioner of lands and works fourteen years earlier. He nursed a continuing contempt for officials who held views more liberal than his own, and he exploited his enduring relationship with Macdonald to undermine them.

Senator and soon-to-be lieutenant-governor Clement Cornwall, an early settler in the Ashcroft area, requested Trutch's assistance in 1880 to secure "the speedy appointment of lands to certain bands of Indians" in the southern Cariboo and "north through which the waggon road runs." The Joint Indian Reserve Commission's (JIRC's) additions to southern Interior reserves had heightened Indigenous people's expectations in adjacent regions, and their agitation had sparked fears among Cornwall's white neighbours. "Although for the past few years such specious promises have been made to the Indians with reference to this important question," Cornwall noted, "yet in many parts nothing whatever has been done and no one can be surprised at the feeling of uneasiness and insecurity which is excited among the Indians."[1]

Trutch shared Cornwall's correspondence with Macdonald, noting at the outset that he was "far from sharing the apprehensions" of "such uprising" or "active disturbance." Trutch also took the opportunity to disparage Indian commissioner Gilbert Sproat: "Almost all the questions at issue with the Indians in this Province are such only as would find easy solution if their adjustment were entrusted to an Agent of acknowledged capability, local experience and established reputation."[2] Trutch likely had himself in mind, or perhaps his brother-in-law Peter O'Reilly. On a separate occasion, he advised Macdonald that Sproat, "acting as uncontrolled and absolute agent of the two governments, has been led into mistakes ... which have occasioned much dissatisfaction amongst the white population of the districts he visited and material wrong to individuals in many instances."[3]

Trutch was not alone in his assessment. Sproat's performance as Indian commissioner regularly raised the ire of provincial cabinet ministers. Sproat knew James Douglas and admired and emulated his land policies.[4] His admiration inevitably led to conflict with provincial officials. Sproat was deeply troubled by what he had seen and learned from his experience with First Nations – small or nonexistent reserves compounded by the loss or alienation of burial grounds, ancestral villages, fisheries, water sources, and previously cultivated lands.[5] He was also troubled by the province's approval of new pre-emptions despite his appeals to desist until land questions had been fully settled.[6]

Sproat was disposed to right wrongs when he found them, gaining him powerful enemies, including prominent members of Parliament. Those parliamentarians included Frank Barnard (representing Yale) and Amor De Cosmos (Victoria). A House of Commons debate in 1880 showed how little their ideas and prejudices had evolved since they'd been leading voices in the BC Legislative Council of 1867 demanding reductions to reserves. Barnard initiated the 1880 debate with a motion cataloguing his dissatisfaction with Sproat. His timing was auspicious: his audience within the house included current and former prime ministers, a former minister of the interior, and a former BC premier (De Cosmos). Each spoke in the wake of Barnard's comments, offering a rare glimpse of competing approaches to Indigenous relations.

Barnard employed a familiar narrative, claiming that before Sproat's appointment in 1877, "we had little or no trouble with the Indians, the settlers agreeing with them and working with them in harmony." He conveniently ignored the turmoil that had led to the creation of the JIRC. In Barnard's view, Sproat "seemed to think that all he had to do was to give the Indians whatever land he fancied, whether it was the property of the Government, or of actual bona fide settlers." First Nations were once again being accused of stripping away lands alienated by settler pre-emptions, as they had been by the Legislative Council of the Colony of British Columbia in 1864.[7]

Barnard was upset that Sproat had set aside First Nation fishing stations, thus impairing the progress of white settlement. For Barnard, fishing was synonymous with indolence. "Securing the fishing station only tends to encourage the Indian in habits of idleness, and seriously retards his civilization," he declared. "We contend that it is wrong to afford Indians an opportunity of following nomadic habits, instead of encouraging them to engage in agriculture, and to settle in the lands allotted to them."

Unlike during the 1867 Legislative Council debate, Barnard's narrative was challenged. David Mills, Premier Elliott's nemesis in 1877, was now, following the Conservatives' electoral victory in 1878, a former minister of the interior. In a direct rebuttal of Barnard's assertions, Mills defended Sproat's work as essential because the amount of land allotted to Indigenous people "was so limited, that it was impossible for them to subsist." He reminded Barnard and Macdonald, also in attendance, "that the Terms upon which British Columbia entered the Union overlooked entirely the Indian claims to the territories where the Indian rights had not been surrendered." Mills reiterated the key point delivered by Governor General Dufferin in Victoria a few years earlier: "I think it is the only instance in the whole history of British colonization in North America, where the Government has undertaken to deal with the land without first securing the extinction of the Indian titles."

De Cosmos's response to Mills touched on familiar colonialist themes. "Up to the time of Confederation," the former premier said, "we had no trouble with our Indians at all. Occasionally, an Indian depredation was committed, but it was soon suppressed ... After Confederation all the Dominion Government was expected to do under the Terms of Union was to deal as liberally with the Indians as before Confederation." He accused the former Alexander Mackenzie Liberal government of going far beyond the spirit and intent of Article 13 in making "Indians a privileged class, in regard to the ownership of land." De Cosmos declared the "proper way – the just way – ought to have been to ignore the so-called Indian title ... That his right to hold all he could use would be respected, but his so-called title to land that he has not made and never could use, would be disregarded."

Alexander Mackenzie, now leader of the Opposition, was surprised to hear De Cosmos, "who was so very zealous of his own rights and the rights of the people of British Columbia, a few nights ago, propound so inhuman a theory regarding Indians." Had the Dominion pursued the course suggested by De Cosmos, "we would have had Indian wars desolating the whole country. I maintain that we have no right to the soil until we arrange with those who inhabited the country originally, and if we have paid too little for the lands that was the fault of the negotiators."

Macdonald also entered the debate, if only to disparage Mackenzie's views on Indigenous rights and title. "The Indians should be protected," Macdonald stated, "but at the same time the progress of any large section of the country should not be impeded by the enforcement of any philanthropic idea of protecting the Indian even against the attempt to win him from his semi-savage customs." Macdonald ignored the unequal treatment of Indigenous Nations east and west of the Rockies with respect to land allocation and treaty negotiations. Perhaps with Trutch's advice in mind, Macdonald offered no defence of Sproat.

One year later, Trutch's continuing role as Macdonald's "confidential agent" was highlighted in another debate when De Cosmos questioned the prime minister (in his role as minister of the interior) about a land dispute between a settler, Alexander Munro, and the Cowichan Nation.[8] De Cosmos believed that a report from Trutch to Macdonald was germane to the dispute and demanded access to it. Macdonald was not sympathetic. The report, he said, was "of a confidential nature, and cannot be brought down"; Trutch had been engaged "to secure a confidential report with reference to all Dominion interests in British Columbia. It would destroy his influence if his confidential report were laid before the House."[9]

Angered by Macdonald's response, De Cosmos declared: "We must infer that Mr. Trutch has been sent out to British Columbia as a spy, with a view of prying into any little matters which may happen in that Province, and reporting to the Government thereon." Better, said De Cosmos, "for the Government to appoint honest, capable and responsible men as its officers, so as to do away with the necessity of appointing a person as a spy." He was far from satisfied with Macdonald's suggestion to "leave the matter before the country and the House." In a final rhetorical flourish, De Cosmos promised to protest "until the time arrives when I shall see spies and confidential reporters ... driven from the shores of British Columbia." He and Trutch may have been colleagues for years, but they were certainly not friends.[10]

This angry exchange drew the attention of the Opposition, including the new Liberal leader, Edward Blake, who suggested that employing a confidential agent to provide secret reports was "new machinery to our system of government altogether" and "rather extraordinary." In his defence, Macdonald replied: "One reason why this report should not be brought down: it is because this report brings up to a considerable degree the delicate question of the relations between the Indians and the Government in British Columbia." Former prime minister Alexander Mackenzie was not persuaded. "That is all settled," he contended. "No, it is not, unfortunately," replied Macdonald. On that point, at least, Macdonald proved correct.

Sproat Resigns and Reserve Creation Returns to Colonial Hands

Beset by criticism from Ottawa and overt hostility from Victoria, Sproat resigned from his post in 1880, just three years into his work as commissioner. His resignation signalled the loss of a rare sympathetic, enlightened, and knowledgeable voice in British Columbia's Indigenous relations. To cap the province's victory, Macdonald instructed Superintendent Israel Powell to consult on all important policy questions with his "confidential agent," Joseph Trutch, and the BC premier.[11] Sproat was replaced by a less controversial figure, at least from a white settler perspective: Peter O'Reilly, the colonial official and politician who had assisted his brother-in-law – Chief Commissioner Trutch – with pre-Confederation reserve creation and reduction.

As Indian commissioner from 1880 to 1898, O'Reilly maintained the same frenetic pace of reserve creation as he had before Confederation.[12] Following Trutch's enduring direction, O'Reilly's focus for reserve creation was minimizing interference with white settlement. Transferring British Columbia's public lands to Canada for reserve creation was no small challenge in an ever-tight-fisted province, but the new commissioner had at least one advantage: he spoke the language of key provincial officials.

When O'Reilly visited the Soda Creek (Xatśūll) First Nation in 1881, Chief Commosaltz complained that the "Queen had sold their land, and had taken the money that had been received for it." O'Reilly refused to acquire lands already alienated by pre-emption, but he eventually allotted 1,100 acres for a Soda Creek reserve. He noted the marginal character of the lands: "It is difficult to conceive anything less suitable for the purpose, it being situated on a steep hill side and containing barely 45 acres for agricultural purposes."[13]

O'Reilly encountered a similar problem in the neighbouring Canoe Creek and Alkali Lake districts, where all potential reserve lands had been sold as pre-emptions by the province.[14] British Columbia's seventh premier, William Smithe, felt free to advise O'Reilly:

> The Indians at Alkali Lake, as well as at Soda and Canoe Creeks, certainly would seem to have urgent claims for relief at the hands of the Dominion Government; and I cannot but think that the Government have not fully realized their responsibilities in respect of the Indians who are in their charge. It is manifestly wrong that the Indians, whose guardianship the Federal Government assumed at Confederation, should be left, in some instances, to starve, simply because the Provincial Government cannot afford to do that which never

> ought to have been expected, never asked for at their hands, that is, to purchase improved property at high prices, and give it to the Dominion Government for Indian purposes.[15]

From Smithe's perspective, problems derived from British Columbia's settlement policies should be resolved by Canada's purse – a theme that would resonate in decades to come. Canada typically relented in the face of the province's intransigence – for example, in one instance, it purchased several preemptions to allot as reserves because the best lands were gone.[16]

A similar story emerged on Vancouver Island, where O'Reilly assured British Columbia's chief commissioner of lands and works that seventeen small reserves on the west coast of Vancouver Island were "except as fishing stations ... very worthless, the land being unsuitable for cultivation. They do not encroach on the claim of any white settler, nor is it likely they will retard settlement at any future time."[17] Concerns about Indigenous people's independence and self-sufficiency – so central to James Douglas's vision – were inconsequential during O'Reilly's leadership. Indigenous people's anger, frustration, and despair with his small, scattered reserves remain to this day.

A Dominion-Provincial Agreement Revealed, with No Indigenous Participation

In its annual report for 1887, Canada's Department of Indian Affairs (DIA) offered some welcome news. Conservative minister Thomas White, the superintendent-general of Indian affairs, declared after discussions with his BC counterpart, the provincial secretary, John Robson, that "there are now no outstanding [Indigenous relations] questions which have not either been settled or which are not in the course of settlement on a basis agreed to by the Dominion and the Provincial Governments." Robson, who would later serve as BC premier from 1889 to 1892, had considerable experience with Indigenous issues going back to the colonial era; he came "vested with the necessary authority to act for his Government in arranging a final settlement of all questions at issue."[18] What neither he nor White possessed was even the remotest concern for the legitimate demands of Indigenous peoples.

The 1887 annual report was an unintended reminder of how little had changed in British Columbia since the late colonial years. White claimed that peace had prevailed across the Dominion in 1887,

> excepting at Kootenay, where the Indians of Chief Isadore's Band, led by the chief, rescued an Indian prisoner who was incarcerated on suspicion of having murdered two white miners about three years before. This act of lawlessness on the part of the Indians occasioned considerable apprehension in the minds of the comparatively few white settlers in that region, and such strong representations were made to the Government that it was decided to dispatch a force of seventy-five North-West Mounted Police.[19]

White added: "To increase the embarrassment, the Indians – Chief Isadore himself being the principal complainant – were not satisfied with the reserve lands allotted to them, which they claimed should have been more extensive and have embraced certain favorite tracts which had not been included in them."[20]

White's scorn for Chief Isadore's complaints was at odds with reports from other officials. A delegation comprising Indian Superintendent Powell, Commissioner O'Reilly, and British Columbia's chief commissioner of lands and works, Forbes George Vernon, toured the Kootenays in September 1887. The men concluded, in O'Reilly's words, that existing reserves were "sufficient, if properly utilized," but "with a view to allaying all feeling of dissatisfaction on the part of the Indians," three new reserves were added, 1,038 acres in total, including the "favorite tracts" identified by Chief Isadore.[21]

Powell's commentary suggests the decision may have been the object of vigorous debate:

> Across the Provincial line ... they [the Kootenay/Ktunaxa] associate with and see the Indians of the North-West [Alberta], who receive annuities and are fed by the Federal Government by which very large reserves have also been set aside. Across the American frontier they have kinspeople who are supplied with splendid lands, grist and sawmills, industrial schools, and so on. Their jealousy and dissatisfaction, therefore, in having their own aboriginal rights ignored, and in not being recipients of any such gifts as those mentioned, are not to be wondered at.[22]

Clearly, Powell had not lost his concerns about the unfair distribution of reserves east and west of the Rockies, which had fuelled his battle with BC cabinets over a decade earlier.

White's claim of "no outstanding questions" in Indigenous affairs contrasted sharply with reports from DIA agents in all corners of British Columbia in 1887. Agent P. McTiernan of the Williams Lake Agency noted that the Bridge River First Nation (Xwísten) was heavily engaged in mining on their reserve near Lillooet:

> Like all landed proprietors, these Indians are naturally jealous of their right and strongly object to anyone except themselves mining on their reserve. I have at various times warned miners to cease their operations and leave the reserve. But the Provincial Government contends that mining is free to all – on a reserve as well as on a whiteman's land – and has so instructed the Government agent located at Lillooet.[23]

In a stark and long-running departure from Governor Douglas's approach to Indigenous gold miners in 1858, British Columbia was loathe to yield subsurface rights even on the smallest of reserves.

Given the paucity of land and resources on many reserves, DIA agents frequently reported that band members were seeking off-reserve employment. Annual reports for 1886 and 1887 contained a strange twist. R.H. Pidcock, Indian agent for the Lower Fraser, raised concerns about "the tax of $3 per head from all Indians found working off their reserves." He stated that the BC government had "collected taxes from some Indians at Yale, Hope, and Cheam. They believe it is the intention of the Government to enforce the payment of $3 from all Indians of eighteen years of age and upwards. This is troubling them very much." The tax was likely part of the shift to race-based employment, but there was no statutory basis for it.[24] A relieved Pidcock reported a year later that "abandonment" of the tax had "allayed" Indigenous people's "fear that they were about to be dealt with unfairly."[25]

Several DIA agents noted persistent discontent regarding the size and quality of reserve lands and a lack of water to sustain crops.[26] And in the southern Interior, some reserve boundaries remained in doubt a decade after the Joint Indian Reserve Commission's recommendations. "The reserves in the Similkameen Valley have not as yet been wholly defined," Laing Meeson wrote, "and not one of them has been surveyed. This unsettled condition of so important a question is highly detrimental to the advancement of these Indians." Not far away, as the Penticton (snpink'tn) Band was preparing to add livestock enclosures and other improvements to its lands, Meeson expressed "doubt as to the limits of this reserve, as it has not been surveyed, and preemption records are being made by settlers on the commonage lying immediately north of the reserve."[27]

Indigenous people's discontent with reserve allocations never disappeared and was highlighted a decade later during the negotiation of Treaty 8 in the northeastern corner of British Columbia. Treaty 8 provided land allocations consistent with Canada's Numbered Treaties east of the Rockies but vastly disproportionate to British Columbia's other comparatively tiny reserves.

Accounting for Treaty 8

Every new Indigenous relations minister in British Columbia is obliged to ask (as I did in 2009): Why did the province, historically resistant to large reserves, approve Treaty 8, which granted 640 acres per family? Given the province's longstanding opposition to large reserves, what made this treaty an exception?

In his 1981 report to Canada's Department of Indian and Northern Affairs, Dennis Madill describes Treaty 8 as happening "almost accidentally." But, given its history, the province seems an unlikely host for accidental reform. Nevertheless, serendipity certainly played a role.[28]

Treaty 8 was, first and foremost, a product of British Columbia's powerful desire to secure a transnational railway. That goal obliged the province, under Article 11 of the Terms of Union Act, to compensate Canada through the creation of the Peace River Block and the Railway Belt, a corridor of approximately twenty miles on either side of the Canadian Pacific Railway main line. With the transfer of the Peace River Block, Canada assumed control over fourteen thousand square kilometres (or 3.5 million acres) of land within British Columbia's borders east of the Rocky Mountains.

Dominion control over the Peace River Block kept opportunities for white settlement to a minimum. The northeast had not experienced the same white-Indigenous tensions as seen in southern British Columbia, including demands from settlers for governmental intervention. The situation changed when the Klondike Gold Rush of the 1890s brought migration of many miners through the North-West Territories (northern Alberta) and the Peace River Block of British Columbia. This migration produced Indigenous complaints of theft and disruption, resulting in "serious Indian resistance ... at Fort St. John in June 1898 when 500 Indians refused to allow police and miners to enter the area until a treaty was signed."[29]

The magnitude of the resistance left the federal and provincial governments with few viable alternatives. Clifford Sifton, minister of the interior and superintendent-general of Indian affairs, supported treaty creation and appointed David Laird, lieutenant-governor of the North-West Territories, to lead the process. Laird embraced the opportunity despite (or perhaps because of) his battles with Joseph Trutch and George Walkem over reserve reform over twenty years before.

Sifton considered whether Treaty 8 should reflect political or natural boundaries. He chose the natural boundaries based on his assessment of the political and cultural ties among Indigenous peoples east of the Rockies: "Had the division line between the Indians been artificial instead of natural such difference in treatment would have been fraught with grave danger and have been the fruitful source of such trouble to both the Dominion and the Provincial Governments."[30] Sifton was undoubtedly aware, from Laird and others, of British Columbia's fierce post-Confederation resistance to reserve expansion, but small and scattered reserves were not going to placate Indigenous leaders in the northeast.

The boundaries of the Peace River Block were not formalized until 1907, but the Dominion took strategic advantage of British Columbia's lingering liability by suggesting in a Privy Council memorandum that "it is not at present clear whether it will be necessary to set apart any land [beyond land in the Peace River Block] for a reserve or reserves for Indians in that part of the province ... covered by the proposed treaty." In short, the memorandum suggested that Canada was promising to solve an "Indian land problem" largely, if not entirely, with Dominion lands, always a seductive suggestion in Victoria. The memorandum was couched in language that would resonate with the BC cabinet. Treaty making was "in the interest of the Province," it argued, because "the country to be treated for should be thrown open to development and the lives and property of those who may enter thereon safeguarded by the making of provision which will remove all hostile feeling from the minds of the Indians and lead them to peacefully acquiesce in the changing conditions."[31]

The Dominion would negotiate Treaty 8 without consultation with the provincial government, but only after it asked British Columbia to "formally acquiesce in the action."[32] Notably, the province declined to respond. It avoided a clash over Indigenous issues by neither openly agreeing nor opposing the treaty.[33] British Columbia's newly minted Charles Semlin government purposefully ignored the proposed treaty. The province wanted peaceful development in the northeast, and overt opposition to treaty making might lead to an "Indian war."[34] In the 1890s, the province had no idea of the potential for oil and gas discoveries in the northeast.[35] Further, the late 1890s were – even by BC standards – a period of political turbulence in Victoria, with six different premiers forming governments within five years. The Peace River Block must have seemed a long distance away, politically as well as physically.

Confirmation of the province's approach came a century later in the Supreme Court of British Columbia when lawyers argued, in opposition to the McLeod Lake Band's petition for adhesion to Treaty 8, that "treaty commissioners were not authorized by, nor did they enter into any obligations on behalf of the Province."[36] The province was happy in 1899 to have Canada make the problem go away and equally happy in 1996 to claim it had played no part in creating Treaty 8. In a province almost entirely devoid of treaties, Treaty 8's formula of 640 acres per family would have been a colonialist nightmare.

At the dawn of the twentieth century, developments in the northeast corner of British Columbia contrasted starkly with the province's approach to treaty making and reserve construction. To the west of Treaty 8 lands, which had 160 acres per person, the McLeod Lake Band had a 286-acre reserve, created in 1892 by Indian commissioner Peter O'Reilly, which provided only 5.4 acres per person. Even amid the rugged expanse of the Rocky Mountains, provincial tight-fistedness prevailed.[37]

The Road to a Royal Commission

The JIRC and its successor, the Indian Reserve Commission, created approximately one thousand reserves between 1877 and 1908, most drawn from provincial Crown lands as anticipated under Article 13 of the Terms of Union. However, tensions reignited early in the twentieth century, putting all of that work in peril. British Columbia had long demanded reversionary rights on reserve lands abandoned or surrendered.[38] The province argued that the Indigenous population had declined substantially while acreage consigned to reserves had grown. In 1907, the BC attorney general, Frederick J. Fulton, stated: "This being the case, it is submitted that the Reserve question should be readjusted, and the surplus lands over what is reasonably sufficient should be surrendered to the Province."[39]

In the first decades after union, British Columbia's insistence on reversionary rights had led the Dominion to avoid any surrenders of BC reserve lands. However, Ottawa was obliged to reconsider its position in 1905 when the Grand Trunk Pacific Railway Company proposed the purchase of Ts'msyen Reserve lands for a railway terminal at Prince Rupert. The Grand Trunk request, reinforced by general settlement pressures, prompted Ottawa to amend the Indian Act in 1906, permitting the surrender of unused reserve lands. In turn, Victoria reasserted its reversionary claim to Ts'msyen (or any other) surplus reserve lands.

Attempts by Ottawa to reach a negotiated solution came to an abrupt halt with BC Order in Council 125, approved by the provincial cabinet on February 28, 1907, and based on a report from Fulton that stated:

> The Dominion are not entitled to hold in trust more lands as Indian Reserves in the Province of British Columbia than are reasonably required for the personal use and occupation of the Indians. It is further abundantly clear that the title of the Indians in these reserves is simply a right of use and occupation, and that the Dominion Government holds no proprietary rights in these reserves ... and that when any Indian Band or Nation abandons or surrenders its right or title to a reserve, the entire beneficial interest in such reserve or portion of a reserve, immediately becomes vested in the Province, freed from incumbrances of any kind.[40]

British Columbia's position, as summarized by Hamar Foster, was that "surrender simply perfected the underlying provincial title, and the land – or, if the sale was complete, the proceeds of the sale – became the property of the province." In short, British Columbia treated Indigenous land rights "as legally non-existent ... beyond the temporary right to occupy them."[41] The Indian Reserve Commission was terminated on April 3, 1908, when British Columbia refused to allot any further land for reserve creation.[42] Victoria and Ottawa were once again at loggerheads.

Indigenous people's anger and activism played an important role in the creation of the McKenna-McBride Commission, just as they had three decades earlier with the JIRC. The early twentieth century saw persistent and growing demands for the resolution of the Aboriginal title question coupled with perennial complaints regarding the quantity and quality of reserve lands. For example, the Secwépemc Chief, Basil David; the Squamish Chief, Joe Capilano; and the Cowichan Chief, Charley Tsilpaymilt, travelled to London in 1906 to appeal directly to King Edward VII on the issues of Aboriginal title and the inadequacy of "lands allotted to our people for their maintenance."[43] Their appeal was heard by the King but directed back to Canada, where it was largely ignored.

Demands for recognition of Aboriginal title were rekindled by the Cowichan Petition of 1909, prepared by lawyers Arthur O'Meara and J.M. Clark on behalf of the Cowichan Tribes. The petition declared that "British Imperial law, and in particular the Royal Proclamation of 1763, recognized Aboriginal title. In failing to respect this, British Columbia had violated that law, and, given the opposition of the provincial government to negotiations, the title question should be referred to the courts – in this case, directly to the Judicial Committee of the Privy Council."[44] A legal review of the Cowichan Petition, conducted by lawyer T.R.E. McInnes on behalf of the Dominion government, confirmed its merits.

A few months later, Canada's deputy minister of justice reached a tentative agreement with his BC counterpart to refer title questions to the Supreme Court of Canada, only to see it rejected by the premier, Richard McBride.[45] McBride feared that reference to the court "would jeopardize the very large sums of money already invested in this province by English and other investors"; hence, Aboriginal title was "too serious a matter to be submitted to any court, however competent from a legal point of view." In turn, the prime minister, Sir Wilfrid Laurier, expressed his regret that the "vexed question" of whether in British Columbia "there is such a thing as the Indian title," had yet to be determined. "This is a fair issue," he said, "and ought to be met squarely."[46]

First Nations fought on despite the power imbalance they faced. In 1910, Chiefs from the Interior stated their case before Laurier, who was visiting Kamloops. They again drew attention to the ongoing disparity between land allocations for white pre-emptions and those for reserves: "We have no grudge against the white race as a whole nor against the settlers, but we want to have an equal chance with them to make a living." The Chiefs expressed confidence in receiving "fair and honourable treatment" from Laurier and "noted of late the attitude of your government towards the Indian rights movement of this country and we hope with your help our wrongs may at last be righted."[47]

White settlement (sometimes in the form of huge ranches in the Interior, such as the Douglas Lake Cattle Company's 110,000 acres) had curtailed Indigenous people's opportunities to hunt, fish, and access grazing lands.[48] "We are being more and more restricted to our reservations which in most places are unfit or inadequate to maintain us," the Chiefs noted. Without Laurier's intervention to "get fair play," they feared "most of us [will] be reduced to beggary or to continuous wage slavery." The Chiefs condemned "the whole policy of the BC government towards the Indian tribes of this country as utterly unjust, shameful and blundering in every way. We denounce same as being the main cause of the unsatisfactory condition of Indian affairs in this country and the animosity and friction with the whites." The Chiefs wanted a "square deal" from the government and Laurier's help to secure it.[49]

Laurier appeared genuinely sympathetic and sincere in his support of Aboriginal title, as reflected in his comments to a delegation in Ottawa on April 26, 1911:

> The matter for us to immediately consider is whether we can bring the Government of British Columbia into Court with us. We think it is our duty to have the matter enquired into. The Government of British Columbia may be right or wrong in their assertion that the Indians have no claim whatever. Courts of Law are just for that purpose – where a man asserts a claim and it is denied by another. But we do not know if we can force a Government into Court. If we can find a way I may say we shall surely do so, because everybody will agree it is a matter of good government to have no one resting under a grievance.

Laurier correctly concluded that the "Indians will continue to believe they have a grievance until it has been settled by the Court that they have a claim, or that they have no claim."[50]

Indigenous leaders renewed their efforts to shift provincial policy at a 1911 meeting with McBride in Victoria. The Interior Tribes of British Columbia, along with the Indian Rights Association and the Nishga Land Committee, made their case for settling the question of Aboriginal title through the courts. "It is a painful matter," their submission declared, "to see our lands sold to speculators whilst many of our people have not sufficient land to maintain their families; and to even these small portions we are told that we have no title." McBride confirmed that the province's disposition to consider the "title question" had not improved in the twenty-four years since Premier Smithe's contemptuous dismissal of the Nisga'a and Ts'msyen delegation in 1887. He declared that "Indians were well satisfied with their position" despite agitation prompted "by the pernicious advice of some unscrupulous whites." Consequently, "Government would not take the [title] question to the Courts feeling that there was no proper case for submission."[51]

The meeting with McBride left Indigenous leaders angry and frustrated. "You know how the BC government has laid claim to all our tribal territories, and has practically taken possession of same without treaty and without payment," Chiefs stated in a subsequent letter to Frank Oliver, Laurier's minister of the interior and superintendent-general of Indian affairs. "You know how they also claim the reservations, nominally set apart for us. We want to know if we own any land at all in this country." The Chiefs also raised questions and concerns about the quantity and quality of reserve lands:

> Why should we be expected to make a good living on four or five acres of land, whilst ... 320 acres was deemed none too much for a white man? A few reserves may appear large on paper, but what amount of good land is in them? Most of them consist chiefly of more or less barren side hills, rock slides, timbered bottoms hard to clear, and arid flats devoid of water for irrigation. We cannot live on and cultivate rocks, side hills and places where we can get no water.[52]

The Chiefs rightly deplored the inequality of opportunity inherent in British Columbia's disparate approaches to the allocation of lands for reserves and lands for pre-emption. Injustice prevailed, even after four decades of provincehood. It would not be relieved by the creation of a royal commission.

6

A Royal Commission Frustrates Hopes

The tension between British Columbia and Canada regarding Indigenous reserves was sometimes masked by shared processes such as the Joint Indian Reserve Commission (JIRC). The disparity between the size of reserves east and west of the Rocky Mountains continued to be a focal point for Indigenous people's discontent. As white settlement grew, so, too, did anger, particularly when small reserves were weighed against much larger pre-emptions, land grants, and timber licences secured by settlers. Over the forty years since Confederation, British Columbia's white population had grown from 8,576 to 336,094 while the Indigenous population declined from 25,661 to 20,174.[1] Whites were now dominant numerically and politically.

The expansion of white settlement brought more land-use conflicts. The Royal Commission on Indian Affairs in the Province of British Columbia (known as the McKenna-McBride Commission) was launched in 1912 with the lofty goal of settling "all differences between the Governments of the Dominion and the Province respecting Indian lands and Indian Affairs generally."[2] The commission was one more attempt by Ottawa and Victoria to resolve conflicting approaches to Indigenous relations; sadly, it soon proved to be yet another failed attempt to reconcile conflict and fulfill the expectations of First Nations.

Commission Accepts a Bold Mandate, Excluding the Title Question

The Dominion general election of 1911 saw Laurier defeated by Conservative Robert Borden, and any inclination to force British Columbia into the courts on the Aboriginal title question evaporated with his defeat. J.A.J. McKenna, a lawyer and career public servant in Ottawa and western Canada, was dispatched to Victoria for one more attempt to persuade McBride to support (or at least allow) a judicial reference on the title question. McBride again rejected the suggestion, contending that "the public interest was paramount, and the question was dropped owing to the seriousness of then raising that question."[3]

McKenna succeeded, however, in securing McBride's support for a joint process "respecting Indian lands and Indian Affairs generally": a memorandum of agreement was signed by McKenna and McBride on September 24, 1912, creating the commission that bears their names. According to Duncan Campbell Scott, a senior Dominion official, the "claim for aboriginal title came within the scope of his [McKenna's initial vision for the] commission, but the Prime Minister of British Columbia [McBride] refused to discuss the question ... Mr. McKenna made an exhaustive memorandum to Sir Richard on that subject, and endeavoured to get him to consent to that, but he would not."[4]

McKenna was soon appointed by Canada to the commission, along with Nathaniel White, a lawyer from Nova Scotia. British Columbia also appointed two commissioners: James P. Shaw, a Conservative member of the Legislative Assembly for Kamloops (successor to Frederick J. Fulton), and Day Hort Macdowall, a former member of Parliament for the North-West Territories (Saskatchewan) residing in Victoria. Edward L. Wetmore, a former chief justice of the Supreme Court of Saskatchewan, was jointly selected by the parties to chair the commission. Reflecting the attitudes of the day, not a single representative was appointed by Indigenous people to represent their interests.

The McKenna-McBride Commission's mandate, like that of the JIRC thirty-six years earlier, was founded on Metlakatla missionary William Duncan's belief that reserves should be custom-made to reflect the "habits and pursuits" of each First Nation rather than constructed around a supposedly arbitrary, population-based formula. Section 2 of the memorandum provided the commission with the "power to adjust [the] acreage of Indian reserves." Reserves that contained "more land than reasonably required" could be "reduced to such acreage as the Commission think reasonably sufficient for the purposes of such Indians." The memorandum promised that reductions would occur only "with the consent of the Indians," a promise both governments would later ignore.[5]

On the other side of the ledger, if the commission determined that an "insufficient quantity of land" had been set aside, it could expand reserves as "deemed appropriate" (subject, as always, to British Columbia's agreement on any subsequent diminution of provincial public lands). Commissioners could also set aside land for "any Band of Indians for whom land has not already been reserved."[6] More than forty years after Confederation, some BC bands remained officially landless, reflecting the long-standing policy that reserve creation should follow white settlement, not precede it.

The commission visited almost all of the sixteen Department of Indian Affairs (DIA) agencies in British Columbia over three years from 1913 through 1915. The one exception was the Treaty 8 area east of the Rocky Mountains. In that case, the commission concluded "that the allotment of lands ... should be in accordance with the terms ... of the said Treaty" – namely, reserves "not to exceed one square mile [640 acres] for each family of five" or "one hundred and sixty acres to each Indian."

The commission initially hoped to address the issue of "landless nomads" west of the Peace River Block, but in 1916, it decided "that the country wherein these Indians are found is so difficult of access, and information as to the location of the Indians so indefinite that visitation to the territory" would be neither practical nor useful.[7] That decision would later carry profound implications for the Tsay Keh Dene Nation (then called the Fort Graham Band, subsequently the Ingenika Band) as the federal and provincial governments struggled to resolve the dispossession and dislocation resulting from the construction of the W.A.C. Bennett Dam and Williston Reservoir.

Commission Hearings Show Colonial Prejudices Are Alive and Well

The commission had two broad audiences during its travels: municipal and business leaders and – invariably in separate venues – Indigenous leaders and band members. Commissioners were solicitous of the former but all too frequently impatient, disrespectful, and contemptuous of the latter. Chair Edward Wetmore often set the tone for hearings in Indigenous communities. Southern Interior First Nations soon experienced his arrogant and confrontational approach.

The commission's 1913 visit to Enderby in the Okanagan Agency got off to a rough start. Some Indigenous leaders viewed the commission and its mandate with considerable suspicion (rightly so, as subsequent history would demonstrate). Among those nursing suspicions was Sam Pierre of the Splatsin (Spallumcheen) Band. In turn, Wetmore revealed impatience bordering on contempt (ironically while lecturing on contempt of court) in a brief exchange with Pierre:

Chair Wetmore: How many acres are cleared on the Salmon River Reserve and under cultivation?

Sam Pierre: I will ask you a question first. What do you intend to do with the land that is already under cultivation? If you tell me your purpose, I will explain it all.

Wetmore: I can't say anything about that until we find out what the character of the Reserve is like.

Pierre: I am in the same fix and would like to know what is going to be done with the land that is already under cultivation.

Wetmore: We are not here to be examined by the Indians. We are here to examine the Indians, and if we cannot find out what we want here we will find it elsewhere. Do you know that we could place you in prison for not answering our questions? We have all the powers of a Court, and we can deal with persons who refuse to answer questions as Contempt of Court, but we don't intend to go that far.

Pierre: I want to find out right here in Court today what is right myself, and what was your object for putting me in gaol.

Wetmore: Because you did not answer our questions. But we don't intend to do that – I am only telling you the powers we have.

Pierre: Well if you will tell us, I will tell you the whole thing.

Wetmore: I won't tell you anything. If you don't want to tell us, we will get the information elsewhere.[8]

Their discussion concluded, and the commission, as Wetmore promised, sought information elsewhere, confirming Sam Pierre's suspicions.

Wetmore next raised his questions with Dominion Indian agent Russell Brown, one of the more than two dozen agents and senior DIA officials examined under oath:

Wetmore: Suppose it was considered advisable to cut off some portion of the Salmon River reserve, what, from your knowledge of the Indians' employment, would you consider the best portion to cut off, taking into consideration a possible increase in the number of Indians?

Brown: If you are going to take into consideration the possibility of an increase in the number of Indians, you cannot afford to cut off any portion of that reserve at all.

Wetmore was unpersuaded: "If it was in the minds of the Commission to cut off a portion of the Salmon River reserve, what portion of it do you say might be cut off with the least likelihood of interfering with their occupation?" Brown assured him that the band's livestock operations utilized the full extent of the reserve.[9]

British Columbia's commissioners were dissatisfied with Brown's unequivocal defence of existing boundaries. Commissioner James P. Shaw challenged Brown's understanding of Splatsin lands: "I have shown you that there is enough land to make 130 acres for a family of 3. Will you therefore explain the discrepancy when you say there is no more land than is reasonably required for Indians?" Brown replied:

> I was taking into consideration both present and future requirements, and allowing for an increase ... I don't think there is any too much land contained in the reserves. I understand that in the [Canadian] Northwest as much as 240 acres have been allowed for each child. If that allowance were to be made here there would not be sufficient land on the reserves to go round.

Day Hort Macdowall followed by suggesting that some of the Splatsin were not born on the reserves but rather "American Indians." Not so, Brown responded: "Since I became Indian Agent there has not been one single application for membership to the band, from any outside Indians."[10]

The relentless search for cut-off lands continued in the examination of T.J. Cummiskey, the DIA's inspector of agencies for the Okanagan and Kamloops districts:

> *Commissioner Macdowall:* Are they using the whole of it [the Salmon River reserve]?
>
> *Cummiskey:* Yes, pretty near all of it.
>
> *Macdowall:* What portion of the Salmon River could be cut off with the least detriment to the Indians?
>
> *Cummiskey:* There is none that you could cut off.
>
> *Macdowall:* If we were going to cut off any, it would be better to cut off what you stated along the west side of the Enderby reserve?
>
> *Cummiskey:* Yes, but I have said already that the Indians at Enderby have no land to be cut off.
>
> *Commissioner McKenna:* Do you make the same answer in regard to the Salmon River reserve?
>
> *Cummiskey:* Yes, I do. They use every foot of land there.[11]

Cummiskey's resistance proved futile in the face of the commission's determination to find reserve reductions, including 1,600 of the 5,625 acres in

Splatsin reserves at Enderby, as well as the band's entire 201-acre reserve near Sicamous, a replacement reserve for lands taken during the 1860s Columbia River Gold Rush.[12]

After completing its deliberations at Enderby, the commission shifted its focus thirty kilometres south to the City of Vernon and the reserves of the Syilx (Okanagan) Nation. Commissioners again sought validation from Brown and Cummiskey for potential cutbacks to reserve lands and again posed hypothetical questions. Wetmore asked: "Supposing the Commission should find that the Okanagan Reserve no. 1 contained more land than was reasonably necessary for the requirements of the Indians, what part of that reserve – in your judgement, could be cut off, which would be as little inconvenience to the Indians as possible?" Brown replied: "If you take the cattle industry as being their principal means of support, I don't know how they could part with any land at all."[13]

When the time came for Inspector Cummiskey's examination, Macdowall renewed the search for reserve reductions. "Now in the Okanagan reserve," he asked, "are the Indians using the whole of their big No. 1 reserve?" Cummiskey patiently explained the extensive agricultural use of reserve lands, including the north end of Indian Reserve no. 1 at Round Lake. Macdowall responded: "If we were to cut any off that reserve, I suppose that is the portion which could be cut off with the least interference with reasonable requirements of the Indians?" Cummiskey was unequivocal: "There is none of it which could be cut off because they are using every bit."[14] These cautions and objections from Dominion officials were not entirely ignored. Despite the efforts of Shaw and Macdowall, Indian Reserve no. 1 survived intact by a vote of three to two.[15] However, the commission recommended that three Okanagan Reserves be eliminated (at Swan Lake, Mission Creek, and Long Lake) and that 1,764 acres be cut off Tsinstikeptum Indian Reserve no. 9.

The drive to reduce the number and size of reserves continued as the commission moved down the Okanagan Valley. Consistent with its work elsewhere, the commission's decisions in the overall Okanagan Agency were notable for their subtractions rather than additions. One new reserve of 2,600 acres was added while a total of 18,536.8 acres were deemed "not necessary to the Indians," including fertile lands sought for fruit production.[16] The commission's visit coincided with a period of boundless agricultural optimism as Okanagan orchards expanded from 7,500 acres in 1900 to 100,000 acres in 1907.[17]

The aggregate area to be retained fell from 146,427.66 to 129,991.41 acres, and from 184 to 163 acres per person, a decrease of well over 10 percent.[18] The Penticton and Osoyoos First Nations saw major reductions to their reserves, particularly those bordering towns and cities. The commission proved to be one more vehicle for achieving the goal, enunciated by Joseph Trutch almost fifty years earlier, of liberating "lands now uselessly shut up in reserves." British Columbia's towns and cities nursed big aspirations as the province's white population swelled.

Reserves Flagged as Barrier to Progress and Growth

The commissioners heard powerful examples of boosterism in Kamloops. The city had grown dramatically since 1865, when Joseph Trutch dispatched his crews to cut back Interior reserves. Back then, it had been little more than "a small village consisting of a fort and a store ... built on the south shore of the Thompson River."[19] By 1913, when it welcomed the commission, Kamloops was the largest city in the southern Interior with a population of close to four thousand. "Progress and growth" was the dominant catchphrase in presentations. Dreams were expansive, as were demands for Indigenous lands.

The Kamloops Board of Trade argued that the "continued use of land on the North Banks of the Thompson River" as "an Indian Reserve is not in the best interests of either the Indians, or the City of Kamloops." It asked the commission to cut off "at least 800 to 1000 acres" of the Kamloops (Tk'émlúps or Tk'émlúps te Secwépemc) Reserve no. 1. Just how such a reduction might serve the "best interests" of the Tk'émlúps was not explained.

The interests of white settlers were ably articulated by Frederick J. Fulton, former MLA, provincial attorney general, and chief commissioner of lands and works. In the last role, he had led British Columbia's Royal Commission of Inquiry on Timber and Forestry in 1909–10.[20] Fulton shared more than a title with Joseph Trutch; he shared at least a few of his predecessor's views. Fulton argued that "while the Indians as the original inhabitants of this province, are entitled to some consideration, still under modern conditions I don't think they should be allowed to hold back the development of the Province." Fulton left no doubts as to where he stood on the commission's core mandate:

> If the Indian lands were being utilized to the best advantage I would not object to the extending of the present holdings, but this is not the fact. As for the Reserves in this locality, not one-half is being properly used ... if there are 500 acres of cultivable land not being used it means a serious loss every year to this Province, because owing to the physical conditions of BC, it is very important to this Province that every acre of land be used. I have seen white settlers come

> here and go back on the ranges utterly disgusted because all the land that might be cultivated was tied up.[21]

The commissioners embraced Fulton's narrative, as their examination of Indian agent John Freemont Smith would make clear.

Chair Wetmore canvassed the physical characteristics of the Kamloops Indian Reserve no. 1 and suggested: "Supposing it was desirable to cut off that portion of the Kamloops Reserve between the village and the river – that sandy portion – I suppose that could be cut off without much detriment to the Indians?" Smith replied that the area produced both revenue and seasonal pasturage for the Tk'emlúps. Far from dissuaded, Wetmore tried a different tack: "Supposing we come to the conclusion that it was proper to cut off a portion of that reserve; what portion could be cut off with the least detriment to the necessary requirements of the Indian?" Smith appeared reluctant to respond. "I might not be in favour of cutting off any," he noted.

Commissioner Macdowall then stepped in to challenge him:

> *Macdowall:* Are they [the Tk'emlúps] using all that Reserve?
>
> *Agent Smith:* No; they cannot.
>
> *Macdowall:* Well then, if they don't use it, how can you say that it is necessary for their requirements?
>
> *Smith:* That is not a fair way to put the question. If they had the facilities it would be to their advantage to use that reserve.
>
> *Macdowall:* What facilities?
>
> *Smith:* Water and irrigation.

When Wetmore asked why the band had not constructed an earthen ditch from a local water source, Smith replied: "The conditions of the Indians, you see, sir, are such that they cannot afford to do it; they have their families to support in the meantime, and they have to have money in order to do that kind of work." Wetmore's response dripped contempt: "Do you think this system of pouring money into the Indians every time they want to have some little improvement done is a good system to adopt?"[22] His question invoked the long-standing colonial myth of the "privileged Indian," but Smith did not rise to the bait. The son of former Black slaves on the Caribbean island of St. Croix, Smith had come to British Columbia in 1872. He built a successful business in Kamloops, won election there in 1902 as one of British Columbia's first Black aldermen, then became an Indian agent in 1912.[23]

Smith demonstrated courage in the face of bullying, but he was not alone in his resistance to reserve reductions. Indigenous leaders frequently and passionately complained of dispossession. Chief Louis of the Tk'emlúps patiently explained his band's efforts, despite scant capital, to utilize their lands to best advantage. Those efforts had sometimes been stymied by adjacent land uses:

> We have tried to cultivate the land which the water cannot reach, and it has been a failure. It gets dried up without irrigation ... There has been a ditch line surveyed to get water for these lands. Afterwards a white man took up a ranch between the reserve and the creek from where the water was to be gotten, and he stopped my water from coming.[24]

His pleas and Agent Smith's supportive testimony were to no avail. The commission recommended that 380 acres be cut off from Reserve no. 1 "immediately opposite the City of Kamloops" and "possessing special value through its close proximity" to the city. "Special value" also reflected Reserve no. 1's appraised value: at $958,580, it was by far the most valuable reserve listed in the Interior. The commission was loath to admit to rebalancing boundaries in the interests of a municipality; instead, it argued that the parcel east of Kamloops was "more adaptable to mixed farming" than the range lands that supported ranching elsewhere, hence "less acreage meets the necessary and reasonable requirements of the Indian occupants."[25] In this and many subsequent decisions, the commission demonstrated devious creativity in manufacturing reasons for reserve reductions, particularly when lands were adjacent to municipalities.

Commissioner (and MLA) Shaw provided a further example of such creativity in a meeting with the Salmon Arm Board of Trade. He asked: "With regard to the Indian reserves in the immediate vicinity, do you think it at all practicable, that the Indians could clear those reserves up, to any extent, within the next two or three generations?" The Board of Trade's answer was predictable: "I think it would be nonsense to expect it."[26] The commission had a remedy for the "unproductive" lands: after "consideration of the reasonable and necessary requirements of the Adams Lake Tribe," it cut off eighty-two acres from Switsemalph Indian Reserve no. 7 on the western boundary of the town of Salmon Arm.

In other Kamloops Agency meetings, commissioners were told that the alienation of traditional hunting, fishing, and harvesting lands had disrupted or prevented the seasonal rounds that had supported Indigenous people's self-sufficiency for thousands of years before contact and white settlement. Chief Andre of the Simpcw (North Thompson) First Nation told commissioners at a hearing in Louis Creek: "You know how poor I am, just like as if I was tied up – therefore I am kind of poor. It seems as though I cannot help myself to better myself, like as if I were afraid all the time. Everything seems to be locked up now, different from what it used to be a long time ago."[27] Similarly, Chief Tawhalst of the Adams Lake Band noted the sharp contrast between his Traditional Territory and reserve lands: "My land is very far away and very deep and very high. My land is lots and the Government has confined me to a small spot and fixed my land so that I could dig in that little spot for a living."[28]

Indigenous people's complaints of being "hemmed in" came as no surprise. In every corner of the province, over three years of hearings, commissioners heard about Indigenous fishing stations, gardens, graveyards, hay meadows, and houses that had been deliberately or inadvertently subsumed in pre-emptions, land grants, and timber licences. The commissioners typically dismissed the complaints, and their decisions rarely remedied even well-documented failings.

As in the Okanagan, reserve reductions in the Kamloops Agency came largely from higher-value reserve lands adjacent to growing towns and cities. Five reserves were reduced by a total of 1,327 acres, "being adjudged in excess of reasonable Indian requirement," and another three reserves of 2,172 acres were cut off entirely as "unused and non-essential to the maintenance of the native population," despite being fishing, hunting, trapping, and timber lands to the First Nations.[29]

Kamloops Agency First Nations submitted sixteen applications for additional lands, but only two were approved: one for 640 acres at Boulder Creek, the most northerly point in the agency, and a second for 900 acres at Zoht Creek near its southern limits. Neither was near a town or city. Applications for additional pasturage from the Neskonlith, Adams Lake, Douglas Lake, and Lower Nicola Nations were all rejected on the grounds of not being "reasonably required," despite being vacant and available.[30] The commission's presumption, deeply embedded in British Columbia's colonial roots, was that only "actual" settlers could make beneficial use of the lands.

White Aspirations Threaten Indigenous Lands

The commission's travels frequently took them through the New Westminster Agency, an area that stretched from the Lower Fraser Valley in the south to Powell River in the north and home of the Tla'amin (Sliammon) Nation. The agency encompassed what is today Metro Vancouver and was home to First Nations who had confronted early and intensive white settlement pressures, such as the Tsawwassen, Tsleil-Waututh, Squamish, and Musqueam. In their early discussions, commissioners frequently heard – as in Kamloops – that white people's aspirations required the diminution of Indigenous lands.

The Vancouver Board of Trade revealed its remarkably expansive aspirations in a 1913 meeting that focused on the goals of its fledgling Harbour Commission:

> *Chair Wetmore:* Do you want the whole [Squamish] reserves?
>
> *H.A. Stone, Board of Trade:* Yes, the whole reserves for the purpose of the development of the foreshore.
>
> *Commissioner Macdowall:* By that you mean that the Dominion Government should purchase these reserves and hand them over to the Harbour Commission as a gift?
>
> *Stone:* Yes, that is about what I mean.
>
> *Commissioner McKenna:* Is there no other valuable land?
>
> *Stone:* Except private property – All the rest is owned by private parties, and it is held at such a high price that we simply could not think of doing anything with it ...
>
> *Wetmore:* To what reserve do you refer to in your request?
>
> *Stone:* All the reserves bordering on the harbour of Vancouver – going out to Point Atkinson on the right and Spanish Point on the left – in fact all the reserves on the North Arm.
>
> *Macdowall:* That's a pretty big order.
>
> *Stone:* Well, this harbour is going to be one of the biggest harbours in the world.[31]

The commission took the jaw-dropping request from the Board of Trade seriously. It resolved to cut 130 acres off the Squamish Nation's Capilano Reserve no. 5 adjacent to what is now the City of North Vancouver.[32]

The commission continued to embrace "progress" elsewhere on the Lower Mainland. It cut off an entire reserve of nearly twenty acres and described it as "three blocks in the City of New Westminster ... originally established to meet camping requirements, no longer existent, of all Coast tribes, in common." Notably, the reserve was described as being "in" rather than "adjacent to" New Westminster. It was assumed to be a part of the city, rather than a vital Indigenous traditional use area that had long predated white settlement.[33] To the commission, a seasonal camping and fishing area was of no consequence when compared with the potential value of urban commercial and residential areas.

Elimination of the "New Westminster" reserve was consistent with amendments to the Indian Act introduced by Frank Oliver, minister of the interior and superintendent-general of Indian affairs, in 1911. One amendment "authorized any company, municipality or other authority with statutory expropriation powers to exercise those powers on reserve." Another allowed relocation of a reserve "within or adjoining a municipality of at least eight thousand people." Neither action required the band's consent or surrender.[34]

In support of his amendments, Oliver claimed: "It is not right that the requirements of the expansion of white settlement should be ignored, – that is, that the right of the Indian should be allowed to become a wrong to the white man."[35] His claim sounds remarkably at odds with the more "liberal" observations of the prime minister, Wilfrid Laurier, but is perhaps consistent with settler sentiment in Oliver's home province of Alberta (created in 1905) or in the City of New Westminster.[36] In New Westminster, a crusade to evict Indigenous people was launched every few years.[37]

Oliver's 1911 amendments followed hard on the heels of a 1910 agreement between Canada and British Columbia to relocate the Songhees Nation from Victoria Harbour to lands near Esquimalt. When asked where his amendments might be used, Oliver replied, "The city we have in mind is Vancouver ... There is a reserve in Vancouver that only differs in degree from the case of the Songhees reserve in Victoria."[38] Oliver had in mind Kitsilano Reserve no. 6, created in 1877 from an eighty-four-acre portion of the Squamish ancestral village of Senákw. In 1913, thirty-six years after the reserve's creation, the Indigenous residents "were forced off the reserve, out of their homes, put on a barge, and sent over to North Vancouver."[39]

As in other agencies with rapidly growing white populations, the commission left the New Westminster Agency with a smaller net area than when it began, reducing the average acreage from an already minuscule 16.45 per person to 16.3. As in Kamloops, the reductions typically came from high-value lands adjacent to municipalities, and First Nations' applications for additional lands in the New Westminster Agency fared poorly. Of the 110 applications submitted, only 15 were approved, and they were generally small additions of 5 to 10 acres (for graveyards, fishing stations, or gardens) to rural reserves.[40]

Reserves Deemed a Barrier to Progress on Vancouver Island

One of the commission's early forays on Vancouver Island was immediately north to the Cowichan Agency, long a hotbed of white-Indigenous conflict. The first stop was a meeting with the Duncan City Council. Mayor Kenneth

Duncan, the son of an early settler family, spoke first, articulating a theme that commissioners heard repeatedly around the province: Indigenous reserves were a barrier to local growth and prosperity. The mayor argued that Duncan was "circumscribed by Indian Reserves and the natural expansion of the City thereby prevented." He wanted one hundred acres of Cowichan reserve lands adjacent to the city.

> *Commissioner McKenna:* What you mean is, that you want the land you have mentioned, thrown open?
>
> *Mayor Duncan:* Well, we hold that the projecting section of this 100-acre tract ... is a distinct detriment to a Civic expansion. Out of the whole 100 acres I don't think that there are more than 9 or 10 acres cultivated.
>
> *McKenna:* Does not the Evans Estate [privately held outside municipal boundaries] also retard the progress of the City?
>
> *Duncan:* We can buy that, but we cannot buy the Indian Reserves.[41]

The notion that "Indian land is wasted land" was evident at the Duncan meeting. Some commission members were quick to sustain and reinforce the persistent colonial narrative of Indigenous "indolence." When good quality agricultural lands were held by Indigenous reserves, as at the Cowichan Agency, they set the table in anticipation of their removal:

> *Commissioner Shaw:* Is it not a fact that the Indians waste a good deal of their time? Is it not a fact that their natural indolence prevents them from working on their own land?
>
> *W.E. Ditchburn, Dominion Inspector of Indian Affairs:* I would not say that. They still have their old customs, and until they are better educated and get rid of them they cannot make much progress.
>
> *Chairman Wetmore:* But the Indians ought not [to] have to be spoon-fed.[42]

Ditchburn was unpersuaded by Wetmore's continuing critique of the "privileged Indian." Like senior Dominion officials elsewhere in British Columbia, he rightly surmised that the commission intended to reduce reserves whenever the opportunity presented itself. He advanced a compelling counternarrative:

> It has been claimed that the Indians of British Columbia do not use their lands and that for this reason the lands should be taken away from them. If the holding of lands unutilized constituted an offence warranting confiscation, then the

> Indians are not the chief offenders in this Province. The commission have now travelled over a considerable portion of Vancouver Island and had seen for themselves that by far the greater portion of the lands is still unimproved. And yet only a very small portion of these lands was contained in Indian Reserves.

White pre-emptions and free land grants were not being revoked by the province if settlers failed to utilize them. Indigenous farmers were being held to a different standard. Ditchburn discouraged the commission from reducing the Cowichan First Nation's lands, "especially in view of the great dissatisfaction obtaining before Confederation as a result of the reserves being reduced in area, [further reductions] would be very hurtful at the present time."[43]

The commission ignored Ditchburn and again advanced novel reasons for reducing or eliminating reserves in the Cowichan Agency. Commissioners noted that the reserves were "either surrounded by white settlement or in direct contact therewith. As a result of this environment, the natural avocation of these Indians, fishing, is now varied by sheep raising and mixed farming (in which, however, comparatively little substantial progress has been made)." Indigenous people were finding work off reserve, they continued, a shift that signalled "land requirements being unmistakably reduced by their present mode of life." The commission concluded that six reserves should be cut off entirely, including the 209-acre Pentledge Reserve of the already land-strapped K'ómoks (Comox) First Nation. At the commission's inception, the Cowichan Agency's reserves covered 19,898 acres, just over 10 acres per person, a small fraction of the acreage enjoyed by settlers. The commission reduced that meagre allocation by a further 575 acres to 19,353 acres.[44] Mayor Duncan's request for 100 acres of Cowichan reserve lands, strongly supported by British Columbia's commissioners, was narrowly defeated by three votes to two.[45]

On the other side of the ledger, the Cowichan Agency First Nations, whose land stretched from Victoria to Comox, directed only eight applications for additional lands to the commission. Of those, seven were dismissed outright as incompatible with earlier land grants for the Esquimalt and Nanaimo Railway, and one from the W̱SÁNEĆ (Saanich) First Nation north of Victoria for 160 acres "per each adult male" was rejected for not being "reasonably required."[46]

The Commission Again Proves Unreceptive to Suspicion or Dissent

The commission's 1913 tour focused on areas of British Columbia that were readily accessible by road or boat. After the meetings in Duncan, commissioners met with the Snuneymuxw First Nation in Nanaimo (the city bore the anglicized version of the Indigenous name). The Snuneymuxw were and are one of the largest First Nations by population in British Columbia. They were marginalized by Nanaimo's early industrial development and (according to the Nation's website) "systematically undermined, ignored and dishonoured by the Crown," resulting in the "smallest reserve land base per person of any First Nation in British Columbia." Based on British Columbia's short history as a colony and a province, Snuneymuxw leaders had good reason to mistrust any governmental process aimed at adjusting reserves.

Louis Good, the Snuneymuxw Chief, was reluctant to answer the commission's questions and (like Sam Pierre of the Spallumcheen) quickly earned the wrath of Chair Wetmore, who issued a familiar threat:

> It is not altogether a matter for the Indians, when they are called before us, to say whether they will give evidence or not, because we could issue a summons and bring them before us and make them give testimony, and if they refused, we could put them in jail ... We don't want to exercise these powers unless we are compelled to do so, and we don't intend to do so now. We want the Indians to testify of their own free will.[47]

Commissioners confronted more suspicion as they moved up the West Coast. At Hartley Bay, 145 kilometres south of Prince Rupert, the commission was greeted by a letter from four Chiefs stating that (in Wetmore's words) they "would not accept anything from anyone until the question of Indian title is settled." In his response, Wetmore declared that the commission's mandate "prohibits us from dealing with the question of title ... if you desire to have some right declared with respect to your title you will have to go elsewhere."[48]

Suspicion and disdain also prevailed on Haida Gwaii (the Queen Charlotte Islands). When a Skidegate councillor, Amos Russ, alluded to a pending title case at the Court of the Privy Council, Wetmore set aside his reluctance to weigh in on the title question:

> For more than 60 years I have been a lawyer and I have been very familiar with the means of bringing cases before the Court of the Privy Council ... There is nothing in that stage, which could get it before the Privy Council at all so you must have been misinformed in some way or another. That is none of my business, I am only telling you this for your information. Somebody is misleading you or you have misunderstood something.

Notwithstanding Wetmore's curt dismissal, the Nisga'a Land Committee had presented, through their London solicitors, a 1913 petition to the Judicial Committee of the Privy Council asserting Aboriginal title based on the Royal Proclamation of 1763. The Privy Council declined to hear the case, turning the matter back to the Canadian government (just as it had with a similar petition in 1906). The Privy Council's reluctance to consider the Nisga'a Petition may have been influenced by the Dominion's duplicitous assurances that consideration of Aboriginal title was indeed within the commission's mandate.[49]

The commission regretted that representations for "more adequate land allotments were hampered by their [Haida] identification with the movement for recognition of Aboriginal Title and their fear that applications for additional Reserves might prejudice action in that connection." To ensure fairness, at least from the commission's perspective, Indian agent Thomas Deasy was asked to tender applications on behalf of the Haida, reflecting their "demonstrated desire" to "enlarge their cultivated areas." Ten of Deasy's thirteen applications were ultimately "not entertained" because of the alienation of the lands through pre-emptions and timber licences.[50]

Despite its stated intentions, commissioners found only 360 acres to supplement Haida reserve lands, raising the acreage slightly from 5.83 to 6.44 per person, which, they acknowledged, was still "very low." However, in "view of the displayed progressiveness" of the Haida and their "practical efforts to develop their holdings and improve their conditions," the commission recommended that Canada purchase additional private lands to extend reserves for farming purposes.[51] Additions might be warranted, but not at the expense of the province, which had sold those same lands into private hands.

Nothing in the commission's first year of operations suggested that it would offer the "fair and honourable treatment" or "square deal" that Indigenous leaders had asked Laurier for three years earlier. And new leadership at the DIA in 1913 did not suggest things would change.

Canada's newly appointed deputy superintendent-general of Indian Affairs, Duncan Campbell Scott, enjoys, at best, a mixed legacy. Despite achieving acclaim as a poet throughout much of the twentieth century, Scott's work in the DIA has rendered him "a man who is now a byword for infamy."[52] Scott told a parliamentary committee in blunt terms: "I want to get rid of the Indian problem. Our object is to continue until there is not a single Indian in Canada that has not been absorbed into the body politic and there is no Indian question, and no Indian Department."[53] He used a variety of coercive measures to break down Indigenous communities, including "enfranchisement" (the right to vote and to obtain title to land formerly held within a reserve), a scheme that proved largely unsuccessful.[54] He worked doggedly to hinder the advancement of Aboriginal title cases, including an extraordinary Indian Act amendment in 1927 that outlawed "raising a fund or providing money for" advancing Aboriginal title. That amendment stood until its repeal in 1951.

The McKenna-McBride Commission, like Deputy Superintendent-General Scott in Ottawa, readily embraced the belief that Indigenous assimilation was laudable and inevitable. From its first hearings in 1913 to its last in 1915, the commission was all too often dismissive and scornful of Indigenous people's submissions.

7

Composition Changes, Disposition Does Not

As it entered the second year of its labours, the McKenna-McBride Commission saw important changes in its composition. A year of travelling and giving improvisational lectures on contempt of court had been more than enough for the chair, Edward Wetmore. He resigned in April 1914. The dominion commissioner, Nathaniel White, was elevated to chair, and Montreal lawyer Saumarez Carmichael became Canada's new representative. The commission's tolerance for dissent did not improve. Whenever the commission was confronted by distrust or suspicion from First Nations, particularly in the form of reluctance to answer questions, commissioners responded with threats and disparagement rather than with empathy or reassurances.

Carmichael all too perfectly captured the combative and arrogant spirit of Wetmore. He wanted his questions answered and was not reluctant to say so. When Chief Edward Spouk of the Gitanmaax Band (near Old Hazelton) proved reluctant to answer questions, Carmichael did not attempt to hide his frustration and scorn:

> There is no use in this Commission, which is a very important Commission and travelling all over British Columbia, wasting its time here if you don't want to talk to us and won't answer the questions that are being put to you ... If you have made up your mind that you are not going to answer any of our questions, then we have nothing more to do but say good-bye and go away, and we won't be back ... If you have made up your mind not to answer the question, that is your funeral and not ours.[1]

Carmichael also took the lead when commissioners encountered reluctance at their hearing in Port Simpson (Lax Kw'alaams). Ts'msyen Chief Joseph expected the commission to "deal with the land question," not simply pose questions about the number of chickens, churches, or rowboats. As in Old Hazelton, Carmichael would have none of it: "You people thoroughly realize, do you, that this will probably be the last opportunity of a Commission coming through to deal with you Indians in the way that we have been trying to deal with you?" When Chief Joseph refused to answer any further questions, White concluded with a further admonition: "If the members of this Tribe later on discover that some of the other tribes have fared better than they themselves at the hands of the Commission, they will have only themselves to blame for not having answered our questions more clearly." He promised that the commission would nonetheless "do all in its power" to "provide for your reasonable and necessary requirements."[2]

The commission's decisions proved entirely at odds with White's promises. It resolved to cut off 11,909 acres from the Naas Agency, with all but 202 acres coming from Ts'msyen reserves. The largest reduction was 10,468 acres on the Tsimpsean Peninsula, described by the commission as "utterly useless for Indian or other purposes, and in reality a detriment to the Indians, in giving a fictitious appearance to the extent and value of their holdings." Here, the commission embodied the spirit of colonial Governor Seymour's advice, offered fifty years earlier, that reserve lands should never "be of such extent as to engender the feeling in the mind of the Indian that the land is of no use to him." From the commission's perspective, the obvious solution to the dilemma of having "utterly useless" land was to cut back the reserve and give the land to the province.

The punitive character of commission decision making was further reflected in its treatment of two Ts'msyen applications for timber supply and hunting areas (each of one square mile). Both were rejected as "not reasonably required" despite being vacant and available.[3]

Acknowledgment But No Action on Indigenous Dispossession

The McKenna-McBride Commission spent much of 1914 and 1915 visiting communities along British Columbia's west coast, home to hundreds of small and scattered Indigenous reserves. Small reserves flowed from the convenient rationale that fishing was – and would remain – the principal occupation of coastal First Nations. Larger reserves were deemed unnecessary and wasteful, given the long-held presumption that only "actual settlers" would make good use of arable land.

The Kwawkewlth Agency on northeastern Vancouver Island and adjacent coastal areas on the Mainland offers a striking example of how tight-fisted reserve policies, combined with generous settler pre-emptions, failed Indigenous peoples. The Tlowitsis First Nation (alternatively described in documents as the Klawatsis or Turner Island) had only one reserve that provided just under half an acre per person, one of the lowest land allocations in the province. Chief Johnnie Clark expressed dismay at the loss of Tlowitsis Traditional Territory:

> No one has been to my Band or my land to sell them; no one has asked me how much, how big or where we want a reserve. I only found out last Saturday that the Government had only reserved one reserve for me ... There are only 26 acres in it. These 26 acres are all I have. I have no other reserve for my Band – only this one little place in this village ... I and my people were born on this land and our people before us, from the beginning. We have not come from a strange country; we are not foreigners. This country is ours. I have been taught and told by my old people that I would be protected by the Government.

As was their wont, commissioners attempted to rationalize the system of pre-emptions, free land grants, and timber tenures that had minimized Tlowitsis lands:

> *Commissioner Carmichael:* Do you understand that when a man comes in here and takes the land, that the Government has given it to him, whether it is right or wrong?
>
> *Chief Clark:* Who gave the Government the right to buy our land and sell it to the white man?
>
> *Carmichael:* When a white man comes on to what you say is your land, do you think that that white man comes there without any authority, or do you think that the Government, rightly or wrongly, gave that white man permission to go on that land?
>
> *Clark:* I think myself that the Government must have given the white man permission. Although my people do not keep any records, they have a way among themselves of knowing what has been done in the past, and my grandfathers have never told me that the land has been taken or bought from us. If my forefathers had ever told us that we had been given a little

> for the land, even an article, today I would not have dared to say a word. But I have not that verbal record from my forefathers.[4]

Chief Clark must have made an impression because the commission was not entirely dismissive of his pleas and took the unusual step of discussing the Tlowitsis's testimony in its agency summary. The commission acknowledged that 0.48 acres per person was "insufficient for the reasonable and necessary requirements" of the Tlowitsis. However, it then claimed to have "diligently, but unsuccessfully, endeavoured to find alternative Crown lands."[5] The commissioners had in fact rejected several Tlowitsis applications for unencumbered lands as "not reasonably required," in one case noting "it would be of no advantage to the applicant Indians."[6] The Tlowitsis predicament was then formally directed to the Department of Indian Affairs for resolution.

At virtually every commission hearing along the Coast, First Nations voiced frustration and anger over the loss of their Traditional Territories. Chief Owahagaleese of the Kwakiutl (Kwawkewlth) First Nation, which had 2.2 acres of reserve per person, described his Nation's dismay at losing both seasonal homes and ancestral villages to pre-emptions: "Although our houses are on their old village sites, the BC Government seems to have been able to sell it right away from under us, and the land that we are living on and the houses we have to live in, we have had to pay rent because it has been sold to white people."[7]

Chief Dawson of the Mamalikulla First Nation (Mahmahlillikullah), which had 6.75 acres of reserve per person, complained that lands and houses occupied during seasonal rounds of fishing and hunting had been subsumed by timber limits, prompting an intervention from Commissioner Shaw:

> *Shaw:* This land is all covered by timber limits owned and paid for by white men, and in that case, we can't give you the land you are asking for.
>
> *Chief Dawson:* The country does not belong to the Government, and they have no business to sell it. What business has anyone to go and sell that land without asking if I had no more use for it? What right have they got to sell it before I was through with it because I was the owner of it?
>
> *Shaw:* The Government has sold this land legally, and it is not for this Commission to question the legality of that sale.[8]

As elsewhere, the commission quickly dismissed Chief Dawson's complaints of dispossession.

The frequency of these complaints demands an explanation, even over a century later. In his 1915 testimony at Kincolith, the Reverend Archdeacon William Collison emphasized the unfortunate gap between the letter of BC law and its application. "Lands to be purchased or pre-empted must be 'no part of an Indian settlement,'" he noted. "While this was the law it was nevertheless a fact that the law was frequently set at nought. Companies, as well as individuals, in many cases took up lands which were old Indian settlements ... and serious complications had arisen in consequence." White responded with reassuring words: "The law is even stronger than that – the law requires that the surveyor who surveys that land must make an affidavit to the effect that there are no Indian shacks or Indian improvements on the lands."[9]

Even so, Indigenous people's testimony consistently suggested (to borrow Collison's words) that "the law was frequently set at nought." It was honoured more in the breach than in the observance. Testimony from Nisg̱a'a member Daniel Guno sheds further light on the issue of unlawful dispossession. Guno had seasonal homes in Aiyansh (for fishing) and Grease Harbour (for gardening and gathering). His Grease Harbour home was under threat from settler pre-emptions:

> When the surveyor came I asked him "what is your business here," and he said "nothing – I have not come to disturb you at all; I simply came because the Government wants to know how many acres there are in this country." Three years ago Surveyor Taylor came along and it was he that surveyed the pre-emptions – I asked him and he told me that the Provincial Government made a law that none of the pre-emptions would come within half a mile of the Indian settlement, and when I heard this I wasn't troubled, but now they grieve me and as it were make fun of me. They [settlers] come and cut down my fences and go into my gardens ... I am no stranger here – this is my own country and the place where I have always lived.[10]

Guno was being pushed off his land despite "laws" that purported to protect him.

The roots of unlawful dispossession lie in the long-standing practice (from colonial times through the first several decades following Confederation) "to lay out on the ground the Indian Reserves synchronously with the settlement of the district by the whites."[11] As noted earlier, one consequence of that policy was that reserves were often created amid competing demands for the most productive lands within a given district. In the face of ongoing racial stereotypes depicting "Indian land" as "wasted land," what did surveyors make of

Indigenous villages, fishing stations, and gardens that were uninhabited during portions of seasonal rounds? "Unoccupied" could far too easily be construed as "abandoned." As Marianne and Ronald Ignace have argued, "the point that Aboriginal people ... had no 'fixed abode' was often reiterated as a way to disqualify the Indigenous peoples on the land from valid occupation and livelihood in, let alone ownership of, their homelands."[12]

Indigenous claims of settler pre-emptions encompassing former village and fishing sites along the coast were credible and, in some cases, verified by Indian agents, prompting a modest concession from BC's commissioners Shaw and Macdowall: if Indigenous occupation was verified, the province would allow the lands to become reserves following "due compensation being made by Canada for the improvements made by the Pre-emptor."[13] As in Haida Gwaii, the remedy for the province's unlawful or inappropriate alienation of Indigenous lands rested in Canada's purse.

The commission's mandate gave equal weight to the expansion and reduction of reserves, but preconceptions about what a particular First Nation could or should be often shaped its decisions. The Kwawkewlth Agency at the time of the commission's visit was an aggregation of ninety-one small and scattered reserves that encompassed 16,601 acres. With a population of 1,183 people, that meant fourteen acres per person. The commission believed the "natural avocation of these Indians is fishing, but progressive members of certain of the Tribes of late have given earnest [expression] of desire to cultivate land." The commission claimed to respect the Kwawkewlth's need for more cultivable land and for additional fishing stations "long used and occupied by the Indians but not heretofore formally set apart for their use and benefit."[14] But its decisions again fell well short of the expectation.

The Kwawkewlth First Nations submitted 187 applications for additional lands. Of these, 106 were rejected because the lands were already taken – either pre-empted or granted by the Crown for other purposes. Among the remaining applications, the commission deemed that 44 parcels, though vacant and available, were "not reasonably required." For example, the Da'naxda'wx-Awaetlala (Knight's Inlet) First Nation's application for a hunting and fishing station on the Asnaakye River was "not entertained, as the land applied for would be of no use to the applicant Indians."[15] The river's vital importance from a "seasonal rounds" perspective was of no consequence to the commission.

The Kitasoo First Nation in the Bella Coola Agency (to the immediate north of the Kwawkewlth Agency) experienced similar treatment. Of the Kitasoo's thirty-two applications for additional lands, sixteen were "not entertained, as not being reasonably required." Twelve others were approved but only after sustained efforts to grind new reserves down to the smallest possible size. An application for a fishing station on Princess Royal Island prompted a discussion with Indian agent Iver Fougner, who had earlier confirmed its historical use and vital importance to the Kitasoo:

Commissioner McKenna: What is the smallest quantity of land that would secure the Indians a piece of land there?
Agent Fougner: I should say five acres.
McKenna: Would it not be less than five acres – they only have one shack there; the occupation of any more land than gives them a landing place and the place where their shack is, with a bit of ground around it, would appear to me to be not of much benefit to them?
Fougner: I would then say one acre.[16]

Tight-fistedness was infectious, even for Dominion commissioners.

The Inescapable Dilemma of Contradictory Rules and Processes

The commission undertook its work at a time of unbridled optimism for forestry. R.E. Gosnell, author of *The Year Book of British Columbia* for 1911, extolled the wonders of the province's forests: "Their present value is enormous, and considering the ever-increasing demand for lumber coupled with the ever-diminishing sources of supply [from external sources], their future worth is inestimable."[17] The flourishing forest industry was very much on the commission's mind as it contemplated applications for additional reserve lands, in some cases adjacent to or overlapping with newly established timber licences. Like agriculture forty years earlier, forestry was seen as the economic mainstay of a growing and prosperous province. British Columbia's forestry sector had grown dramatically from 27 sawmills in 1881 to 224 in 1911.[18] The commission was not about to circumscribe that bright future by expanding Indigenous reserves. Such concerns were highlighted in a Kitasoo fishing station application at Eagle Bay, which was supported by Agent Fougner's recommendation for the creation of a five-acre reserve:

Commissioner McKenna: Suppose that piece of land is in an area covered by a timber limit or a timber licence, do you think the location of sufficient importance to the Indians to warrant the Commission asking that it be set aside subject to the timber licence?

Agent Fougner: Yes.

McKenna: And do you think five acres is the smallest quantity they will require there?

Fougner: For fishing purposes only – of course they could do with less.

McKenna: So that if it were a timber limit they would be satisfied with a couple of acres?

Fougner said yes, despite abundant evidence of historical Kitasoo occupation of the site.[19]

The province often inhibited future reserve expansion by creating non-Indigenous timber tenures while Ottawa restricted Indigenous logging on their own reserves. Kitselas Chief Samuel Wise complained to the commission:

> We believed what the Government said when the Government men says "this is your reserve, and no one else's," but when we start to make a little money, perhaps selling timber or fish, what at once that same Government come upon us and put us in gaol and we have to sit down and cry because we cannot dispose of anything on these reserves without being put in gaol.[20]

The Tseshaht First Nation provided a compelling example of the dilemma noted by Chief Wise. Their Reserve no. 1 near Port Alberni became the object of the commission's attention in 1914 when Indian agent C.A. Cox's testimony set the stage for later decisions:

Commissioner McKenna: When you were examined at Nootka the other day, you stated that No. 1 Reserve of the Sechart [Tseshaht] Tribe near Alberni, was the only one that was not absolutely required for the use of the Indians unless they were inclined to log it off. Did you mean by that that it would be useless to them unless they were allowed to log the timber off?

Agent Cox: I meant by that that if they were allowed to log the timber off, they might show some aptitude for farming after it was cleared, and therefore it would be of some use to them for that purpose.

Commission Shaw: Under the present regulations, can they log it off?

Cox: No.

Commissioner McKenna: Would you say under present conditions in view of the fact they cannot log it off, is it reasonably required for their use?

Cox: They cannot make any use of it the way it is at the present time. It is very heavily timbered, as you saw when passing through it.[21]

The commission subsequently resolved to cut off blocks of 240 and 600 acres from the Tseshaht's existing reserves because it had found "few evidences of cultivation." In short, the Tseshaht were being punished for not making agricultural use of reserve lands they were not allowed to log for revenue or clear for farming.

First Nations were equally constrained when it came to fisheries. The provincial government had allowed coastal First Nations only very small reserves based on the argument that their principal occupation was fishing. But, in subsequent years, federal regulations curbed Indigenous fisheries. Commissioner Shaw explored constraints on Indigenous fisheries around the Nass River with Indian agent C.C. Perry, asking why white men held all 175 independent licences for the region:

> *Commissioner Shaw:* Did the Indians apply for any of these?
>
> *Agent Perry:* No, because they were for white men, and the Indians know they could not get them if they did apply ... Under the regulations of the [Fisheries] Department, Indians are not allowed to have independent licenses.
>
> *Shaw:* Do you think that a hardship is worked on the Indians from the fact that they are not allowed to take out independent licenses?
>
> *Perry:* Yes, I certainly do, and on this account I asked Ottawa if they would issue twenty as an experiment. Mr. Scott, the Deputy Superintendent-General took up the matter with the Fisheries Board and they declined, and his recommendations were turned down on the grounds that the Indians could get all the employment they wanted at the canneries. The Indians are well able to provide their own boats and gear, and in my opinion if they were granted independent licenses, they would get a better price for their catch.[22]

The province's meagre reserves, in combination with the Dominion's "whites only" fisheries, effectively undermined prospects for Indigenous independence and self-sufficiency, as had been articulated by James Douglas several decades earlier.

First Nations Deemed Squatters on Their Own Lands

Themes explored in coastal communities re-emerged as the commission travelled through the Mainland. In its Lytton Agency summary, the commission noted that many First Nation applications for additional lands "were for small parcels adjacent to established Reserves, which had been utilized by the applicant Indians for garden or orchard purposes as containing better soil or being in a more favourable position as regards water than the lands of the nearby Reserves." As elsewhere, more favourable (and often scarce) agricultural land was placed in pre-emptions, with more marginal lands consigned to reserves. Commissioners promised "insofar as possible" to protect these "progressive and industrious Indian squatters" in "their opportunities to self-support by their own activities as farmers and orchardists."[23]

By using the term "squatters," the commission validated the specious notion that Indigenous people had somehow avoided cultivating the better soils around them before colonization. Evidence suggested otherwise. During a commission meeting with the Xaxli'p (Fountain) First Nation, for example, Indian agent H. Graham described areas adjacent to Indian Reserve no. 1 that were traditionally cultivated by Nation members, but were now subsumed by a recent pre-emption.[24] The Xaxli'p First Nation was one more victim of British Columbia's long-standing policy of laying out "Indian Reserves synchronously with the settlement of the district by the whites." Even in 1878, when Gilbert Sproat undertook his duties as sole Indian commissioner, he found along the Fraser River "the greatest problem to be [white] squatters on Indian lands in the Railway Belt, but he reported that he had exhausted every effort ... to provide for the Indians without unnecessarily disturbing any of those settlers."[25] Forty years later, Indigenous farmers displaced by those settlers were now deemed "squatters" by the commission.

The commission's goal of supporting Indigenous self-sufficiency conflicted with its decisions at the Lytton Agency, where First Nations made 158 applications for additions to their often small and scattered reserves. Many applications were "not entertained" because the land applied for was deemed unavailable. In other cases, the land was "vacant and available" but deemed "not reasonably required." An application from the Boston Bar First Nation (which only had six acres per person) for range rights outside the reserve was refused even though the lands were available. Similarly, the Boothroyd Band's request for 160 acres to connect Reserve no. 1 and Reserve no. 4 (and provide farmland and pasturage) was deemed "not reasonably required," even though their existing reserves provided only six acres per person.[26] The commission's decisions were invariably guided by the presumption that five white men briefly visiting a region knew what was best for Indigenous peoples who had occupied those lands for hundreds or thousands of years. Indigenous people's appeals for greater self-sufficiency were routinely ignored.

Indigenous people's complaints about marginal or unproductive reserve lands were expressed in every corner of the province, no matter how remote. At hearings in the Bella Coola Agency, the Ulkatcho First Nation described their main reserve of over four thousand acres as "all rock and gravel" on which "nothing at all could be grown" but on which they were to provide for five hundred horses.[27] The reserve had been laid out in 1901 by Peter O'Reilly's successor, Arthur Vowell, "in a region that he thought was worthless."[28] In the Stikine Agency, the commission noted that the Tahltan's two reserves together covered 415 acres (just under two acres per person) and contained "only a few acres of cultivable land of very indifferent quality, and the so-called Meadow Reserve being merely a muskeg swamp around the edges of which a limited quantity of wild hay can be cut."[29] Even in the more remote corners of British Columbia, tight-fistedness prevailed.

Commissioners Judge Indigenous People's Character

In its agency summaries and formal decision making, the commission attempted to maintain a veneer of respect and objectivity. However, where commissioners heard evidence of Indigenous people's social and economic dysfunction, they presumed the cause was a failure of character (such as indolence) rather than the product of governmental policies that had thrown their ways of life into disarray. The largest reserve reduction in the Williams Lake Agency was foreshadowed by the claim that its occupants were "poor and lazy."[30] In another striking example, the commission described the Blackwater Nation, devasted by smallpox and reduced to only a few members, as "lazy, improvident and non-progressive." The commission responded by reducing their north-central reserve by 409 acres on grounds of the "practical extinction of the Blackwater Tribe."[31]

The commission's claim did not prevent the Blackwater Nation from tendering five applications for additional lands. Four were "not entertained, as not reasonably required," and the fifth application for two acres of graveyard was approved, perhaps with unintended irony.[32] When it encountered a similar situation on Vancouver Island, the commission cut off reserves of forty-eight and fifty-five acres from the "virtually extinct Klaskino Tribe," leaving one reserve of twelve and a half acres, "which is ample for the Indian requirement."[33]

In one of the final stops of its three-year marathon, the commission met in Old Hazelton with representatives from the Kispiox and Kuldoe Bands. The final exchange between Kispiox Deputy Chief William Jackson and Commissioner Macdowall reflected the ongoing collision of world views:

Deputy Chief Jackson: We are asking to get back the land of our grandfathers – we want our places, and we want our places to be free as they were before; as our fathers had a free living in their own land, we want to be in the same way. Where we catch fish, where we hunt and where we get berries, we want to use as our fathers did. God gave us this land where we were brought up, and it was free. There was no one bothering us and we want the land just as it was before the white men came to this country.

Commissioner Macdowall: You need not speak to us about holding this land the same as your grandfathers did – the world moves along, and you in your lifetime must move with it. It is for the sake of your grandchildren that we are here; to preserve something for them. The world will be different for your grandchildren than what it is today, and if you think of them at all you should select a piece of land for them – if you are not willing to do that, we might as well not talk to you at all.

Jackson: What is moving this world?

Macdowall: You will have to go to a wiser lot of men than the Kuldoes to find this out – but you will have to move with the world. If you don't, you will be wiped out ... We are sorry that you have not seen fit to answer our questions, and all that remains to be done is to wish you Good-Bye.[34]

Three years on the road had done nothing to improve the commission's disposition or its appreciation for the First Nations of British Columbia. After hearing thousands of stories in virtually every corner of the province, the commission could muster nothing more than contempt for Indigenous people's ideas and customs.

The McKenna-McBride Commission Opens a Decade of Conflict

Across three years of hearings, First Nations consistently emphasized that their connection to their unceded Traditional Territories was central to their past, present, and future lives. British Columbia's small and scattered reserves had robbed them of the opportunity to survive and thrive on the lands of their ancestors. The commission was not entirely oblivious to Indigenous appeals for more land. In aggregate, the commission recommended that more lands be added to reserves (87,291 acres) than subtracted (47,058 acres). Unfortunately, those figures tell only part of the story.

By the commission's own accounting, the value of the recommended cut-off lands ($1,385,308) greatly exceeded the value of the lands added ($444,838), particularly given that the latter figure included lands previously acquired by

Canada for reserve purposes.[35] As detailed above, the commission frequently heard and often supported appeals from city councils and boards of trade for reserve land adjacent to towns and cities, land that had a far higher monetary value than the rural, remote, and often marginal lands recommended as additions to reserves.

Reflecting its long history of tight-fistedness, the province regarded even modest additions to reserves as far too generous. Delays ensued as the provincial government did nothing.[36] Back-and-forth discussions between Victoria and Ottawa consumed weeks and months and then years.

Potential reserve reductions within the Railway Belt (the twenty-mile corridor on either side of the Canadian Pacific Railway main line given to Canada to compensate for construction costs) were the subject of fierce and protracted debate. Ottawa took the position that the McKenna-McBride agreement did not apply to those lands and refused to accept any reserve reductions proposed by the commission. Victoria disagreed, prompting another joint review.[37] The BC cabinet ratified the McKenna-McBride commission's report (including Railway Belt cut-offs and reserve reductions) by an Order in Council in July 1923. Ottawa's approval followed a year later, but it was subject to no cut-offs or reserve reductions in the Railway Belt or Peace River Block lands under its control.[38]

Aggrieved by the report's adoption despite their widespread opposition, and seeking a broader resolution of the Aboriginal title question, the Allied Tribes of British Columbia pressed Ottawa for an opportunity to air their grievances.[39] Hearings were finally held in March and April 1927 with a special joint committee of the Senate and House of Commons. The committee proved entirely dismissive of the case for Aboriginal title:

> Indians were consenting parties to the whole policy of the [BC] government both as to reserves and other benefits which they accepted for years without demur ... The fact was admitted that it was not until about fifteen years ago that aboriginal title was first put forward as a formal legal claim by those who ever since have made it a bone of contention and by some a source of livelihood as well.

The committee reserved its harshest vitriol for the Allied Tribes' lawyer, Arthur O'Meara. It "regretted the existence of agitation" by which "the Indians are deceived and led to expect benefits from claims more or less fictitious. Such agitation, often carried on by designing white men, is to be deplored, and should be discountenanced."[40]

The committee's rejection of Aboriginal title was supported by advice from the deputy superintendent-general of Indian Affairs, Duncan Campbell Scott, who quoted Joseph Trutch's emphatic dismissal of Aboriginal title as colonial chief commissioner in 1870 and as lieutenant-governor in 1872.[41] In the final paragraph of its report, the committee made a suggestion that was undoubtedly music to Scott's ears:

> [The] decision arrived at [dismissing Aboriginal title] should be made known as completely as possible to the Indians of British Columbia by the direction of the Superintendent General of Indian Affairs in order that they may become aware of the finality of the [committee's] findings and advised that no funds should be contributed by them to continue further presentation of a claim which has now been disallowed.[42]

That suggestion set the stage for a 1927 amendment to the Indian Act that prohibited raising money or engaging legal counsel to defend Aboriginal title, enforced by fines of up to two hundred dollars or imprisonment for up to two months, a prohibition that remained in effect until 1951.[43] By drastically interfering in Indigenous people's ability to exercise their political and legal rights and criminalizing fundraising, the provision made it impossible to defend Aboriginal title and other rights.[44]

The question of reserve adjustments as recommended by the commission was raised again in 1929 in the context of negotiations between Canada and British Columbia on the return of the Peace River Block and Railway Belt lands to provincial control. By 1929, the BC government was well aware of oil and gas production in neighbouring Alberta and undoubtedly hoped to replicate that success. Lands east of the Rocky Mountains, including the massive Peace River Block, held promise in that regard. In the 1920s, the BC government drilled five or six test holes in the Peace River area.[45] In 1930, during the dark days of the Great Depression, the prospect of British Columbia regaining developmental control over 3.5 million resource-rich acres must have been hugely alluring. The Peace River Block held far greater economic potential in 1930 than it had when transferred to Canada in 1883.

The Canada-BC Agreement of 1930 (based on a memorandum of agreement of the previous year) facilitated the "re-transfer" of the Peace River Block and Railway Belt lands back to the province. Fifty-five commission cut-offs were reduced to thirty-six, and the cut-off acreage was reduced from about 47,000 to 36,000. As the Union of British Columbia Indian Chiefs notes, those cut-offs were imposed "*without* the consent of the Bands concerned and in most cases were directly against requests for more land"; they were contrary to the commission's mandate as set out in 1912.[46]

As was so often the case in Canada-BC relations, the term "agreement" proved to be a misnomer. The province did not drop its claim to Railway Belt cut-offs until 1934, nor did it relinquish its claims to minerals and timber on reserves until July 23, 1938, when approximately one thousand reserves created through the Indian Reserve Commission were officially conveyed from the province to the Dominion.[47] Sadly, the issue of control over natural resources would return in a different form as Canada and British Columbia negotiated replacement reserves for First Nations dispossessed and displaced by post–Second World War industrial development.

8

Dispossession and Despair

Several thousand Indigenous Canadians served in the armed forces during the Second World War only to return, at its conclusion, to a nation where they still did not possess the right to vote, except under the coercive "enfranchisement" provisions of the Indian Act.[1] This irony prompted postwar reviews of Indigenous people's citizenship rights, and substantive reform slowly followed. Indigenous people were granted the right to vote in BC provincial elections in 1949 and in federal elections in 1960. In 1951, Parliament repealed some oppressive sections of the Indian Act, including, most notably, bans on engaging legal counsel for Aboriginal title cases and fundraising to sustain these activities.[2] These reforms, while vitally important, proved to be only small steps on the road to reconciliation. Postwar recognition and respect for Indigenous rights and title to their lands proved far more difficult to secure.[3]

Among the returning veterans was Abel Peters, a Cheslatta Nation member from north-central BC, about two hundred kilometres west of Prince George. Peters enlisted in the army as a private in the 102nd Northern British Columbians in 1943. On June 6, 1944, Rifleman Peters was thrust into battle with the Canadian D-Day forces who landed at Juno Beach. Years later, he told a friend, "All he could hear was noise and bombs and bullets and he knew people were dying around him and just kept walking straight ahead and he didn't know how he got to the beach without getting killed."[4] His luck did not hold. One month later, he was shot by a German sniper near Cannes Airfield and suffered serious wounds to his head and left arm. After a lengthy convalescence, Peters returned home to Cheslatta Lake intent on fulfilling his dream of building a home and raising a family.[5] Postwar economic development all too quickly rendered that dream a nightmare.

In British Columbia, Indigenous peoples paid an extraordinary price for postwar economic and industrial expansion. The persistence of colonial policies and prejudices was reflected in the dispossession and dislocation of two Indigenous Nations: the Cheslatta Carrier Nation and the Tsay Keh Dene Nation (Ingenika). In their collisions with this drive for growth, Indigenous peoples lost not only their homes but also their livelihoods and connection to the lands of their ancestors.

British Columbia's Dream Becomes Canada's Problem and Cheslatta's Nightmare

British Columbia's enthusiasm for major hydroelectric development and the Aluminum Company of Canada (later called Alcan and Rio Tinto Alcan) had deep roots, as indicated by internal correspondence among Alcan executives about the premier, Duff Pattullo, on November 4, 1941:

> As you have already been informed, the Prime Minister of British Columbia called on 3rd November to attempt to interest the management of the Aluminum Company of Canada Ltd. in the underdeveloped water powers in his Province. He plainly indicated that the Provincial Government would do almost anything to get the Company to establish itself there.[6]

But Pattullo's Alcan initiative was derailed with the formation, one month later, of a Liberal-Conservative coalition government and his unceremonious ouster from the premier's office.[7]

Discussions aimed at attracting Alcan to British Columbia were revived a few years later, this time led by E.T. Kenney, minister of lands and forests in the coalition government. In a letter to the president of Alcan on June 16, 1948, Kenney underlined the province's determination to secure Alcan's interest and investment:

> In order to enable you to carry on in engineering studies to determine the feasibility of such a project from your Company's point of view, may I offer you the following assurances for your further guidance:
>
> 1 We will place a departmental reserve in favour of such extensive investigations to be carried out on the following watersheds ... together with the necessary Crown lands in the vicinities of such possible power sites.

2 Should you decide to proceed with your proposed project, we shall be glad to issue to you water licences on such of those power sites as you may select as being suitable for your requirements.
3 If ... your engineering studies demonstrate that our existing laws would not economically permit further development, I shall be glad to discuss ways and means with my colleagues, having in mind the amendment of such laws whereby such a project might be economically pursued to the mutual advantage of our Government and your Company.[8]

In short, the BC government was indeed prepared to "do almost anything" to secure Alcan's investment, including providing Crown lands, issuing water licences, and amending provincial laws.

Cheap power was the goal, enabled by the Industrial Development Act of March 1949.[9] The province and Alcan signed an agreement in 1950, providing Alcan with the right to store, divert, and use water under the Water Act and purchase and occupy as much Crown land as was required for the project. According to Kenney, British Columbia offered "the perfect setting" for Alcan: "The combination of aluminum and hydro power ... go together as naturally as ham and eggs or Blondie and Dagwood." The project was "an augury" that British Columbia would become "the leading industrial province in Canada" and that Kitimat would grow to be the province's third-largest city of "perhaps 50,000 people."[10]

But the project's great promise was threatened by a stipulation that "plans must be submitted to various government bodies," including the federal Department of Fisheries. Just six weeks after the Alcan agreement was signed, Kenney complained to a federal MP that "it is rather exasperating after all the groundwork that has been done to find the Federal Fisheries obstructing" the project. He was "amazed at the deductions" drawn from "meagre information." If Fisheries persisted with their "fanciful objections," Alcan had advised that the project would be over "as far as they are concerned."[11]

The fate of Alcan's Kemano project and its impact on the Cheslatta First Nation were not determined until fifteen months after British Columbia and Alcan signed their agreement. In late July 1951, the Indian commissioner, W.S. Arneil, notified the Indian Affairs Branch (IAB) in Ottawa that Alcan had advised that, should Fisheries' issues be resolved, portions of two Cheslatta Reserves would "likely be flooded," with a more precise determination to follow.[12] Eight months later, Fisheries and Alcan reached an agreement to mitigate the impact of warmer, shallower waters on migrating salmon: a reservoir for strategic cold water release, which involved flooding Murray and Cheslatta

Lakes.[13] Alcan also advised the IAB that flooding would consume several Cheslatta Reserves, nine hundred acres, forty buildings, and two graveyards.[14] The Department of Fisheries' solution became the IAB's problem and Cheslatta First Nation's nightmare.

Before their forced relocation, the Cheslatta occupied reserves adjacent to the Cheslatta and Murray Lakes, located south of Burns Lake in north-central British Columbia. They had enjoyed continuous occupation of the region for thousands of years, as corroborated by a rich body of archaeological evidence and oral histories.[15] Prior to the Alcan project, the Cheslatta drew their livelihoods from ranching in combination with trapping, hunting, and fishing. Their isolated reserves could not be accessed by road, and IAB records suggest that only one First Nation member, veteran Abel Peters, spoke fluent English.[16] Government and corporate decisions soon breached their seclusion without the prior knowledge or consent of the First Nation.

Nothing in the archival record suggests that IAB officials ever considered opposing the Alcan plan. The absence of opposition was notable but not surprising. Fisheries had filed an objection to issuing Alcan's provincial water licence based on the threat posed to migrating salmon. Opposing the proposed solution, and at least temporarily blocking the massive project, would have been challenging indeed. The superintendent of reserves and trusts, D.J. Allan, likely reflected the prevailing the sentiment at IAB headquarters in Ottawa. "I do not assume we should stand in the way of a development such as that proposed by the Company," he suggested to Arneil, "even though it may mean the Indians will lose two or three small Reserves."[17] Nor does evidence suggest that the IAB considered utilizing any leverage they possessed in Alcan's regulatory approval processes. Harry Swain, a former federal public servant, recalls that "quick capitulation to Fisheries was a long-standing [IAB] posture ... We were told that Fisheries management was more important, more critical to good fed-prov relations, especially in BC."[18]

Shortly after official authorization of the reservoir plan and confirmation that reserve flooding would occur, the provincial comptroller of water rights contacted Arneil regarding the impact on the Cheslatta. Arneil responded that negotiations underway with Alcan "will ensure that the rights of the Indian owners ... will not be adversely affected through the raising of the lake."[19]

A discomfiting "government knows best" attitude permeated the IAB's approach from late July 1951 (when Alcan first flagged the possibility of flooding two reserves) to March 1952 (when it confirmed that seven reserves would be inundated). The IAB appeared far more preoccupied with preparing mutually acceptable appraisals with Alcan than with preparing the Cheslatta for the physical and social consequences of flooding. Archival records reveal that at least four months before a final decision was rendered on the Murray and Cheslatta Lakes reservoir, the IAB agreed to a compensation plan with Alcan without consulting the Cheslatta.

On October 12, 1951, Alcan advised Arneil of its desire "to agree on compensation in the field for all of the various items concerned."[20] Two weeks later, after a joint field visit to the affected reserves, Arneil wrote to Superintendent Howe of the Vanderhoof Agency, expressing concern that Alcan and the IAB might have emerged with differing appraisals. He urged Howe to contact Alcan "to arrive at mutually acceptable values."[21] Howe's response was reassuring: "The only difference is in the valuation of the whole acreage of each Reserve on our lists, whereas [Alcan] only appraised the acreage which may be flooded ... Otherwise, our appraisals are identical."[22]

Even though reserve relinquishment would mean the evacuation and relocation of the Cheslatta, Alcan hoped to pay only for the area flooded and not the broader area where occupation would be prohibited. The company's approach was reflected in the lower valuation figures it tendered in community meetings with the Cheslatta, without objections from the IAB.[23] Arneil was undoubtedly relieved to advise IAB headquarters on December 5, 1951, that valuations "have been made and compensation agreed upon."[24]

As discussions between Alcan and the IAB proceeded, the Cheslatta were never warned that dispossession and dislocation from their lands might be imminent. Officials reported no interactions, adverse or otherwise, with First Nation members during their October visit. The IAB concluded that given Alcan's letter of March 27, 1952, confirming that extensive flooding would occur, a meeting with the Cheslatta "was necessary to inform the Indians of this sudden turn of events."[25] This "turn of events" would see the Cheslatta immediately dispossessed of their homes, reserves, and livelihoods by a process from which they'd been excluded, for a price they had no role in negotiating.

The Cheslatta Learn Their Fate

On April 3, 1952, Superintendent Howe arrived at Cheslatta Lake to advise the First Nation of Alcan's plans and deliver the bad news: the company "had received instructions from the Fisheries Department at Ottawa to build a dam at the outlet of Murray Lake, in order to catch this spring's run-off."[26] Cheslatta Lake would rise approximately ten feet in ten weeks, prompting "the urgent necessity for evacuation at the earliest possible date."[27]

Not surprisingly, Howe reported, the Cheslatta "were shocked to learn that they should be asked to move on such short notice and at the outset were not prepared to move under any circumstances." Immediate removal held dangers of its own because the reserves were served by pack trails and wagon trails that were impassable at the time, according to the IAB's regional supervisor. He advised that the move could be made over the ice on Cheslatta Lake, but removal would have to occur before the ice broke up and "each family had the necessary sleighs and horses to make the move." The implication was clear: move quickly or face the double jeopardy of drowning. In the IAB's telling, the Cheslatta could then look forward to being established in a place "better than their present holdings in an area served by roads, schools, doctors ... and other amenities of life not now enjoyed on their isolated Reserves." Officials were surprised and frustrated when Alcan's offer of $107,830 was not immediately accepted. The Cheslatta "wanted additional compensation in cash, due to the short notice given and the additional difficulties they would have moving at this time of year due to poor travel conditions."[28] The meeting ended without resolution.

Not everyone at IAB's Ottawa headquarters was sympathetic to Alcan's position. One official, in a note to Commissioner Arneil, stated "that neither the Indians nor the Department should be at all backward in seeking compensation" from Alcan. The company should do more than "merely pay for buildings and improvements at their present-day valuation"; they should "pay and pay well for the serious disruption their plans will make in the livelihood of these Indians."[29] This bolder stance was not replicated among IAB officials in British Columbia, who may have felt greater pressure not to "stand in the way."

Two weeks later, a second meeting was held with the Cheslatta, this time with Alcan representatives present. Superintendent Howe was also joined by W.J. MacGregor, regional supervisor of Indian agencies. E.A. Clark reiterated Alcan's offer as previously conveyed by IAB officials in April and "outlined why none of the requests [for additional compensation] could be considered by the company." Alcan's offer, he said, was "fair and just" and "the result of a joint appraisal" with the IAB, suggestions that were confirmed by Howe.[30] The Cheslatta, in Howe's view, had "countered with fantastic and unreasonable demands, which were definitely out of the question."[31] Negotiations again stalled.

Alcan's hard-line stance was bolstered by new information that was overtly at odds with the "urgent necessity for evacuation." At a closed meeting with IAB officials, the company shared that "conditions in the Cheslatta watershed" suggested that "the level of the lake would not rise as rapidly as was first anticipated." They were, therefore, inclined to hold firm. That loss of urgency, in the IAB regional supervisor's words, "would allow us time to have another meeting later with the possibility that the Indians would reduce their demands." The next morning, Alcan representatives reiterated that there would be "no further concessions" and then departed.[32]

IAB officials stayed on for what they described as "exhausting and gruelling sessions, which lasted for three days and nights. Finally, on the last day, when we were just about to give up, the Indians compromised and agreed to surrender the Reserves for a definite sum for each individual owner of land and improvements." Total compensation was $129,000, including $109,450 for individual holdings and $3,500 for emergency moving expenses.[33]

Their strategy relied on several deceptive tactics: exaggerating the urgency of the threat and the need for evacuation (even though Alcan had admitted that the water was rising more slowly than expected), offering the Cheslatta what seemed like fair compensation (even though it was based on lands flooded, rather than all reserve lands lost), and promising them better lives in a new location that hadn't even been chosen yet.

Despite their success, MacGregor noted that "it was most frustrating attempting to negotiate with these Indians. They have lived in an isolated area all their lives, with the result that they are a backward group, have had little supervision and, consequently, little knowledge of the Indian Act and Departmental policies." His words say far more about the IAB of the early 1950s than about the Cheslatta; not even encyclopedic knowledge of the Indian Act and departmental policies would have saved the Cheslatta from the disdainful racism inherent in both. MacGregor also complained that "the interpreter, Abel Peters, son of the Chief, and a veteran of the Second World War, was very difficult to deal with, being against any sort of compromise while at the same time not being able to give any basis for the demands he supported."[34] After recovering from wounds suffered in France, Peters had just completed a new house, which he was now being asked to give up, along with the lands of his ancestors.

Officials with the IAB enjoyed a much more comfortable relationship with Alcan and vice versa. In a letter of late May, E.A. Clark noted Alcan's appreciation of the IAB's "most helpful assistance and cooperation in all this Cheslatta business."[35]

Replacement Lands Sought beyond Cheslatta Traditional Territories

The loss of reserves raised an obvious question: Where should the Cheslatta be relocated? IAB officials knew very well the long and painful history of reserve creation in British Columbia. The superintendent of reserves and trusts in Ottawa flagged the issue for Arneil and suggested that IAB "make it a condition of our consent that the Company arrange to secure from the Province other lands in the district for reserves ... It would have the advantage of getting around the executive stop order on new Indian Reserves."[36] Arneil responded that Alcan had been informed of the order, and "they are prepared to either acquire such lands on our behalf or to persuade the Provincial authorities to waive the Executive Order in these cases."[37] As events quickly unfolded, the latter course was never pursued.

Confirmation of pending reserve flooding left the IAB with an estimated ten weeks to come to an agreement with the Cheslatta and relocate them. The severely compressed timeframe and the province's prohibition on the creation of new reserves on Crown lands effectively ruled out replacement reserves within the Cheslatta's Traditional Territories, a situation that had longer-term implications for the Nation.[38] Lessons drawn from the McKenna-McBride Commission some forty years earlier were not lost on IAB officials: purchasing private lands was a quicker and simpler route to reserve creation than seeking Crown lands from tight-fisted provincial governments. The IAB's solution drew on that experience. Canada would purchase existing fee-simple farms and ranches with Alcan funds and then convert those lands to reserves.

The IAB's readiness to relocate the Cheslatta outside their Traditional Territories meshed with Ottawa's postwar belief that marginalized citizens in remote settings could build better lives through relocation to areas with "modern" infrastructure.[39] In one grim example, the Royal Commission on Aboriginal Peoples described the 1964 amalgamation and relocation of the Gwa'sala and 'Nakwaxda'xw First Nations (from Takush and Bahas, respectively, both on the central coast across the Queen Charlotte Strait from northern Vancouver Island) to the Kwawkewlth's Tsulquate Reserve adjacent to Port Hardy.[40]

The Gwa'sala-'Nakwaxda'xw, like the Cheslatta, were offered no genuine choices. In the commission's words, "Coercion – in the form of withheld or eliminated funding for housing, schools and services – coupled with promises of improved housing, health and education facilities, and economic opportunities, ensured Aboriginal 'consent.'" The IAB failed miserably in fulfilling its promises to the Gwa'sala-'Nakwaxda'xw. The commission noted that when "100 people arrived in Tsulquate in 1964, only three houses were ready to be occupied, and 20 to 30 people were forced to cram into a single dwelling. Some families resorted to living on their boats. However, safe anchorage had not been provided, and many boats were soon damaged or destroyed." Meanwhile, the IAB burned their former central coast villages to the ground to discourage any thoughts of returning.[41]

The Cheslatta experience mirrored that of the Gwa'sala-'Nakwaxda'xw. Superintendent Howe noted in late May: "These Indians are still in a very unhappy frame of mind over being uprooted and hastily evacuated from their old established homes and reserves. They are living in shacks and tents and their belongings are scattered all over the country."[42] Any potential return to Cheslatta Lake was out of the question. Despite a plea from the local Indian agent, "Cheslatta villages were bulldozed and burned before most families could return for their belongings."[43]

Howe pushed hard to expedite the Nation's re-establishment, fearing "an ugly and undesirable situation may develop."[44] By "ugly and undesirable," he undoubtedly meant a public relations situation for the IAB. The Cheslatta were already in such a situation, thanks to the government's indifference to their plight. Within a few short weeks, the Cheslatta's world had been overturned and uprooted. Two months later, Howe reported that options to purchase had been secured on several properties, but the Cheslatta remained in shacks and tents awaiting permission to occupy them. "It is a very unsatisfactory state of affairs," he wrote, "and if something is not done in the near future, the Department will be subjected to adverse publicity and unfavourable criticism."[45]

After frustrating delays, most of the Cheslatta settled in the Grassy Plains and Uncha Lake areas, about fifty kilometres north of Cheslatta Lake. By then, some Nation members had begun to suffer long-term health problems, including tuberculosis, because of prolonged exposure to the elements.[46] Marvin Charlie was eight years old when the Cheslatta were relocated. He told the Royal Commission on Aboriginal Peoples in 1993 that "due to wet weather and wet bedding, some of our people got TB, and some of them died from TB. I was one of the victims who was ill from TB, and stayed in a hospital for five years."[47]

The change proved traumatic and destructive for the Cheslatta. Their website offers a poignant summary of their experience:

- 18 days notice to Cheslatta to move
- 120,000 acres flooded
- 3 villages burnt to the ground
- Over 60 graves washed away.

The Cheslatta do not mince words in describing the consequences of their sudden dispossession and dislocation: "Depression overwhelms the lost people and soon alcohol, drugs and hopelessness begins to consume the Cheslatta, one at a time."[48]

The year 1952 brought dramatic and unexpected change for the Cheslatta. It was also a year of remarkable political change, signalled by the surprise election of an upstart Social Credit provincial government led by British Columbia's twenty-fifth premier, W.A.C. Bennett, a prominent Kelowna businessman and former Conservative (and coalition) MLA. Bennett and his new party secured only a minority of seats in 1952, but he would win an unprecedented seven consecutive provincial elections and govern continuously until his defeat in 1972. His relentless passion would be building or expanding the province's infrastructure – from roads and dams to schools and hospitals – funded largely by tax revenues generated through natural resource development and exploitation. Bennett changed the face of British Columbia in countless ways, but improving the province's relationship with First Nations was not among his priorities.[49]

Cyril Shelford, the newly elected Social Credit MLA for Omenica, described the Alcan project as "a terrible tragedy" in his maiden speech in the legislature. He deplored its destructive impact on First Nations and the environment, including lakes "filled with standing trees, floating trees, sticks, branches, and such like."[50] The *Vancouver News-Herald* offered a different perspective: "Why should there be any loss as Mr. Shelford fears? The new lake will be much larger, with a greater mileage of shoreline ... Fish may be counted upon to take care of themselves and actually increase in numbers."[51] The fish would certainly have nothing to fear from fishers. As the new Social Credit forest minister, Robert Sommers, pointed out in his critique of the former Liberal government's policies and practices, most of the land flooded by the Alcan project had not been cleared.[52] Sadly, the same mistake would be repeated by the Social Credit government a decade later when it created Williston Lake – one of the world's largest human-made reservoirs – behind the W.A.C. Bennett Dam.

9

Refugees on Their Own Lands

The Tsay Keh Dene Nation (Ingenika) was, like the Cheslatta a decade earlier, uprooted by a massive project that soon became a cornerstone of the province's economic development. The Tsay Keh Dene's dispossession and dislocation graphically demonstrated just how readily governments subordinated Indigenous people's interests to their own and, similarly, how officials imposed their own judgments in place of respectful engagement with First Nations. A decade after the dislocation of the Cheslatta, the federal government's focus continued to be accommodating the province's bold aspirations for economic expansion rather than protecting the Indigenous people threatened by it. The provincial government continued to operate according to the enduring premise that Indigenous issues were Canada's to resolve, without resorting to British Columbia's public lands. Despite the devastating impact that the W.A.C. Bennett Dam and Williston Reservoir would have on the Tsay Keh Dene, the province remained remarkably petty, cavalier, and miserly in its approach to reserve replacement.

The Rocky Mountain Trench, home of the Tsay Keh Dene, had been the object of an engineering assessment for hydroelectric development since at least 1958. A report of that year undertaken for the Wenner-Gren British Columbia Development Company described the area, north of Mackenzie, as "virtually uninhabited and almost completely unexplored."[1] The BC Electric Company also surveyed the area, and an internal report noted "a total white population" of seventy-six but made no reference to the region's Indigenous inhabitants.[2] In the wake of Premier W.A.C. Bennett's controversial expropriation of BC Electric in 1961, and the company's subsequent transformation into a Crown corporation, dam construction became an urgent political priority.

Even as expropriation hearings were underway in Victoria, Bennett expressed his hope "that BC Electric directors will call tenders right away for a pilot tunnel and reservoir clearing."[3] The fate of the Tsay Keh Dene was sealed long before they were advised of a future dam and reservoir that would consume their homes, reserves, and livelihoods.

Did the federal Indian Affairs Branch (IAB) fail to protect Tsay Keh Dene interests by giving up whatever political leverage it enjoyed too early and too easily, just as it had a decade earlier with the Cheslatta? On March 21, 1962, the Indian commissioner wrote the superintendent of the Stuart Lake Agency suggesting that "Indians be advised to object to granting of a water licence to BC Electric." Ottawa ramped up stakes with the BC comptroller of water rights, asking that the licence be withheld pending assessment of "the extent to which Reserves and the Indian economy will be involved and to make representations to you in this connection." The request became a formal objection to the water licence, which gained the attention of BC Electric. At a meeting of senior officials from the IAB and BC Electric a few weeks later, BC Electric promised consultation and compensation "to settle trapline and land claims" issues.[4]

The IAB's opposition appeared to soften after the meeting. Speaking to the water comptroller's licence hearing in late June 1962, IAB spokesman R. Kendall commended BC Electric "for its constructive attitude" and stated "that the Indians are 'all quite anxious to see that progress is being made.'" The meeting notes suggest that Kendall did not object to the project but raised specific objections with the comptroller.[5]

A conditional water licence was issued to BC Electric (thereafter BC Hydro) on December 21, 1962, and the province's determination to find a replacement reserve and deal with compensation issues evaporated. Its consultation with the Tsay Keh Dene was cursory and fragmented. A cultural chasm fostered misunderstanding and miscommunication.[6] Land issues remained unresolved for years. In September 1966, Canada (now represented by the renamed Department of Indian Affairs and Northern Development, or DIAND) reached a tentative agreement with BC Hydro on replacement reserves, only to have the agreement founder months later over the long-standing issue of subsurface mineral rights.

The issue was not finally resolved until January 1969, when DIAND accepted new reserve sites "under protest, due to Mineral rights being retained by the Provincial Government."[7] In short, the Tsay Keh Dene were hurriedly uprooted by a provincial megaproject and dispossessed of their homes, livelihoods, and reserves, but the province was nevertheless determined to quarrel over the subsurface mineral rights below these small replacement reserves.

As it had been for almost a century, British Columbia was loathe to share wealth on even the smallest pieces of ground.

British Columbia Devastates Lives First by Fire and Then by Flood

Miscommunication – or an absence of effective communication – made retreating from rising floodwaters in 1968 an extraordinarily painful event for the Tsay Keh Dene. Some had returned from seasonal rounds of hunting, fishing, and gathering earlier in the year to find their homes burned to the ground. "We lost everything we had not taken with us," Elder Jean Isaac noted. "We had pictures, pots, pans, traps and guns under the floorboards for safe keeping. They were all destroyed by the fire."[8]

Officials claimed their actions had been necessary to reduce debris in the rising waters, a dubious claim given the huge impact of unharvested trees surfacing on the Williston Reservoir. The reservoir was inundated by thousands of unharvested trees that formed massive packs that inhibited water travel. One pack at Finlay Reach (near the northern end of the reservoir) was of particular concern. It covered an estimated two thousand acres and contained, according to the *British Columbia Lumberman* magazine, "an estimated 2.1 million cunits of trees ... several times the annual cut of most BC logging companies."[9]

Seasonal fluctuations in the reservoir's water levels eroded sand and gravel beds, exacerbating the loss of hunting, fishing, and trapping resources that had long sustained the Tsay Keh Dene. Another Elder, Francis Isaac, noted, "We were never really told how high the water would come." Disbelief that the Finlay River would somehow be transformed into a massive lake was not relieved by advice that the lake would reach "the 250-foot level." A reporter from the *Mackenzie Times* asked: "How were the people of the valley to know what a 250-foot lake would look like?" Bill Bloor, the storekeeper at Finlay Forks, witnessed the flood's impact first-hand:

> One evening as the waters were coming up, I went over to where the Natives were.
>
> They had campfires lit, all in a row. They were seated around these campfires. It was as though I had come to a funeral. Like a vigil, they were watching

> what was happening. The older people were weeping. They were saying, "No more good land." They knew it was no longer safe. It was a very, very sorrowful sight.[10]

The Williston Reservoir disrupted long-established social and economic relationships among the three Tsek'ene-speaking Nations along the Finlay River: the Tsay Keh Dene, the Kwadacha to their north, and the McLeod Lake Band to their south. "We were one big family," according to Kwadacha Nation Elder and former councillor Mary-Jean Poole. "'One people' they'd say."[11]

Former Kwadacha Chief Emil McCook made his living operating riverboats up and down the Finlay River until it was inundated by the reservoir: "I went into the lake three times. We had riverboats swamped. We lost everything on them in the lake. Suddenly we can't use our highway." The loss of Finlay River connections produced physical isolation and, according to Susan McCook, "the emotional sadness, the lifestyle change, the separation of peoples."[12]

Governments simply ignored the loss of community connection. Former BC minister Ray Williston was asked in a 1975 interview whether the construction of the Bennett Dam and the reservoir that bore his name had had negative consequences. "No," he replied, "it was an absolute wilderness and there were no people, no nothing. Outside of Fort Ware [Kwadacha, seventy kilometres north of Ingenika Point] where there were a few Indians and so on, there was nothing in the whole area."[13] The BC government recognized neither the Indigenous peoples of the Rocky Mountain Trench nor their plight.

How the Tsay Keh Dene Became Refugees on Their Own Land

As the water rose in the Williston Reservoir, so, too, did confusion over where the Tsay Keh Dene would relocate. The Tsay Keh Dene became, in the words of Chief Gordon Pierre, "refugees on our own land."[14]

The Chief's words were apt; in 1968, the Tsay Keh Dene became refugees and remained in that predicament for another twenty-one years. Some set up camp at Ingenika Point, just beyond the reservoir's high-water mark, and across the water from Finlay Forks, where about thirty Nation members worked at the Carrier Lumber sawmill. The absence of housing necessitated the "temporary" use of nine "10 x 24 bunkhouse-type dwellings" provided by DIAND. One official, after a 1971 visit, described the dwellings as "one room plywood shacks with no insulation and primitive wood-burning stoves. There is no electricity, running water, sewage disposal facilities or garbage pick-up."[15] Others moved to the replacement reserve at Parsnip River, where DIAND had constructed five houses and planned to build more. Some moved north to Fort Ware.

In a look back at the Nation's relocation, the DIAND district manager wrote (with either withering sarcasm or unintentional irony) that "the planning was good other than being unacceptable to the vast majority of the people."[16] At a meeting with First Nations in 1965, three years before forced displacement, Superintendent Presloski had suggested they "give consideration to various provincial facilities and utilities such as access to roads, schools, power, postal services, telephone communications, job opportunities and various other necessities." He then went on to suggest "that careful consideration should be given to such matters as fishing, hunting, trapping, timber and semi-isolation which are still dear to many Indians."[17]

Presloski's suggestions were well intentioned, and his various goals were not necessarily incompatible. But in trying to merge the advantages of urban and rural life, DIAND failed to achieve either in the new Tutu Creek and Parsnip River Reserves.[18] Hunting, fishing, and trapping were sorely limited, while proximity to the town of Mackenzie spawned a host of social problems, similar to those experienced by the Cheslatta. In short, "Their social and cultural lifestyles were radically altered with no serious thought given as to the long-term implications of these community disruptions."[19] Gordon Pierre was a Grade 9 student at the time. He recalled, "It didn't feel like home. It wasn't our territory."[20]

Growing disenchantment at Parsnip River and Tutu Creek led many Elders and their families to abandon the new reserves and, with no governmental sanction or support, return in April 1970 to their Traditional Territories. In Jean Isaac's words, "We wanted to be near a river again. To get back to what was left of our land." Their destination was Ingenika Point. By 1970, the sawmill at Finlay Forks had been forced to shut down because of rising waters, but the temporary DIAND dwellings remained. By 1977, all but one family had settled there.[21]

The move to Ingenika Point left the Nation devoid of resources and support. To add insult to injury, as the Tsay Keh Dene settled on a small fragment of their Traditional Territory, they were characterized as "squatters on Crown lands" as the two governments quarrelled over the perennial issue of reserve creation. The Nation was caught in an intractable Catch-22 situation: British Columbia refused to create a new reserve at Ingenika Point; Canada was reluctant to provide program support to a First Nation living on "provincial" lands. The Nation possessed no internal funds to rebuild the community. Total compensation from the province to the Tsay Keh Dene for dam impact was approximately $35,000 – primarily for lost traplines.[22] The Band "endured hardship beyond imagination," in the words of Ed John, a lawyer for the Tsay Keh Dene at that time, as they awaited resolution.[23]

Diaspora and the Dilemma of the Landless First Nation

DIAND initially believed that settlement at Ingenika Point would be temporary. After canvassing First Nation members in 1970 and again in 1971, the superintendent of the Lakes District, A.C. Roach, determined that the majority "strongly prefer Ingenika, but dissatisfaction would probably arise within 2–3 years after relocation [to Ingenika Point] because of isolation from services and employment." Roach believed the First Nation would eventually embrace the new reserves at Parsnip River and Tutu Creek, but "only by first moving to Ingenika will the Indians satisfy their remaining nomadic instincts."[24] Nevertheless, he wanted to establish a reserve quickly at Ingenika Point and allow DIAND to legally spend money on housing and related infrastructure: "This can be done by outright purchase, the province granting the Indians a Reserve site, or an exchange of land." BC Hydro responded on behalf of the province with an offer of 500 acres at Ingenika Point, contingent on the return of the Tutu Creek Reserve's 92.3 acres to the province. The First Nation met on April 16, 1971, and resolved that a minimum of 5,000 acres of additional reserve land would be necessary to compensate them for their losses. Negotiations stalled.[25]

To break the impasse, in 1973 DIAND British Columbia advanced an innovative proposal: treat the Tsay Keh Dene as a Treaty 8 band, opening the door to a much larger reserve allotment. The proposal was well grounded in history. Dominion officials, including Indian commissioner David Laird, had concluded in 1910 that "the Sekanis of the Fort Grahame-Finlay River area [as the Tsay Keh Dene were earlier known] should be brought into treaty," but an adhesion agreement was never completed.[26] The opportunity to re-address the question over sixty years later excited no enthusiasm at national headquarters: "Although the Ingenika band may have inhabited an area covered by Treaty #8 in 1899, the policy of the Canadian Government at the present time is not to renegotiate the treaties or make new ones."[27]

Would a creative local solution be sacrificed on the altar of federal policy? Despite Ottawa's response, DIAND's BC regional director two months later wrote to the provincial deputy minister of lands, forests and water resources and noted that since "there is some doubt as to whether or not the Ingenika band can qualify for a land grant under the terms of Treaty 8, we would like to discuss the acquisition of a large tract of land to be converted to Reserve status." The letter requested an early meeting with the deputy to discuss "the ways and means by which both Governments can accommodate those people in their desire to preserve their nomadic lifestyle."[28]

Internal correspondence among DIAND officials in Ottawa expressed growing frustration with their provincial counterparts. Among the remedies they contemplated was "that the Band make a direct submission to the Provincial Premier [Barrett] on the matter." Roach argued: "If we can be confident that such a submission would indeed receive the personal attention and consideration of the Premier himself, we would assist the Band accordingly." He was less than optimistic, however, as "past submissions have not gone beyond the Director of Lands for British Columbia and this route has thus far been unproductive." He asked DIAND's regional supervisor of lands to arrange a "top level discussion involving the Band Council, Provincial Government Leaders and Departmental Officials ... Nothing less than this will be anything more than a repetition of past efforts."[29]

Subsequent discussions led to a meeting between federal and provincial district-level officials and thirty-six Nation members at Ingenika Point in February 1974. Officials heard the Tsay Keh Dene's story of fragmented consultations, minimal compensation, diminishing water quality, the loss of rivers for trade and travel, and lost opportunities for fishing, hunting, and trapping. Officials were impressed by the Nation's stories and the living conditions the residents were enduring. The meeting was held in a newly opened school building, constructed only months earlier by volunteers from the Nation and BC Indian Missions. Officials noted that the community had installed a diesel-powered generator at the school. The generator produced "the only electric light in the community" despite its proximity to a major hydroelectric dam.[30]

The same officials met again the next day in Prince George, this time without the Nation. Their discussions reflected a deep concern that the Tsay Keh Dene were victims of an impasse between governments: "As a consequence the matter demands immediate corrective action." They offered two recommendations to Victoria and Ottawa: first, "that various government agencies brook no delay in dedication of an Indian Reserve at Ingenika," and second, that "a parcel of land of adequate size be set aside for Indian Reserve." Officials defined "adequate" as "the area between 2 Mile Creek to 8 Mile Creek," an area akin to the five thousand acres requested by the Tsay Keh Dene. "The social disruption to the band has been enormous following the creation of Lake Williston," officials noted, and the larger area would be required to restore traditional opportunities to hunt, fish, and trap.[31]

Officials had listened respectfully to the First Nation. Was the spirit of Trutch at last giving way to that of Douglas? The answer came six months later in a letter from BC Hydro to the Band council. Hydro offered "about 500 acres" subject to the release of the Tutu Creek Reserve. The Tsay Keh Dene rejected the offer, just as they had three years earlier in 1971.

Events elsewhere in Canada, most notably the recent James Bay and Northern Quebec Agreement, prompted a more aggressive approach from the federal government, encouraged by bipartisan support from Frank Oberle, the Progressive Conservative member of Parliament for Prince George–Peace River. Oberle "felt that Indian peoples' lifestyle had been drastically changed and using the James Bay settlement as an example, felt that negotiations should be reopened and decided by the Courts."[32] DIAND's Judd Buchanan responded to Oberle's initiative, ordering a detailed file review to prepare for legal action. In March 1975, DIAND officials advised the Ingenika Band council that the file review could "support the Band seeking a legal settlement which might possibly be based on the precedent set recently on behalf of the Indian people of the James Bay area."[33]

After considering DIAND's offer, the Chief politely declined it. A DIAND official summarized the exchange:

> The people appreciate and trust the good wishes and motives of Indian Affairs but their experiences and association with other agencies has left them quite cold and suspicious. They do not believe the total system cares or is interested in their predicament and consequently treat all offers of legal assistance with disdain.[34]

Not surprisingly, a decade of deflection and obfuscation by government officials had come home to roost. Years passed, but the Tsay Keh Dene's land tenure remained unresolved. BC Hydro made offers in 1979 and again in 1982, and the First Nation rejected both.[35] The land offered grew to nine hundred acres, but it was now contingent on the return of both the Parsnip River and Tutu Creek Reserves to the province.[36] Parsimony persisted, obstructing any kind of agreement.

New Players Open New Doors

One positive development was the creation of a Native Affairs Secretariat within British Columbia's Ministry of Intergovernmental Relations in 1987, a significant shift after more than a century of dismissing Indigenous relations as a federal responsibility. What prompted this shift? Had British Columbia at long last moved beyond ignoring "the Indian land question?" The secretariat was led from the outset by Assistant Deputy Minister Eric Denhoff. In his view, British Columbia in the latter 1980s was "a province in transition when it came to recognition of Indigenous rights and title," particularly in its shift "from its historical position of fobbing all responsibility for Indigenous issues off on the Government of Canada."[37]

Indigenous relations was elevated again, in 1988, with the creation of a Ministry of Native Affairs. British Columbia was not alone in embracing a new approach. For example, Ontario had officially designated a minister responsible for Native affairs in 1985 followed by a Native Affairs Directorate two years later.[38]

From an operational perspective, the secretariat expanded the government's capacity to respond to Indigenous issues beyond the legally focused Ministry of the Attorney General. That capacity proved integral to progress on the Tsay Keh Dene file. Soon after the secretariat's creation, Denhoff met with Grand Chief Ed John. The latter raised "a host of title and rights related issues," Denhoff recalls, among them the "Ingenika/Bennett dam issue and the travesty that had occurred." Denhoff promised that he and his minister, Stephen Rogers, would fly to Ingenika to meet the community. They did, and in Denhoff's words, Rogers "was so devastated by the poverty and the ramshackle mess of the folks stuck there with no federal or provincial services, he authorized me to start negotiating internally within government to put together a package to take to Cabinet and to push the feds for involvement."[39]

The Tsay Keh Dene's situation became a prominent media issue in 1987, providing further impetus for resolution. The *Vancouver Sun* on April 16, 1987, reported that the Tsay Keh Dene were threatening to block logging roads in a bid for governmental action on the "deplorable conditions" in which they lived. Chief Gordon Pierre described a "life of squalor": poor housing, lack of potable water, and an inadequate sewer system were the most pressing problems, all linked to the absence of reserve status.[40] Two months later, the *Vancouver Sun* featured a high-profile special report on the plight of the Tsay Keh Dene. Multiple articles by journalists Terry Glavin, Tom Barrett, and Bev Christensen caught the provincial government's attention.[41] A briefing note from the Ministry of Intergovernmental Relations argued that new forest tenures in the area should not be granted until the issues were resolved, "otherwise the Ingenika people could be left with new wilderness reserves located in the middle of denuded forests. This may spell the final ruin of a formerly self-sufficient people."[42]

MLAs from both sides of the legislature visited Ingenika Point in June and "were all shaken and shocked by what [they] saw there." Among them was Stephen Rogers (for his second visit), who remained anxious to know "how this particular Indian band managed to fall through the cracks of the social nets that we have."[43] Rogers was instrumental in securing an agreement that brought long-overdue infrastructure support to the Tsay Keh Dene in 1989. His initiative met with some resistance in the cabinet, but according to Denhoff, he "really didn't give a crap about what skeptical colleagues thought, nor did he have time for the political and bureaucratic resistance to fixing an obvious wrong. So, once he was convinced, he had enough clout with his colleagues and Premier to push one-off initiatives like this along." In Denhoff's words, Rogers "was very good at conveying the narrative of this community that had been absolutely devastated by the dam creation and ignored by everyone."[44]

According to Ed John, in his capacity as lawyer for the Tsay Keh Dene, "Rogers expressed the need to do something constructive in short order. The unclean water source at Ingenika made an impression on him ... He was genuinely concerned about what he saw."[45] Denhoff followed up with a letter to Owen Anderson, DIAND's director general for the BC region, expressing British Columbia's commitment to resolving the Ingenika situation, including an enhanced land package. To reinforce the province's good intentions, Denhoff offered emergency assistance to address housing and water issues and $100,000 for community facilities.[46]

Denhoff's letter led Anderson to visit Ingenika Point in 1987. Like those who preceded him, Anderson was struck by the First Nation's plight:

> We were all most impressed by the environmental damage wreaked by the creation of Williston Lake: the fish stock parasitic because they cannot adapt to still, low-oxygen water; the continuous erosion of the sand and gravel beds caused by 40-foot seasonal changes in the height of the water; sandstorms brought on by heavy occasional winds over the resulting sand bars; dangerous debris in the water; loss of valuable hunting and trapping.[47]

Anderson promised Chief Pierre that "action would be forthcoming very soon." Like British Columbia, Ottawa offered immediate "good faith" assistance: five mobile homes for "elders who the Band feels should not suffer another winter in their uninsulated cabins," five new homes, repairs to twenty-seven others, and access to potable water from a new well.[48]

Despite the officials' good intentions, negotiations were tough and protracted. British Columbia had proven to be a prickly, unpredictable negotiating partner on more than a few occasions since Confederation. Distrust was evident. In a letter to Denhoff written on May 16, 1988, Manfred Klein of DIAND claimed that to save time, "we have declined to put forward our preferred position – i.e., the Province/BC Hydro pay for everything – but have chosen instead to convey our rock bottom compromise position." After seven pages reiterating why the province or BC Hydro "should really pay the total cost," Klein noted that "senior officials were struck by the plight of this isolated band" and hence were prepared to offer 50 percent of infrastructure costs.[49]

Three months later, Denhoff sweetened the negotiating pot on behalf of the province with promises of $500,000 in cash, $500,000 in land, and $350,000 in social, educational, and environmental programs.[50] Federal officials were hopeful but cautious. At a meeting at Ingenika Point, federal and provincial officials shared their perspectives with Grand Chief Ed John, the Carrier Sekani Tribal Council, and over thirty First Nations members. After Chief Pierre summarized the challenges facing the Tsay Keh Dene, DIAND's deputy minister Harry Swain stated that the "federal government has been wanting to act on this for some time now and considers, of course, that the province has some duty in this regard. We have made some approaches and offers to them." He looked forward to reciprocal support from the province.[51]

Denhoff responded by listing the recent initiatives undertaken by the province and its willingness to do more in partnership with Canada. His minister, he added, had taken the Ingenika situation to treasury board and cabinet "to do some things until the land question was settled." Owen Anderson was diplomatic but firm in his response: "I had asked [BC] for a 50/50 share of the costs. The province has come back with a serious opening offer. It's not 50/50 but it's not 100/0 either." He was appreciative of the "serious response" from British Columbia and believed "we do indeed have the basis for negotiations."[52]

First Nations members spoke emotionally and powerfully, underlining the urgent need for an agreement. "This negotiation has been going on for years and years," one member stated. "It started when I was a little girl and I'm 25 years old now. We don't ask for much. This land belongs to us. We have lived off it forever. I think we should get a reserve." Another added, "Everything we ask for they say no because we are not on-reserve. Why can't we get a reserve?" Their appeals prompted Swain to reply:

> I resolved that I was going to stay quiet about this [British Columbia's long-standing resistance to new reserve creation] but the conditions are not forgotten outside and they are known in Ottawa. For the first time we have the

> province willing to give the land. They will provide the land for the federal government to make it into a reserve."[53]

Denhoff believes that British Columbia's long-standing resistance to creating new reserves helped to move the initiative forward:

> I convinced them in advance that they should agree to create a reserve if BC would provide the land and some cash, and since BC had never done anything remotely like that in a hundred years or something, they thought it was an easy give they'd never have to honour, and agreed instantly. When we actually got the land and our cash, they were quite stunned and had to spend a lot of time convincing Ottawa to move it through. By then, we'd created pretty strong messaging around it at both the bureaucratic and political levels, so they were cornered and, to be fair, did more or less the right thing.[54]

From Canada's perspective, it was British Columbia that was finally compelled to do "the right thing" for the Tsay Keh Dene after years of delay and obfuscation.

DIAND wanted an agreement but not until the province was irrevocably committed to it. After difficult but productive discussions with the federal Treasury Board, Swain said he "put together the federal purse ($13 million), agreed with Owen on what could reasonably be demanded of the province, and off we went." British Columbia undoubtedly moved further than anticipated but not without resistance from the cabinet. Jack Davis, minister of energy and minister responsible for BC Hydro, wrote Jack Weisgerber, the newly sworn minister of Native affairs, on September 8, 1988: "It is all wrong. Land was set aside and other contributions made by Hydro, years ago. The reservoir issue was settled insofar as Hydro's flooding was concerned ... It should not be used as a convenient milk cow by Native Affairs or any other Ministry."[55]

Despite resistance, a tripartite agreement was signed on August 5, 1989, a vital first step in what has proven to be a long and continuing journey toward reconciliation. The Tsay Keh Dene received 3,300 acres, $10.2 million from Canada, $2 million from BC Hydro for community infrastructure, and guaranteed employment on a provincial $10 million fish and wildlife enhancement program for Williston Reservoir. Construction of the contemporary Tsay Keh Dene Village followed the 1989 agreement. After more than twenty years of dispossession and dislocation for the Tsay Keh Dene, the tripartite agreement brought, in Swain's words, "a new reserve, a new village, a modest timber license, a contract to remove deadwood from the Williston Reservoir, and even a four-wheel drive road into the village. To this day, I'm still pleased with what we accomplished."[56]

For the Tsay Keh Dene, the destructive changes of the 1960s had come with blinding speed, but restitution was painfully slow. A generation grew from infancy to adulthood before the provincial and federal governments finally addressed the harms created by British Columbia's relentless pursuit of economic development.

The Tsay Keh Dene Nation continues to work tirelessly on multiple fronts to remedy these harms. In 2010, after protracted litigation, the Tsay Keh Dene reached a $22 million final settlement with BC Hydro and the province.[57] Since that time, the Nation has also concluded forestry and mining agreements with the province and private-sector companies.[58] They are continuing their journey toward reconciliation through Stage 4 negotiations of an agreement in principle at the BC Treaty Commission.

The Cheslatta Carrier Nation has also worked tirelessly toward resolving issues, including a 1993 settlement agreement with Canada. In 2019, after another set of protracted negotiations, the Cheslatta signed a settlement agreement and an interim reconciliation agreement with British Columbia involving both cash and land. More recently, the Cheslatta and Rio Tinto Alcan signed a "new day" agreement setting out a range of training, employment, business, and environmental stewardship opportunities.[59] The Cheslatta are pursuing broader reconciliation through Stage 3 negotiations of a framework agreement in the BC Treaty Commission process. The Cheslatta and Tsay Keh Dene stories are studies in courage, patience, and determination. Their stories are far from over.

10

A Slow Shift in Indigenous Relations

As British Columbia celebrated a century of provincehood in 1971, the Cheslatta and Tsay Keh Dene were mired in deplorable situations created by government actions (and subsequent inaction) that would take decades to resolve. The colonial policies and prejudices that fostered their dispossession and dislocation still held sway. The province continued to resist using public lands to create or expand reserves. Conversely, when reserves stood in the way of development, British Columbia presumed that the broader public interest trumped Indigenous people's interests and concerns. Governments changed; long-standing policies did not.

Had he been alive in 1971, Joseph Trutch would have gazed across the province and felt profound satisfaction. Great cities and prosperous towns had grown up around the small and scattered reserves he'd been instrumental in creating. In rural and remote corners of the province, First Nations had proven to be no barrier to the development of mines, timber and pulp mills, and hydroelectric dams. The 1970s would see vital shifts in the federal government's approach to Indigenous rights and title, largely prompted by Indigenous people's political and legal activism. British Columbia remained resistant to such reforms.

W.A.C. Bennett's Social Credit government was defeated in 1972 after an uninterrupted twenty-year reign. The incoming NDP government of Dave Barrett changed the face of the province in many ways over the next three years, from introducing the Agricultural Land Reserve to creating the Insurance Corporation of British Columbia. Such bold policy initiatives were not undertaken in Indigenous relations, which the Barrett government would tackle with "affirmative action and economic development, not comprehensive treaties." Despite the inclusion of Frank Calder – Atlin MLA and Nisga'a leader – as a minister without portfolio in Barrett's first cabinet, substantive action on treaty making would not be realized until the election of another NDP government in 1991.[1]

The Barrett government was defeated in 1975 by a resurgent Social Credit party led by Bill Bennett. Like his father, the younger Bennett led a government focused on economic and resource development, and it would make its mark on Indigenous relations largely through its spirited defence of the status quo. In 1978, over a century after George Walkem's cabinet had explicitly set out British Columbia's post-Confederation position on the expansion of First Nations reserves, Bennett's cabinet declared its opposition to the federal government's interest in exploring potential treaty discussions with the Nisga'a Nation.

In *Response of the Government of British Columbia to the Position Paper of the Nishga Tribal Council*, the Bennett government cast the province's small and scattered reserves as an unqualified success: "The selection of these reserves was made over a period of years jointly by Canada and British Columbia with such care and precision that, ultimately, the province conveyed to Canada almost 1,700 reserves for continued Indian use, whether for settlements, burial grounds, fishing stations, berry patches, and so on." British Columbia had created more reserves than the rest of Canada combined, the response declared, while acknowledging that the five hundred reserves elsewhere were "generally larger, reflecting a basic difference in the policy under which they were established as well as distinctions in the topography and land use."[2]

This rosy description of British Columbia's postcolonial reserve policies was largely at odds with the historical record. The ongoing disparity in reserve size east and west of the Rockies had in no way been relieved by "care and precision" in the province's reserve selection, given that this process had been largely aimed at ensuring that prime farmlands were showcased in settler pre-emptions and not "trapped" in reserves.

Cabinet documents from both 1875 and 1978 feature finger wagging at the supposed impracticality of enlarging Indigenous lands through treaty or any other means. "The enlargement of past Reserves is in many instances practically impossible, as they are surrounded by white settlements," the 1875 report declared, when British Columbia's total white population was about ten thousand. The same argument was employed a century later: provincial lands "available for Indian use have been reduced over the course of the years by settlement, development, and resource extraction. This fact of history cannot be reversed and must be accepted by all parties to these discussions," even in the sparsely populated Nisga'a territory of northwestern British Columbia.[3]

Similarly, both documents emphasized that fulfillment of Indigenous people's aspirations would be achieved off – not on – reserves. The 1875 report claimed that Canada's proposal for larger reserves would promote a "concentration of the Indians upon Reserves," thereby undermining their opportunity to enjoy the social and economic advantages of a growing province. That argument was also redeployed a century later: "In summary, the Province holds the view that a symbolic, one-time settlement of Indian land claims – a settlement which may preclude or diminish any future extension of programs and services to native peoples by the Province – would result in the furthering of the social and economic isolation of our native peoples."[4]

The Bennett government's words were deliberate: should the Nisga'a or any other First Nation succeed on the "land claims" front, they would pay the price of exclusion from provincial programs and services. The policy lesson was also clear: reserves had contributed to Indigenous people's social and economic isolation, so alienation of more provincial lands for treaty purposes would only exacerbate their isolation. The province would not "contemplate providing extraordinary benefits to the Nishga people at the expense of others, whether Indian or non-Indian." The government feared that setting this precedent would all but guarantee that "no Band will be satisfied to accept less."[5]

The Bennett cabinet correctly discerned that the federal position on Aboriginal title was shifting in the wake of the Supreme Court of Canada's *Calder* decision a few years earlier and was troubled by suggestions from Ottawa that the province should play any part in negotiating and settling land claims. British Columbia's response emphasized that the province had "not altered its stance with respect to denial of the existence of aboriginal title," and added, for clarity, that "if any aboriginal title or interest may once have existed, that title was extinguished prior to the union of British Columbia with Canada in 1871." If Canada chose to think otherwise, the "responsibility to extinguish that title" rested solely with the federal government.[6] British Columbia's core message on Indigenous lands continued to be "there is no problem and if there is a problem it is a federal responsibility."[7]

Calder Prompts a Shift in Canada's Approach to Indigenous Relations

The Bennett government's concern was sparked by the influential 1973 Supreme Court of Canada decision *Calder v Attorney-General of British Columbia.*

According to Jim Aldridge, legal counsel and treaty negotiator for the Nisga'a, the roots of *Calder* lay in Premier Smithe's harsh rebuke of the Nisga'a and Ts'msyen delegation that visited Victoria in 1887:

> The chiefs went home and started organizing. The organization took place around what was referred to then and continued to be referred to by the Nisga'a as "the resolution of the land question." The concept of land claims was not part of the vocabulary, rather it was "the land question." And to that end, the Nisga'a formed the Nisga'a Land Committee in the 1890s. The Nisga'a Land Committee was the first modern political organization created for the specific and express purpose of pursuing a resolution to the land question.[8]

The Nisga'a had unsuccessfully petitioned the Judicial Committee of the Privy Council in 1913 but continued to battle until 1927 amendments to the Indian Act "effectively made pursuing the land question a criminal offense."[9] Repeal of that amendment in 1951 renewed the Nisga'a's efforts. When attempts to pursue a negotiated solution in the 1960s proved fruitless, the Nisga'a turned to the courts.

The initial results were not encouraging. Thomas Berger, who led the Nisga'a's legal battle from its inception, described the political context:

> We weren't expected to go very far. Prime Minister Trudeau came to Vancouver in 1969 while this case was before the courts and he was asked: "What do you think of the whole subject of Aboriginal rights?" His answer was, "We will not recognize Aboriginal rights, because no society can be built on historical might-have-beens."[10]

Frank Calder, president of the Nisga'a Tribal Council, and the Nisga'a argued that title to their traditional lands had never been extinguished by treaty or any other means, but their argument was rejected in a unanimous decision of the BC Court of Appeal in 1970. The decision reflected the prejudices of colonial British Columbia a century earlier, depicting the Nisga'a at the time of white settlement as "a very primitive people with few of the institutions of civilized society, and none at all of our notions of private property."[11] The Nisga'a then sought a declaratory judgment from the Supreme Court that their Nation held "the aboriginal title, otherwise known as the Indian title ... to their ancient tribal territory."[12]

The Nisga'a were determined that the court should hear their case despite the doctrine of sovereign immunity that then prevailed.[13] The decision to launch an appeal to the Supreme Court, without the consent of the provincial government by way of fiat (formal decree), was a testament to the Nisg̱a'a's courage and determination in their long-standing battle for recognition of Aboriginal title, even at the risk of standing alone. The Nisg̱a'a pressed forward despite opposition from some First Nations, who worried that a loss could jeopardize the fight for Indigenous rights. British Columbia resisted the *Calder* case at every stage, even after the NDP took power and Calder was appointed a minister without portfolio.[14] Change in the partisan composition of government in 1972 did not fundamentally alter its position on Aboriginal title.

Calder was the first in a series of game-changing decisions from the Supreme Court and a watershed moment in the evolution of Indigenous policy. Justice Pigeon, as Berger notes, "refused to decide the matter on the basis that we had not used proper procedure to come to court."[15] The balance of the court produced three separate judgments; notably, six of the seven justices "were of the view that Aboriginal title was – and, by inference, always had been – part of the law of Canada."[16]

The court was divided, however, "on the question of whether, as the lower courts had said, the general legislation passed by the colony of British Columbia had the legal effect of voiding Indigenous title." Three justices held that it did, but a powerful dissent authored by Justice Emmett Hall (and supported by two of his judicial colleagues) argued that Aboriginal title still prevailed.[17] Hall asserted, in a rebuke of the court's arguments, that "evidence must be approached in the light of present-day research and knowledge, disregarding ancient concepts formulated when understanding of the customs and culture of our original people was rudimentary and incomplete and when they were thought to be wholly without cohesion, laws, or culture, in effect a sub-human species."[18]

In the wake of *Calder,* Trudeau sought advice from the Department of Justice: "Who was right? Mr. Justice Hall or his opposing colleagues on the Court? Had Aboriginal title been extinguished in these non-treaty areas of Canada?" The department and its chief legal adviser, Gerard La Forest, concluded that Hall was right.[19] And Hall's dissenting opinion was deemed "sufficiently persuasive" to shift thinking within Trudeau's Liberal government. In a sharp departure from its 1969 "Statement of the Government of Canada on Indian Policy" (also known as the 1969 White Paper), the government acknowledged that Indigenous rights and title exist.[20]

The federal government's shift ended a century of vacillation on whether treaties should address unextinguished Aboriginal title, but it did nothing to change British Columbia's opposition.[21] For his part, Frank Calder believed the Supreme Court's divided opinion opened the door to Aboriginal title negotiations in British Columbia, so he saw it as the "number one victory of the Calder case."[22]

Constitutional Patriation Brings Recognition of Indigenous Rights and Title

The Trudeau Liberals were defeated by Joe Clark's Progressive Conservatives in the 1979 election but returned to power in 1980 after Clark's minority government was defeated in a vote of confidence. Trudeau returned with a majority government and a paramount goal: patriation of the Canadian Constitution (meaning the formal transfer of authority on all constitutional matters from Great Britain to Canada's federal and provincial governments) and inclusion of a charter of rights and freedoms within it.

Among the most heavily debated issues on the road to patriation was constitutional recognition of Indigenous rights. British Columbia's Social Credit government was, unsurprisingly, among the most vociferous critics. Mel Smith, British Columbia's deputy minister of constitutional affairs in the early 1980s, participated in the federal-provincial conference of November 1981, an event that produced substantial agreement on Trudeau's constitutional package – minus recognition of Aboriginal title and treaty rights (incorporated into section 35 of the draft Constitution Act).[23]

According to Smith, recognition of Aboriginal title and treaty rights came about because of bilateral discussions between the federal government and Indigenous leaders, and the provinces played no role in the process.[24] Closed-door negotiations at the November conference produced a tentative agreement between Ottawa and all provinces except Quebec but only after section 35 language was dropped from the deal at the insistence of Premier Bennett.[25]

Barry Strayer, an assistant deputy minister at the federal Department of Justice in the early 1980s, offers a detailed account of the twists and turns on the road to patriation in *Canada's Constitutional Revolution*. He notes that Trudeau had returned to office in 1980 with only two seats west of Ontario, both in Manitoba, a serious challenge given the British Parliament's preference for a constitutional package with "sufficient" provincial support or consent.[26] Trudeau sought support for his initiative from, among others, Ed Broadbent and his federal NDP caucus, which included twenty-seven MPs from Western Canada. In return for their support, the NDP demanded the inclusion of provisions recognizing Indigenous rights and title. Trudeau agreed and included a version of section 35 in his initial patriation proposal but dropped it when faced with unrelenting provincial opposition at the November conference.[27] Resolution of one problem produced another for Trudeau: the NDP caucus promptly withdrew its support for his patriation package.

In Mel Smith's reckoning, two factors led to section 35's return to constitutional discussions: "fierce lobbying" from Indigenous organizations and a "compromise" proposal from Alberta's premier, Peter Lougheed, to add the word "existing" to the phrase "aboriginal and treaty rights" in section 35. According to Smith, the addition was an improvement, "but no serious analysis was done as to what the clause meant ... The fact is that the premiers and the Prime Minister had a political problem and including the amended clause, whatever it meant, was deemed to be the way to solve it."[28] British Columbia was, in Smith's words, "backed into" accepting section 35 and would minimize its importance in subsequent federal-provincial-territorial discussions.[29]

Some British Columbians strongly disagreed with the Social Credit government's position on section 35. Thomas Berger, a judge for the Supreme Court of British Columbia from 1981 to 1983, passionately supported inclusion and put his judicial position in jeopardy by speaking out publicly. "The native peoples have not come this far to turn back now," he told the *Globe and Mail.*[30] Ian Waddell, NDP MP and justice critic, noted that the justice minister, Jean Chrétien, "felt intense pressure from Aboriginal protest groups."[31] Waddell and his NDP colleagues quickly threw their support behind the Indigenous campaign for reinstatement of section 35.

Strayer also notes the key role that Indigenous people's resistance played in influencing the outcome of Canada's constitutional drama. Indigenous lobbying and demonstrations, he suggests, were not unwelcome in Ottawa: "The federal government stood ready at all times to see section 35 restored, and Cabinet confirmed that position on November 19."[32] Among the key initiatives was the "Constitution Express," led by George Manuel, president of the Union of British Columbia Indian Chiefs.[33] He and other Indigenous leaders and organizations from across Canada worked tirelessly and effectively to secure what became section 35(1) of the Constitution Act, 1982, despite ongoing resistance from the BC government.

Over a Century after Confederation, the Treaty Settlement Door Slowly Opens

Bill Bennett retired in 1986, and his successor, Bill Vander Zalm, also appeared to be unreceptive to treaty making. However, the creation of the Native Affairs Secretariat within the Ministry of Intergovernmental Relations in 1987 was an early sign of pending, if tentative, change. Eric Denhoff's role as the secretariat's assistant deputy minister was intended to be narrow in scope, confined primarily to identifying economic development opportunities for First Nations. "When I took the job under Vander Zalm," Denhoff told journalist Justine Hunter, "it was a firing offence to meet with any First Nations on the topic of treaty making."[34]

Vander Zalm's position shifted after visiting Indigenous communities and learning more about their history. "It was apparent the real problem was that here in BC, because we don't have treaties, there was no relationship," Denhoff argued. Jack Weisgerber, appointed as British Columbia's first minister of Native affairs in 1988, came to a similar conclusion: "What we found, almost without exception, was that the First Nations were so angry because BC wouldn't engage in treaty making. You couldn't get a conversation going on economic initiatives because they were so frustrated."[35]

In his first years as premier, Vander Zalm offered up process and good intentions, but First Nations wanted more substantive action. Early throne speeches promised "a new, mutually productive relationship with the native Indian people of our province" through structures such as a "Premier's Council on Native Affairs" and a "First Peoples' Traditions for Tomorrow Council." All fell short of Indigenous people's expectations. The slow pace of reform sparked road blockades in several corners of the province during the summer of 1990. To de-escalate tensions, Vander Zalm and Weisgerber met with Indigenous leaders in mid-July and offered their commitment "to address BC's unresolved Indian land question."[36]

Their commitment predictably led to concern and resistance both within and outside the Social Credit government. Indigenous people's goodwill evaporated after Weisgerber commented on Aboriginal title in the *Vancouver Sun:* "The question was, 'Does this mean you recognize aboriginal title?' The answer was 'no.' What I am going to have difficulty getting people to understand is that you can deal with the land question without recognizing, as a starting point, aboriginal title."[37]

For his part, Vander Zalm attempted to frame the question by providing historical context and less-than-subtly shifting the blame onto the federal government:

> In the past we've consistently said it's a federal matter. When BC entered into Confederation, the terms of Confederation provided that it be a federal matter and we've stuck to this stubbornly. Unfortunately, that's not resolving anything

> because the federal policy is not getting at it quick enough. The system as we know it, as we see it today, and the policies that are in place federally, aren't working. It's taking too long.[38]

Clarification of the province's position brought immediate accusations of a "double cross" and a resumption of blockades. A yawning gap persisted between governmental policy and Indigenous people's expectations. "All through this period and beyond," Denhoff notes, "increasing pressure from Ottawa, Indigenous leaders, churches and the opposition continued."[39]

Turbulence in British Columbia Mirrored in Canada

Indigenous people's anger and discord were evident elsewhere in Canada in the summer of 1990. A dispute arising from a proposed golf course expansion on contested land at Oka, south of Montreal, produced a violent seventy-eight-day standoff between Kanyen'kehà:ka (Mohawk) warriors, Quebec's Sûreté du Québec, the RCMP, and the Canadian Armed Forces. The open conflict finally ended following Ottawa's commitment to purchase the lands under dispute.[40] The Kanyen'kehà:ka conflict, and blockades in British Columbia, undoubtedly played a role in Prime Minister Brian Mulroney's establishment of the Royal Commission on Aboriginal Peoples on August 21, 1991. Sadly, the commission would not bring an end to land-based confrontation and violence.[41]

The Royal Commission on Aboriginal Peoples was successful, however, in drawing broader public attention to the issue of Indian residential schools, an issue all too often ignored. British Columbia was home to 18 of Canada's over 130 residential schools.[42] The royal commission powerfully summarized the legacy of these schools: "Bad policies always claim victims. But the effects of bad education policies seep through the decades, from child to parent to family to community, and from one generation to those that follow."[43]

Commission hearings drew testimony from many former students, among them Jeannie Dick of Canim Lake: "The intent of the residential school policy was to erase Aboriginal identity by separating generations of children from their families, suppressing their Aboriginal languages, and re-socializing them according to the norms of non-Aboriginal society. The repercussions of the often-brutal enforcement of measures to achieve assimilation are still being felt in the lives of former students." Chief Cinderina Williams of the Splatsin First Nation characterized residential schools as a multigenerational tragedy in her 1994 testimony:

> When these children returned home, they were aliens. They did not speak their own language, so they could not communicate with anyone other than their own counterparts. Some looked down on their families because of their lack of English, their lifestyle, and some were just plain hostile. They had formed no bonds with their families, and some couldn't survive without the regimentation they had become so accustomed to.[44]

Residential schools added one more layer to the economic and social dislocation produced by over a century of destructive public policy from federal, provincial, and colonial governments. Loss of language and culture in residential schools exacerbated other historical losses – from voting rights and commercial fishing licences to resource development opportunities. The commission's 1996 recommendations would be pivotal in generating governmental action through the Indian Residential Schools Settlement Agreement and the Truth and Reconciliation Commission.[45]

Change was coming to Indigenous relations in the late 1980s and early 1990s – even in British Columbia – but it was court decisions that put pressure on the province. In 1984, a Musqueam fisher, Ronald Sparrow, was arrested by Fisheries and Oceans Canada officers for using a net that was longer than permitted under his food-fishing licence. The Musqueam Nation defended Sparrow, arguing that their Aboriginal right to fish had never been extinguished by a treaty. The department's charges against Sparrow were upheld in British Columbia's lower courts but subsequently rejected in the BC Court of Appeal.

A key passage from the Court of Appeal's decision underlined the ongoing and critical importance of *Calder* in Canadian jurisprudence: "Six judges of the Supreme Court [of Canada] having joined in rejecting the view that aboriginal title can exist only if conferred by a treaty, statute or agreement, there can be no justification for continuing to treat that view as binding."[46] The BC Court of Appeal's 1987 decision in *Regina v Sparrow* was subsequently "confirmed and strengthened" on appeal to the Supreme Court of Canada in 1990, undermining British Columbia's existing interpretation of *Calder* and obliging "the province to face reality."[47]

Why would a case about the constitutional right to fish have vital implications for broader Indigenous rights and title? Section 35(1) of the Constitution Act, 1982, recognizes and affirms the "existing aboriginal and treaty rights of the aboriginal peoples of Canada." Did those rights include – in the absence of treaty, statute, or agreement – Ronald Sparrow's right to fish? As historian J.R. Miller notes:

> In the course of ruling on that question, the high court also laid down criteria to determine if an Aboriginal right, including title, had been extinguished. In essence, it declared that title could be nullified only by legislation that had explicitly declared extinguishment as its purpose, had a legitimate public policy reason for overriding the right, and encroached on the Aboriginal right only so far as was necessary to achieve that policy goal.[48]

From Joseph Trutch's assertion in 1867 that "Indians have really no right to the lands they claim" to the Bill Bennett cabinet's continued "denial of the existence of aboriginal title" over a century later, BC governments were quick to disparage the concept of Aboriginal title, but none had undertaken legislative initiatives that met the *Sparrow* test.

By 1990, the "Indigenous land question" could no longer be capriciously dismissed by the province, and it was never far removed from the BC cabinet table. Eric Denhoff, deputy minister of Native affairs, was frequently in demand at cabinet or premier meetings and felt that Indigenous issues "really consumed the government for some time." Some of his visits to cabinet were less than pleasant, particularly meetings focused on the province's potential participation in treaty making. On one such occasion, he was "roundly attacked, quite vehemently, by several ministers." According to Denhoff, a touch of levity from Premier Vander Zalm saved the day: "Now, now everybody, we all know Eric's a bit of a liberal here but he's just trying to present us all the options so we can get our minds around this!"[49]

Resistance to treaty making was deep and entrenched, but according to Denhoff, "as tensions, roadblocks and lawsuits grew and started to become a threat to the economy, provincial politicians started looking for different answers." After protracted debate, the cabinet recognized that "Canada could not on its own resolve modern treaties since virtually all the available Crown land was held by the Province!"[50]

Overcoming long-standing opposition to treaty making within the caucus, the cabinet, and industry required a concerted effort from government and Indigenous leaders. "Eventually a joint task force with BC Indigenous leaders was struck to recommend how treaty discussions could move forward," Denhoff notes, "and once Cabinet accepted the report, the die was really cast. The BC government changed its 125-year policy and started treaty making."[51] However, vital questions remained unanswered: What operational model should be adopted? Who would pay and how much? Who would set the goals, and how would they be prioritized? What would be the mix of cash and land?

The 1991 Throne Speech, the last from the Vander Zalm premiership, promised two important steps forward on treaty making: "The first land claims framework agreement in the province's history, with the Nisga'a Tribal Council" and a tripartite task force (with the First Nations Summit and Canada) "to determine how best to proceed with other pending aboriginal claims." After a protracted controversy unrelated to Indigenous issues, Vander Zalm resigned on March 29, 1991.[52] His successor, Rita Johnson, and her Social Credit government were soundly defeated by Mike Harcourt's NDP several months later. A new and dramatic chapter in British Columbia's history of Indigenous relations was about to unfold.

11

The Nisg̱a'a Canoe Finally Reaches Home

Mike Harcourt's NDP government laid out its goals for Indigenous relations boldly in the 1992 throne speech. Lieutenant-Governor David Lam gave voice to commitments that had been anathema for over 120 years when he said, "we recognize aboriginal title and the inherent rights of aboriginal people to self-government." He added that an agreement on a new treaty commission had been negotiated.[1] The speech contained no reference to the Nisg̱a'a Tribal Council or to the Vander Zalm government's promise to institute the "first land claims framework agreement in the province's history." However, the Nisg̱a'a were far from forgotten, and the goal of completing British Columbia's first modern treaty was high on the new government's agenda.

The speech's brevity and optimistic tone masked daunting challenges. British Columbia's long-standing dismissal of Indigenous issues as a "federal problem" left the province poorly equipped to enter the realm of treaty making. A briefing note from the Ministry of Finance and Corporate Relations from May 1992 reflected these concerns, stating that the Ministry of Aboriginal Affairs was entering negotiations "without established policy or provincial experience in the area." It faced daunting challenges, including developing a "comprehensive provincial policy related to aboriginal people" and identifying "the significant financial, legal and intergovernmental implications of all component policy options." Finance was particularly concerned that Aboriginal Affairs was entering negotiations without a clear understanding of the "likely cost to government of land claims ... expected to be in the range from \$4.5 to \$14.5 billion in 1991 dollars." For context, the Ministry of Health (by far the largest of all ministries) had a 1992 budget of about $6 billion: the "financial implications of policy decisions must be well understood," the note emphasized, "given potential costs of settlements."[2]

Political momentum continued despite these issues. Prime Minister Mulroney, Premier Harcourt, and Indigenous leaders "ushered in a new relationship between natives and government" with the signing of the British Columbia Treaty Commission Agreement in 1992. The agreement confirmed important details regarding the size and function of the commission, but critical financial questions remained unresolved. Journalist Deborah Wilson believed the commission's work would be hobbled until the federal and provincial governments reached an agreement on apportioning settlement costs, specifically in relation to cash and land.[3] Apportionment raised a host of thorny questions, particularly given there was early interest in treaty making from First Nations in both urban and rural settings, where land values varied widely.

British Columbia and Canada reached a cost-sharing agreement in June 1993. In it, British Columbia's Aboriginal affairs minister, Andrew Petter, noted, "The federal government will give up mostly money while the province will give up mostly crown land." British Columbia would pay an estimated 17 percent of the "cash costs" of settlements, Canada about 83 percent.[4] "Estimated" was the key word to describe the agreement, which, *Vancouver Sun* columnist Vaughn Palmer noted, was "only a memorandum of understanding and not legally binding on either government."[5] Estimates of cost distribution sustained the launch of the BC Treaty Commission on September 21, 1992, but the devil was indeed lurking in the details. Allocation of costs and credits became an immediate issue in the Nisg̱a'a Treaty negotiations.

The *Vancouver Sun* reported the pending collapse of those negotiations on July 14, 1995, citing differences between the federal and provincial governments over resource values attached to settlement lands.[6] The province had substantially increased stumpage fees on Crown lands since 1993 and wanted the foregone revenues from stumpage on treaty settlement lands credited to British Columbia's side of the Nisg̱a'a ledger. As Palmer noted, "The resource revenue that the province would lose handing over that land to the Nisg̱a'a was now calculated to be $70 million, nearly five times as much as the $15-million figure that had been estimated just a few months earlier!"[7]

At that point, Jean Chrétien's Liberal government was in the throes of a program review, which involved deep and painful cuts to most ministries.[8] Bad timing moved British Columbia's resource demands from being unwelcome to unacceptable. A high-stakes standoff ensued. Fortunately, a timely intervention by British Columbia's chief negotiator, Jack Ebbels, and his deputy minister, Philip Halkett, "resolved to pitch the cabinet for a final push to get a deal. It meant persuading a beleaguered [BC] government to make several key concessions."[9]

The federal government was also anxious to sustain the treaty process. "While issues surrounding cost sharing caused an unfortunate delay in efforts to reach an agreement in principle with the Nisga'a, we are committed to getting back on track and are eager to make up lost ground," said Ron Irwin, the federal Indian affairs minister. Senior officials from both governments were "hauled back from their summer holidays to hammer out a cost-sharing agreement." Premier Harcourt's deputy minister, Doug McArthur, joined the discussions, underlining their critical importance.[10]

Further obstacles stood in the way of an agreement in principle. A provision for a treaty-protected commercial fishery drew loud opposition from, among others, the Treaty Negotiation Advisory Committee (an amalgam of thirty-one associations representing third-party interests). The BC Liberal leader, Gordon Campbell, joined the chorus: "I think this process is doomed to create the kind of fear and anxieties that you see when these announcements or leaked documents come forward. People in the North feel left out of this discussion."[11] The fishery controversy emerged as Premier Harcourt was preparing to leave office in February 1996 following his resignation over the Nanaimo "Bingogate scandal." Ron Irwin hoped an agreement in principle could be reached before Harcourt left office "because this thing with the leadership and a possible election throws all negotiations off."[12]

If Irwin needed additional impetus, he'd certainly got it via a presentation from Campbell to the federal Liberal caucus when it met in Vancouver a few days earlier. "My goal wasn't to go in there and make friends," Campbell noted. By all accounts, he achieved that goal. Irwin was reportedly "almost apoplectic" on hearing Campbell's opposition to a "race-based fishery." In Campbell's own words: "The BC public would be glad to accept a deal that reflected a few basic principles, like one law for all British Columbians. If Mr. Irwin thinks he can convince British Columbians that there should be special rights for one set of people, beyond what is already allowed in the Constitution, I think he is kidding himself."[13]

Ironically, Campbell's rhetoric heightened the urgency for moving treaty negotiations along. "Marathon talks at a Vancouver hotel" in February 1996 ended in a historic agreement in principle with the Nisga'a that provided $190 million, 2,000 square kilometres of land, broad self-government powers, and a guaranteed 18 percent of the Nass River salmon fishery. "Today we make history," said Irwin. "This agreement in principle forms the fundamental basis on which Canada, BC and the Nisga'a people are forging a new relationship based on partnership and mutual respect."[14] For the Nisga'a Tribal Council's president, Joe Gosnell, the agreement in principle marked a special moment in his Nation's remarkable 120-year struggle for recognition of its title rights: "At 8:27 a.m. our canoe arrived. The journey our ancestors began more than a century ago ended."[15]

Critics quickly and predictably panned the deal. "This treaty will haunt Canadians for generations to come," the federal Reform Party's John Duncan argued. "If this is a model framework for future negotiations, Canadians will be saddled with an unfunded liability of terrifying magnitude." Gordon Campbell set out policy markers he would follow for the next several years: "There are two obvious and glaring problems with it. The first one is there is a racially based commercial fishery which I don't think most people will find acceptable. And two, there is virtually no certainty created by this agreement."[16] He had the opportunity to set out his ideas explicitly during the 1996 provincial election.

Gordon Campbell Follows the Path of Greatest Resistance

Prior to winning the leadership of the BC Liberal Party in 1993, Gordon Campbell had enjoyed considerable political experience as a councillor and mayor in the City of Vancouver and as chair of the Greater Vancouver Regional District (now Metro Vancouver). He understood the critical importance of building a winning coalition in a province where the centre-right was frequently divided. After four decades of minor-party obscurity, the BC Liberals formed the Official Opposition in 1991. They were joined on the Opposition benches by remnants of the formerly dominant Social Credit party, renamed and reinvigorated as the Reform BC party. Reform BC fell far short of Campbell's Liberals in funding and membership but enjoyed strong rural support; they were, in short, the dominant centre-right threat to Campbell's hopes of winning the 1996 election.

The platform Campbell constructed for the campaign aimed to capture support from the populist right, including Reform BC and its more successful federal cousin, the Reform Party of Canada. That platform, titled "The Courage to Change," offered two paragraphs on Indigenous relations under the headline "Better Jobs and Expanded Opportunities." It argued that "treaty settlements are essential for all British Columbians. For aboriginal peoples, settlements represent an opportunity to take control of their communities [a reference to the intrusive Indian Act] and to provide for their future." For other

British Columbians, treaties would bring the "certainty necessary to create a more prosperous province."

The platform emphasized that certainty was one of the four principles that "should apply to land claims." The other principles were similarly purpose-driven. The suggestion that "treaty negotiations must be open" was aimed at assuaging local governments' demands to be included in treaty discussions. The assertion that "treaty settlements must recognize existing property rights including leases and licenses" was a nod to all Crown land tenure holders and the BC Fisheries Survival Coalition's concerns regarding "race-based fisheries." The fourth principle was a familiar Campbell adage: "When negotiations are complete there must be one law for all – one law for taxation, the environment and on conservation law."[17]

The notion of "one law for all" was both controversial and deeply ironic given British Columbia's history of excluding First Nations from (among other things) pre-emption, voting, public education, and commercial fishing. Indigenous relations was not the focal point of "The Courage to Change" or the broader election campaign. Both centred on Campbell's vision for smaller government. The platform featured at least seven references to it, along with promises such as reducing the size of the legislature from seventy-five MLAs to fewer than sixty and cutting personal income taxes and government spending by 15 percent.

Campbell's pitch fell short with the electorate. The BC Liberals won the largest percentage of the popular vote but fewer seats than the NDP.[18] Campbell blamed his loss on Reform capturing 9 percent of the vote.

My entry into provincial politics in 1996 gave me first-hand knowledge of what a vote split meant at the polls. I had the lowest winning percentage among BC Liberal MLAs in 1996 with slightly less than 35 percent, and the dominant threat to my victory in Shuswap was the Reform BC candidate, with 23 percent of the vote. However, a split vote on the right flank was only part of the story.

The NDP's new leader, Glen Clark, proved adept at exposing the potential downside of smaller government: loss of rural seats in the legislature, the diminution of health services, the abolition of the homeowner grant, and more. The NDP's majority win rejuvenated Clark's drive for a final agreement with the Nisg̱a'a.

The Drive to Complete the Nisg̱a'a Treaty

The pre-election initialling of the Nisg̱a'a agreement in principle left more than a few thorny details to be sorted out. Two years after his election as NDP leader and premier, Glen Clark grew increasingly concerned with closing the deal. Just a few years after the *Sparrow* decision, the Gitxsan and Wet'suwet'en peoples secured another important victory for Indigenous rights in the nation's highest court with the 1997 *Delgamuukw v British Columbia* decision. *Delgamuukw* reconfirmed that the province did not have the right to extinguish Aboriginal title and, further, that the province had a duty to consult with First Nations before undertaking activities that could undermine their rights or future ability to access the land and its resources. "When Delgamuukw came out," Clark noted, "many aboriginal people were euphoric, as if they had won everything."[19] He praised the Nisga'a's determination to achieve a final agreement, despite prevailing sentiment.

Clark was also concerned with the polarization of public opinion in the wake of *Delgamuukw*. He saw a window to achieve "a historic breakthrough" and directed Jack Ebbels, the deputy minister of Aboriginal affairs, to engage full-time in the talks.[20] Backed by an enhanced cabinet mandate, Ebbels secured a final agreement after intense negotiations during the spring and summer of 1998.

As the government and the Nisga'a prepared for a public announcement of the draft final agreement, Campbell suddenly seized the spotlight. After catching wind of Ebbels's negotiating success, Campbell secured a copy of the draft agreement and leaked it to the media on July 21, 1998. Before then, only the NDP cabinet and the Nisga'a Tribal Council had seen the document, although it was slated for public release within weeks. Campbell argued that the public had the right to know: "This is a major initiative and I don't think it's something that should be managed in terms of public relations." In a scathing response, Nisga'a president Joe Gosnell described Campbell's action as "unfortunate, ill-timed and reprehensible. The political grandstanding is an insult to the Nisga'a nation. I ask the leader of the Opposition, is this his way of contributing to the building of a new relationship?"[21]

Campbell's bombshell release of the final agreement was accompanied by a predictable critique. The Nisga'a Treaty model, he argued, would create a "racially based government, that is a recipe for significant long-term problems. It is not entrenched equality, it's entrenched inequality."[22] He demanded that the agreement either be returned to the bargaining table for revision or subjected to a province-wide referendum: "There is no question we are creating a whole new third order of government, we are creating new rights, we are entrenching inequality based on race. Those things are all fundamental to the constitution."[23]

Campbell then raised the stakes with a call for a national referendum on the treaty or its ratification under the terms of the Constitution Act's amending formula – namely, approval by seven provinces making up more than 50 percent of the population.[24] When his suggestions failed to gain traction, he landed on what became a longer-term BC Liberal pledge: a province-wide referendum on the principles that should underpin treaty making. "It's not wrong," he argued, "for every citizen to be included in looking at the principles that are going to be involved in every treaty as we move forward." Glen Clark was unpersuaded by Campbell's sundry suggestions: "If he changes his position many more times he's going to get whiplash. It's hard to comment on a moving position."[25]

Debate on the Nisga̱'a Treaty (formally, the Nisga̱'a Final Agreement Act) soon moved into the legislature. In his second reading speech, Campbell again pulled out some well-tested, Reform-style objections to the package, all variations on his "one law for all" theme. His speech echoed George Walkem's 1875 claim that large reserves would foster economic and social exclusion for Indigenous people. For Campbell, the Nisga̱'a Treaty would exacerbate – not relieve – such exclusion: "The myth is that the treaty will break down the barriers that exist under the reserve system; but in reality, it will reinforce those existing barriers and erect new walls that will cleave our province into 50 or 60 'gated communities.'" A referendum on the principles backstopping the Nisga̱'a Treaty was required, he said, to reflect a broader governmental "vision for treaties." In anticipation of a key staple in his 2001 campaign, Campbell suggested that British Columbians wouldn't "need to vote on all 700 pages of the treaty ... But we do need a vote on the key principles at stake, like the principles of equality, certainty, finality, affordability, fairness and workability."[26]

Campbell's ongoing critique of the Nisga̱'a Treaty changed no minds within the legislature, but it did set the stage for responses framed around certainty and investment. Premier Glen Clark, in his welcome to Chief Gosnell, emphasized that the "full and final settlement" of land claims within the Nisga̱'a Treaty would provide "the certainty British Columbia needs to attract new jobs and investments." Gosnell himself, in his Address from the Bar of the House, directly tackled the issue of economic certainty flowing from the treaty:

> Clause by clause, the Nisga̱'a Treaty emphasizes self-reliance, personal responsibility and modern education. It also encourages, for the first time, investment in Nisga̱'a lands and resources and allows us to pursue meaningful employment for our own people from the resources of our own territory. To investors, it provides economic certainty, and it gives us a fighting chance to establish legitimate economic independence, to prosper in common with our non-aboriginal neighbours in a new and, hopefully, proud Canada.[27]

Gosnell's powerful words were respectfully received in all corners of the legislative chamber, but debate unfolded along predictable partisan lines, embracing questions about process, principles, and the agreement's content.

I had the unenviable task of speaking on the Nisga'a Final Agreement Act directly after Chief Gosnell's address. I began with the obvious: "I certainly won't be able to achieve the dignity and grace that Dr. Gosnell was able to provide for us in this Legislature." My remarks focused on Chapter 11, titled "Nisga'a Government," and its implications for future treaty agreements in British Columbia. My concern was the absence of provisions for non-Nisga'a residents within treaty boundaries to enjoy a vote on fourteen areas of public policy where paramountcy would reside in the Nisga'a Lisims government.[28]

Was this a legitimate concern? Perhaps but what I would come to appreciate during debates on the Tsawwassen Final Agreement a decade later is that every treaty is built on compromise and accommodation achieved over years of hard negotiation. The breadth and depth of modern treaties give rise to many questions in areas such as treaty boundaries, fishery allocations, and the scope of governance. Every response to every question potentially invites debate and division. Looking back, I regret casting my vote against the Nisga'a Final Agreement Act. I believe the Opposition's "right and duty" to question and oppose specific elements within a treaty agreement must always be weighed against the broader and higher goal of advancing reconciliation and remediating past injustices through treaty making.

I suspect that I am far from alone among my former BC Liberal colleagues in experiencing regret. In 2007, Gordon Campbell offered an admission which could not have flowed easily from his lips: "A lot of the things I was concerned about in 1998, the observations about the Nisga'a treaty, were not correct. Frankly the Nisga'a treaty has done quite well for the Nisga'a people and I think it's done well for British Columbians."[29]

When the debate finally concluded on April 22, 1999, the Nisga'a Final Agreement Act was approved by a vote of thirty-nine to thirty-two, precisely along party lines. The act then moved on to consideration by the federal Parliament, where it suffered a rough ride. The Reform Party of Canada formed the Official Opposition when the act was introduced later in the year. As Nisga'a lawyer Jim Aldridge noted, Reform "was feverishly opposed ... introducing 474 amendments to the three-page statute ... and required votes on them. This went on for three nights, every amendment was voted down, which led to the only time that my clients stepped off the absolute high road, when they had some T-shirts printed up saying: 'Nisga'a 474: Reform: 0.'"[30]

The governor general, Adrienne Clarkson, gave royal assent on April 13, 2000. "A generation of Nisga'a men and women has grown old at the negotiating table," Chief Gosnell wrote of that long-awaited event, but he also reflected on the Chiefs who paddled to Victoria in 1887 and the "century of darkness" that followed. Those Chiefs "died before they could see their dream realized," he wistfully noted, but "perhaps a child somewhere will hear that the canoe returned to the Nass Valley, more than a century later, carrying justice for the Nisga'a and honour for us all."[31]

In a celebration of the successful completion of the Nisga'a Treaty on May 12, 2000, the new NDP premier, Ujjal Dosanjh, declared that it symbolized "a new era of recognition, respect and reconciliation between the aboriginal and non-aboriginal residents of BC."[32] His declaration proved premature. Gordon Campbell offered a competing vision in his 2001 election platform, titled "A New Era for British Columbia," which contained over two hundred commitments across a broad range of policy areas, including Indigenous relations.

The platform offered a more extensive and nuanced assessment of Indigenous issues than its predecessor had. Two paragraphs from the 1996 platform became a full page in 2001, along with eleven platform commitments. The most controversial was a "one-time, province-wide referendum" to give "all British Columbians a say on the principles that should guide British Columbia's approach to treaty negotiations."[33] This was a nod to populist antipathy toward treaty making, which was reflected in Reform British Columbia's 1996 campaign platform, "Voters' Warranty." Other "New Era" promises, like "protect and promote aboriginal languages" and "create a permanent First Citizens' Forum," were aimed at reassuring mainstream voters.

Absent from the "New Era" document were the overt promises of smaller government that had dogged the 1996 campaign. Instead, BC Liberals promised "a vision for hope and prosperity," and the electorate delivered them a massive majority.

12

A New Era Brings Hope and Vexation

Gordon Campbell and the BC Liberals won a massive majority in the 2001 election. His strategy of uniting the centre-right proved successful. Reform BC's vote declined from over 9 percent in the 1996 election to less than 1 percent in 2001, and they failed to elect even a single member to the legislature. The NDP captured two seats and formed a tiny but vociferous Opposition to a BC Liberal government that held seventy-seven seats. High hopes were fostered by Campbell's extensive and ambitious "New Era" election platform, which contained over $2 billion in election promises scattered across every corner of government. Indigenous relations was by no means at the top of the new premier's agenda in 2001. First out of the gate, one day after inauguration, was a dramatic tax cut of 25 percent. The tax cut was initially popular but held short- and long-term adverse consequences for the government, including programs serving Indigenous people.[1]

Premier Campbell took his over two hundred platform promises seriously. Ministerial responsibility for each of those promises was confirmed through mandate letters from the premier. Ministers never needed to look far for reminders of their responsibilities. "The New Era" was framed and mounted on the wall of the cabinet room, immediately behind the premier's chair. Promises related to Indigenous relations were divided between the attorney general, the designated lead on treaty negotiations, and the Ministry of Community, Aboriginal and Women's Services, which I had the honour of leading.[2]

Campbell had an immediate problem to shed before moving forward on Indigenous relations: a constitutional challenge he had initiated against the

Nisga'a Treaty, launched while in Opposition.[3] The Supreme Court of British Columbia rejected the challenge in July 2000, upholding the treaty's constitutional validity, but Campbell signalled his intent to appeal.[4] After the election, the attorney general, Geoff Plant, abandoned the lawsuit, noting, "Now that we're in government, it's not possible to sue ourselves."[5]

The platform's commitment to conducting a provincial referendum on "principles that should guide British Columbia's approach to treaty negotiations" could not be jettisoned so easily. An all-party committee of the legislature (unsurprisingly disparaged and boycotted by the NDP) was soon dispatched to consult British Columbians and draft referendum questions. Campbell saw no potential harm in the process: "Our Constitution guarantees aboriginal rights. There's nothing a referendum can do to take those away." He suggested that public engagement through the committee hearings would create "some public literacy around the issues that we confront."[6]

Indigenous leaders uniformly condemned the referendum as divisive and racist. Bill Wilson of the First Nations Summit was bluntly critical: "I think it's a colossal waste of time and money. We think this is a morally repugnant exercise that is dredging up racism around the province." Hupacasath Chief Judith Sayers described it as the "single most destructive process I've seen in my lifetime."[7] Critics disparaged every aspect of the referendum's design, content, and delivery, particularly its cost – several million dollars – which would come as the government was imposing cuts to social programs.[8]

The referendum was conducted by mail-in ballot in April and May 2002. Just under 36 percent of eligible British Columbians completed ballots. The low participation rate reflected boycotts from numerous organizations. Voters were asked to reply to eight yes-no statements. Results ranged from 85 percent "yes" on statement one, "Private property should not be expropriated for treaty settlements," to 94.5 percent "yes" on statement four, "Parks and protected areas should be maintained for the use and benefit of all British Columbians."[9]

Campbell was undoubtedly relieved to have the referendum commitment completed. It was an obligatory political nod to former Reform voters rather than a meaningful guide to future treaty making, especially as it came at the cost of heightened tensions with Indigenous leaders. To improve relations, Campbell acted on a recommendation from the legislature's 2001 committee on treaty principles: a "statement of regret" regarding the past treatment of Indigenous peoples. That recommendation found expression in the 2003 Throne Speech: "Your government deeply regrets the mistakes that were made by governments of every political stripe over the course of our province's history." The response to the provincial apology was respectful but guarded. Grand

Chief Ed John of the First Nations Summit stated: "Actions speak louder than words and we will pay attention to how the intentions in the speech are reflected by the actions of the government."[10] Campbell hoped the apology would trigger a vital reshaping of not only his government's Indigenous relations but also his government's political fortunes.

The lieutenant-governor, Iona Campagnolo, delivered the Throne Speech amid intense political turbulence. Outside the legislature, thousands gathered to protest a broad range of service reductions flowing from the 2001 tax cuts. The Throne Speech aimed to signal a shift in tone and direction. Along with an obligatory reference to "affordable treaties that will provide certainty, finality and equality" came a promise of "bold new steps to advance issues that are common to most treaty tables, such as governance, certainty, and access to fish."[11]

The promise of treaty-based fisheries surprised some observers. Columnist Michael Smyth recalled Campbell's 1997 condemnation of race-based fisheries as "morally, ethically and legally wrong": the Throne Speech, Smyth argued, "revealed a government in full retreat from its own rhetoric." Campbell paid a price for this shift. The BC Fisheries Survival Coalition, the most vociferous opponent of treaty-based Indigenous fisheries, called it "the biggest betrayal of a promise in our history."[12]

Campbell supported the tripartite treaty process, notwithstanding his earlier opposition to portions of the Nisg̱a'a Treaty, and he recognized that treaties were unlikely to progress without "access to fish" provisions. The shibboleth of race-based fisheries was thus unofficially consigned to the annals of history. He was also keen to advance a new vision centred on Indigenous communities as partners in economic growth. Energy development – notably run-of-the-river projects – was frequently touted as a potential source of jobs and revenues for Indigenous peoples. "The emphasis will be on providing jobs and opportunities in the here-and-now," as Vaughn Palmer suggested, "not on the longer-term pursuit of treaty negotiations."[13] Treaty making was not cast aside, but its longer-term character did not meet the needs of a "premier in a hurry."

Premier Campbell Impresses and Surprises with a New Relationship

Gordon Campbell was attracted to big and bold initiatives in all areas of public policy, from tax cuts and smaller government to health care and carbon taxation. Indigenous relations proved no exception. During the 2005 provincial election campaign, media reports suggested that senior officials were "quietly circulating the plan for a dramatically different relationship with first nations."

Weeks later, that plan was formalized as the New Relationship agreement, an ambitious attempt to reconcile competing visions for the management of the province's public lands. Among the big and bold commitments was a promise to develop "new institutions or structures to negotiate government-to-government agreements for shared decision-making regarding land-use management, tenuring and resource revenue and benefit-sharing." Such provisions would recognize the "economic component of aboriginal title."[14]

The New Relationship did not emerge from a vacuum. A unanimous Supreme Court of Canada decision in 2004, titled *Haida v British Columbia (Minister of Forests)*, had confirmed the province's duty to consult and accommodate Indigenous interests on lands over which the Haida Nation claimed title. The Supreme Court's *Haida* decision, backstopped by *Delgamuukw* in 1997, demonstrated that economic certainty would never be found in the absence of a constitutionally defensible consultation and accommodation framework. The province needed "to sit down and figure out what we thought the courts were telling us ... And it was pretty clear the First Nations had been unhappy that we had not worked with them to develop a shared understanding of what those obligations are," Attorney General Plant told columnist Les Leyne of the *Victoria Times-Colonist*. "Our continued attempts to discharge what we considered our obligations to be, unilaterally, was still running into trouble in the courts."[15]

The big and bold agreement surprised many British Columbians, among them the BC Liberal caucus and most members of the cabinet. As journalist Paul Willcocks noted, "It's not really the government and First Nations that have agreed. So far it's been the premier's office and First Nations, and that is worrying some people. The policy shift was made without any real participation by the cabinet, MLAs, ministries, industry or municipalities."[16] How far knowledge of the clandestine discussions extended is unclear. The premier and attorney general were directly engaged in negotiations, but if other ministers were aware, that awareness did not reach the Ministry of Sustainable Resource Management, where I became minister in January 2004. Caucus did not receive a full briefing on the agreement until July 2005, shortly before its release to the public.[17]

A key element in my mandate at Sustainable Resource Management was negotiating a Great Bear Rainforest conservancy on the central coast. Negotiations were intense and complex, involving First Nations, environmental organizations, industry, and local governments. Negotiations were occasionally fractious but more commonly respectful, collegial, and constructive. Remarkably, a draft agreement was reached and presented to the cabinet a few months before the provincial election of May 17, 2005. I thought the timing was entirely fortuitous: the government had forged a land-use agreement in an area of British Columbia that had national and international significance, and it had done so with groups often at loggerheads with the Campbell Liberals. A high-profile celebration on the eve of the provincial election would, I thought, be a great way to kick off a campaign. I was surprised – astonished, in fact – by the lack of enthusiasm our draft agreement generated from the Premier's Office. Rather than embracing a remarkable political opportunity, the Premier's Office's response was (at least from my perspective) a mix of quibbles and red herrings.

Why did the premier not share my enthusiasm? The most probable answer: Campbell was deeply enmeshed in negotiating the New Relationship and did not want that work disrupted – even by something as benign as a Great Bear Rainforest agreement.

The BC Liberal's 2005 platform, titled "Real Leadership, Real Progress," had plenty to say about Indigenous relations, despite making no reference to the New Relationship. "Real Leadership" touted the successful completion of 2001 commitments and a bevy of new agreements in revenue sharing, economic development, treaties, and forestry. Commitments to the co-management of parks and the collaborative management of resources suggested that "one law for all" was now but a distant memory.

What accounts for the remarkable shift in Campbell's approach to Indigenous relations? An article from columnist Justine Hunter in the *Globe and Mail* of October 13, 2007, titled "How Campbell Changed His View," canvassed this question. Premier Campbell cited a 2004 meeting with Phil Fontaine, National Chief of the Assembly of First Nations, as a pivotal moment in his transformation: "He was the one who opened the door, who said we can do something that would be pretty significant for first nations across the country, certainly in British Columbia, and I felt that was a very strong and powerful message."[18]

As a cabinet minister during this period, I saw Campbell's perspective on Indigenous relations shift before his meeting with Fontaine. To his credit, Campbell met regularly with First Nations leaders, heard their powerful stories of dispossession and injustice, and learned (as I did) from them. Campbell became a more confident leader after his massive victory in 2001, much less concerned with how his actions might be viewed by the political right. I have been an unstinting critic of Campbell on several fronts, including Indigenous relations, but I think he genuinely saw an opportunity for transformational change in that realm.[19]

"Real Leadership" revealed a premier determined to reshape the public's perception of his leadership on Indigenous relations and other public policy fields. The Gordon Campbell of 2001 had been intent on reducing and remaking government; the 2005 version was intent on delivering the fruits of his reforms to all British Columbians, including First Nations. After four years of "New Era" political turbulence, Campbell was returned to office on May 17, 2005, with a much-reduced majority of forty-six seats to the resurgent NDP's thirty-three.

In the weeks and months that followed, much of Campbell's legacy in Indigenous relations was established. The New Relationship won praise from Indigenous leaders. Grand Chief Ed John described it as "a turning point in the relationship between the Crown and First Nations."[20] To give practical expression to the New Relationship, and to relieve public angst over the billion-dollar sale of BC Rail assets to the Canadian National Railway, Campbell announced the creation of a $100-million New Relationship Trust fund. The trust would be managed and directed by First Nations representatives to benefit First Nations. The stage was now set for an equally ambitious initiative that would engage the federal and provincial governments and Indigenous leaders.

The Kelowna Accord Provides a Rare Moment of Tripartite Commitment

Gordon Campbell was not the only politician with Indigenous relations on the agenda in the mid-2000s. Prime Minister Paul Martin was also seeking a new relationship with Canada's First Peoples. That common interest produced a fortuitous alignment of political agendas and political power that culminated in the Transformative Change Accord, commonly known as the Kelowna Accord, in November 2005.

Many of the accord's core themes – "quality-of-life priority areas," including health, education, housing, and economic development – had their roots in the Canada–Aboriginal Peoples Roundtable, which began in April 2004 and comprised eighteen months of consultations with over one thousand invitees. All five national Indigenous leadership organizations were engaged in its work. Sectoral tables led by the relevant federal ministries were tasked with developing strategic plans and goals in those priority areas.[21]

Grand Chief Ed John was among the participants and noted: "It didn't just happen overnight. Roundtables convened across the country. A lot of preparation work went into those tables."[22] With the federal-provincial-territorial-Indigenous conference slated for Kelowna, Campbell enjoyed the fortuitous position of host and cochair. In the weeks prior to the conference, he met with other provincial premiers as well as Indigenous leaders in hopes of building a consensus and a successful outcome.[23]

Those efforts – and a congenial atmosphere fostered by the promise of $5.085 billion in new federal funding – produced a groundbreaking agreement aimed at addressing compelling challenges among Indigenous peoples, many directly linked to persistent colonial policies and prejudices. In 2005, for example, national unemployment stood at 7 percent for all Canadians but 19 percent for Indigenous people (29 percent for those on reserve). In the realm of education, the lasting impact of residential schools was clear: 19 percent of non-Indigenous Canadians aged twenty to twenty-four had not completed high school, compared with 44 percent of Indigenous people. Similarly, in health care, Indigenous infant mortality was nearly 20 percent higher than that for other Canadians.[24]

The conference reached a successful conclusion. "We walked away with an agreement," said Ed John. "The commitments Paul Martin made were important to us."[25] Leaders departed Kelowna on a wave of high expectations, but political developments soon tempered those hopes. Parliament dissolved just days after the conference concluded, and the subsequent election produced a Stephen Harper minority Conservative government skeptical of the Kelowna Accord.

In his postelection analysis, columnist Gary Mason anticipated a constructive and collegial relationship between Harper and Campbell but noted one potential exception: the Kelowna Accord. Some Conservatives were less than subtle in dismissing the accord as the last gasp of a discredited Liberal prime minister. "Something crafted at the last moment on the back of a napkin on the eve of an election" was how Conservative MP and soon-to-be minister Monte Solberg characterized the accord.[26] That comment, Vaughn Palmer noted, "was especially hurtful to aboriginal leaders, who spent 18 months working on the accord, often to the detriment of pursuing other objectives with senior governments."[27] Conservative dismissal of the accord also grated on Campbell, unsurprisingly given his investment in building a consensus around it.

As premier, Campbell was rarely given to openly challenging federal policy (something he was much more willing to do while in the Opposition). He departed from the path of quiet diplomacy when confronted by the Harper government's first budget, which contained no acknowledgment of, nor funding for, the ambitious goals set out in the Kelowna Accord. "I characterized that agreement as Canada's 'moment of truth,'" Campbell told the legislature. "It was our time to do something that has eluded our nation for 138 years. It was our chance to end the disparities in health, education, housing, and economic opportunity ... Any unilateral reversal will invite consequences that only make us poorer as a nation."[28]

Campbell's statement produced at least a diplomatic acknowledgment from the Harper government that there were gaps in Indigenous services that needed to be filled. British Columbia's minister of Aboriginal relations and reconciliation, Tom Christensen, called his federal counterpart, Indian Affairs Minister Jim Prentice, and was assured that "the federal government is committed to meeting the objectives that all premiers and aboriginal leaders came to agreement on last fall."[29] Diplomacy produced reassuring words and gestures, but details on funding and timelines were saved for a later date. An inspired attempt at federal-provincial-Indigenous policy reform foundered and was soon lost in the fog of competing political objectives.

Amid the Kelowna Accord controversy, quiet progress was being made on the treaty front. Agreements appeared to be near conclusion with the Lheidli T'enneh near Prince George, the Maa-nulth on western Vancouver Island, and the Tsawwassen on the Lower Mainland. The Tsawwassen First Nation had certainly come a long way between 1874 (when Superintendent Israel Powell and his survey crew awaited provincial authorization to expand their reserve) and 2007 (when they awaited ratification of their treaty by British Columbia and Canada).

Tsawwassen Treaty Ratification Proves Controversial

The Tsawwassen Treaty broke new ground in British Columbia's history of Indigenous relations. It was the first to emerge from the modern treaty process, as the earlier Nisga̱'a Treaty had been negotiated outside the parameters of the BC Treaty Commission. Tsawwassen was also British Columbia's first "urban" treaty, engaging a host of complex issues that required resolution. Ratification of the treaty produced difficult and divisive politics in the local, provincial, and federal spheres. Tsawwassen leaders faced persistent and often vociferous objections to their treaty model. Their journey from negotiation to ratification is a study of patience, determination, and courage.

A potential Tsawwassen Treaty raised a novel question: Should farm properties within the Agricultural Land Reserve (ALR) and under the purview of the Agricultural Land Commission (ALC), but proposed for inclusion within treaty settlement lands, be subject to the same processes as nontreaty parcels also located within the same municipality or regional district? Normally, without treaty negotiations, even ALR lands of average quality have very little chance of being approved for exclusion by the ALC, an independent administrative tribunal.

In 1999, the possibility of potential ALR exclusions emerged in the Tsawwassen Treaty discussions, prompting alarm from the City of Delta, home to some proposed treaty settlement lands. As provincial negotiator Gerry Thorne succinctly noted: "The reserve is small and there's no room for expansion, yet it's surrounded by [ALR] land which the [Tsawwassen Nation] says it needs for growth and as an economic base. We've got to find a solution and it's not going to be easy."

The creation of small reserves in colonial times had modern ramifications.

Tsawwassen Chief Kim Baird was clear throughout negotiations that excluding treaty lands from the ALR was critical. She noted in 1999: "We need a sustainable economic base, and if all we are left with is agricultural land [not developable for other economic activities] then we'll need a lot more land than we are seeking now."[30] Her position on ALR exclusion was unchanged seven years later: "If we can't do that [exclude some ALR lands], I don't think we can have a treaty. That would be a deal-breaker."[31] Chief Baird believed that the use of those lands for higher-value development would be vital to the achievement of the Tsawwassen's independence and self-sufficiency.

The BC Liberal government recognized that ALR exclusions would be crucial to success not only to Tsawwassen but also to future treaties. But what of the independence and integrity of the ALC and its processes? As matters came to a head in 2004, responsibility for the commission resided with me as minister of sustainable resource management.

Our solution was embodied in the Agricultural Land Commission Amendment Act, passed in 2004 and also known as Bill 27, a stark departure from the "one law for all" theme that Campbell had propounded a decade earlier. Bill 27 set out the provisions under which treaty-based exclusion applications might proceed directly to the commission without prior consideration by the local government in which the subject parcels resided. In the case of Tsawwassen Treaty settlement lands, existing processes would have routed applications through the City of Delta, where the government anticipated antiexclusion sentiment.

The introduction of Bill 27 in the spring of 2004 prompted debate at Delta City Council. A resolution opposing the bill was moved by Councillor (and subsequently NDP MLA) Guy Gentner and supported by, among others, Councillor (and later Independent MLA) Vicki Huntington, the latter noting, "It appears Minister of Sustainable Resource Management George Abbott is delegating authority to First Nations similar to a local municipality."[32] Huntington's assertion was accurate but only in relation to First Nations that had reached the agreement in principle stage of treaty negotiations.

Bill 27 also produced questions from MLAs on both sides of the legislature, most asking why access to a commission ruling would be provided before, rather than after, treaty ratification. My answers consistently emphasized that the status of land (meaning its inclusion or exclusion from the ALR) could "become a very important component as the First Nation looks at the land quantum associated with a potential treaty." Direct access to the ALC, I argued, would "give them a great deal more certainty and, hopefully, produce the positive outcome that our government looks forward to."[33] The questions did not lead to open dissent, and Bill 27 enjoyed unanimous support at all stages.

Three years later, with a much-expanded NDP caucus forming the Opposition, issues pertaining to the ALR re-emerged during the debate on the ratification of the Tsawwassen Final Agreement. That debate proved to be challenging for MLAs on both sides of the aisle. The treaty would see two hundred hectares (just under five hundred acres) of active farmland removed from the ALR. For some MLAs, such as North Delta's Guy Gentner, the agreement created "a collision course" between "two core values," preservation of farmland and advancement of treaties. For her part, the NDP's leader, Carole James, chose to draw a line in the sand in support of the agreement: "When there is a caucus position, all of caucus is expected to hold that position."[34] Her position on Tsawwassen as leader of the Official Opposition offered a stark contrast to Gordon Campbell's unrelenting opposition to the Nisg̱a'a Treaty a decade earlier.

To her credit, James recognized an uncomfortable truth that Campbell and the BC Liberals (including me) had chosen to ignore in the context of the Nisg̱a'a Treaty debates in the latter 1990s: the benefits of advancing reconciliation and remediating past injustices through treaty making can be all too easily lost in the cut and thrust of parliamentary debate and tactical partisan positioning. In the case of Tsawwassen, James and her caucus could just as easily have voiced support for treaty making while demanding an alternative (and undefined) treaty model emphasizing the preservation of farmland.

James chose not to follow that path, but some in her caucus were not easily dissuaded. The NDP MLA for Maple Ridge–Pitt Meadows, Michael Sather, was adamant: "Yes, I will be voting against the treaty. I think it's atrocious we would take some of the best farmland in North America out of the ALR." Corky Evans, MLA for Nelson–Creston, had been agriculture minister during the NDP government's controversial exclusion of Six Mile Ranch near

Kamloops in the 1990s, a step he now believed was a "stupid thing" to do: "I was part of an unfortunate decision once and I guess my worst nightmare would be to be a participant in another one."[35] Evans and Gentner left the House as the votes were conducted; as promised, Sather voted against the treaty and was suspended from caucus.

Three BC Liberal MLAs also voted against the agreement, but without disciplinary consequences, as it was deemed a free vote by caucus. Blair Lekstrom, MLA for Peace River South, framed his concerns around the "one law for all" theme. He argued that the "law-making authority that's given within this document is beyond what I accept as far as a treaty ... In some cases, these laws and the law-making authority matches that of the province and the federal government. In others, it supersedes it." He highlighted the treaty's "preferential harvesting agreement for wildlife and fish," reflecting the race-based fisheries arguments of the 1990s. He also disagreed with treaty provisions that would give "away subsurface rights, something that other British Columbians don't have and don't enjoy."[36]

Dennis MacKay, MLA for Bulkley Valley–Stikine, emphasized similar themes. "This treaty will give them ... a race-based fishery," he argued, "and I cannot and will not support it." His speech resurrected a dominant theme of the 1875 Report of the Government of British Columbia on the Subject of Indian Reserves: that reserves inhibit the entry of Indigenous people into the broader economy and society. "The problem, as I see it," he said, "is the isolation of living on a reserve. They live on a reserve though it separates them from the rest of us in society." He was alarmed not just by the Tsawwassen but by all future treaties: "Stop and think for a moment what we're going to do as we go through this treaty process over and over again ... Call it a reserve; call it treaty lands. It's going to isolate them from the rest of us." MacKay declared that he would not "support any legislation that attempts to keep this invisible wall between all of the people of this great province and country."[37]

The federal government's ratification of the Tsawwassen Final Agreement prompted dissent, led by Conservative MP John Cummins, who represented the treaty area within the House of Commons, Delta–Richmond East. Cummins was unrestrained in his criticism, which revolved around the recurrent theme of "one law for all." A familiar target was race-based fisheries. The agreement would provide the Tsawwassen with a 0.7 to 3 percent share of various salmon species in the Fraser River fishery, a provision he deemed "simply not acceptable."[38]

Cummins believed treaties such as Tsawwassen would create "fiefdoms or kingdoms" in which a "double standard" would prevail: "If you're the white farmer here, you're going to be forced to farm it. But if you're an Indian under treaty you can do whatever the hell you want with it."[39] The Conservative Indian affairs minister, Jim Prentice, was not swayed by Cummins's arguments. Parliamentary ratification of the agreement was successful. In his final missive, Cummins declared: "Mr. Prentice is totally lacking in common sense" and "has broken faith with the people of this province who elected Conservatives in the election earlier this year."[40]

Cummins enjoyed greater support from local government than he did within Parliament. Opposition to agricultural land exclusion brought Delta's mayor, Lois Jackson, into the fray. "Some of that land has been farmed for a long, long time," she said. "It's some of the best land we have."[41] On another occasion, she was even more blunt, suggesting that "if they want this land, they should farm it, just like everyone else."[42] Chief Kim Baird framed the treaty in a different light: "The treaty represents our final break from the Indian Act – through self-government, not assimilation."[43] The treaty brought the opportunity to make choices too long denied.

The Ghost of Indian Superintendent Israel Powell Appears at Musqueam

In July 1874, Israel Powell's survey crews stood by at Musqueam as well as Tsawwassen. Like the Tsawwassen, the Musqueam would wait over a century to see their land expanded. That expansion would not result from treaty negotiations but rather a combination of factors, most notably court rulings and fortuitous timing in relation to the 2010 Winter Olympics and Paralympics. The Musqueam Reconciliation, Settlement and Benefits Agreement Implementation Act of 2008 initiated the transfer of several properties to the Nation: the University of British Columbia golf course lands (which had been sold by the province to UBC in 2003 for $11 million), the Bridgepoint casino lands in Richmond, and portions of the Pacific Spirit Regional Park (within the Metro Vancouver park system).

The Musqueam had vigorously opposed earlier transfers of those lands and, when their objections were ignored, launched legal challenges. In March 2005, the BC Court of Appeal unanimously ruled that the province had not met its legal obligations to consult and accommodate the Musqueam in its sale of the UBC golf course. The court suspended the sale for two years (then extended until January 7, 2008) to allow the parties to negotiate an agreement. The Musqueam scored an additional legal victory in July 2005, this time in the BC Supreme Court, which ruled that the province should have consulted with the Nation prior to the relocation and expansion of the casino lands at Bridgepoint.

The province, in short, found itself on the losing end of two important legal cases at a time when it was attempting to secure Indigenous peoples' participation in the 2010 Winter Olympics. Negotiations were completed just before the January 2008 deadline. Musqueam members voted 98 percent in favour of the package, which included $20.5 million in cash along with extensive high-profile lands.[44] In return, the Musqueam dropped their lawsuits against the province. "Litigation is always the last resort for us," Chief Ernest Campbell noted. "This is a great example of what can happen when both sides are there out of honour, respect and good faith."[45]

The Greater Vancouver Regional District (today known as Metro Vancouver) opposed the agreement and launched a lawsuit against the province. Portions of Crown land (or at least what the province argued was Crown land) subsequently known as Pacific Spirit Park had been transferred to the district for one dollar in the 1980s, despite objections from the Musqueam. Metro Vancouver characterized the province's return of the parcels to the Musqueam as "expropriation without compensation." Metro Vancouver chair Lois Jackson pointed to the BC Liberal government's 2002 referendum on treaty negotiation and the public's 95 percent support for the principle that "parks and protected areas should be maintained for the use and benefit of all British Columbians." She argued: "I don't think we ever thought this land would be on the table for the taking to resolve land claims or treaties. It's a precedent, and we'd like to know where this is headed. Are we going to lose more of our parkland?"[46] When the BC Supreme Court dismissed Metro Vancouver's claim in 2009, Gordon Campbell was spared from an embarrassing walk down memory lane to the dark days of the 2002 referendum.[47]

The 2010 Winter Olympics opened provincial and federal doors to other reconciliation initiatives. Enthusiastic participation by the four host First Nations who lived in the Vancouver to Whistler corridor (Musqueam, Squamish, Tsleil-Waututh, and Lil'wat) was essential if British Columbia and Canada aimed to show their best face to the world. Olympics-related agreements saw extensive provincial land transfers, monetary support for new home construction on reserves, and new recreational and cultural amenities.[48] From Canada, the Departments of National Defence, Public Works, and Fisheries and Oceans offered up over thirty hectares of high-value but surplus property in Vancouver and West Vancouver.[49] The remarkable parsimony that had pervaded Dominion and provincial policy earlier in our history was set aside, at least temporarily, in the hopes of winning Olympian lustre.

The political stage was crowded in the run-up to the 2010 Olympics. Campbell's Liberal government introduced North America's first revenue-neutral carbon tax to mixed reviews in the summer of 2008. A few months later, an international economic recession hit British Columbia on the eve of the 2009 provincial election. During the same period, Indigenous issues with their roots in the New Relationship and the Kelowna Accord once again came to the fore in another bold Campbell initiative, the Recognition and Reconciliation Act.

13

Recognition, Reconciliation, and Recoil

Four years before the 2010 Olympics, Premier Campbell enjoyed praise from many Indigenous leaders following the completion of the New Relationship agreement and the Kelowna Accord. For Indigenous leaders, those agreements contained future promise as well as present benefit. Grand Chief Stewart Phillip, the firebrand leader of the Union of British Columbia Indian Chiefs, reflected such hopes when he spoke to the BC Liberal annual convention in November 2006. He praised Premier Campbell as "an exceptional, extraordinary, visionary leader in this province."[1]

But appreciation soured as expectations went unfulfilled. One year after his effusive speech praising Campbell, Phillip stated: "In the beginning, there was great hope, based on the statements from the Premier, that we were going to make some significant progress through the New Relationship. However, that has not been the case." Great hopes had given way to "tremendous frustration and anger welling up in our communities as a result of the lack of progress." Others weighed in with scathing comments. "I think the Premier ... suffers from attention deficit disorder," said Stól:ō Chief Doug Kelly. "He gets a new project in his mind and it might last to the end of the week or it might last to the end of the day. And that's what the New Relationship is suffering from."[2]

The First Nations Leadership Council – which included the First Nations Summit, the Union of British Columbia Indian Chiefs, and the British Columbia Assembly of First Nations – met with Premier Campbell and the Aboriginal relations minister, Mike de Jong, in February 2008 and asked the province to convert the high-level principles of the New Relationship agreement into a practical, workable statute.[3] Campbell formally responded on February 20: "I believe it would be a mistake to commit to a timetable for the introduction of legislation. If we do so and not meet it, we would appear to fail."[4] He did agree to engage former attorney general Geoff Plant to assess the potential for future legislation.

Four months later, on the third anniversary of the public announcement of the New Relationship, Vaughn Palmer suggested that reconciliation had been "replaced as a top-of-mind concern for the premier by other enthusiasms – the conversation on health, then the climate action plan."[5] Campbell was, indeed, heavily invested in those two "enthusiasms." Multiple legislative initiatives had the Ministry of Health, which I had the honour to lead from 2005 to 2009, running flat out. Meanwhile, the Ministry of Finance was putting the final touches on what would be North America's first revenue-neutral carbon tax. However, Indigenous relations was never far from the premier's agenda, and his interest was undoubtedly reinvigorated by high-profile developments on the national stage, most notably the launch of the Truth and Reconciliation Commission of Canada (TRC) in 2008.

The TRC had its roots in the report of the Royal Commission on Aboriginal Peoples, which over five years from 1991 to 1996 brought public attention to the "lasting harm that was done by the residential schools. A growing number of Survivors and their descendants came forward to tell their stories and demand action."[6] The establishment of the TRC was one element in a broader legal settlement between residential school Survivors and "parties responsible for creation and operation of the schools" – namely, the federal government and church organizations. Settlement also brought a commitment for a public apology, subsequently delivered by Prime Minister Harper in the House of Commons in 2008, emphasizing the vital importance of reconciliation.[7]

Discussions between Campbell and the First Nations Leadership Council, which commenced in the latter months of 2008, also drew on the theme of reconciliation. Those talks showed promise, prompting references in the Throne Speech of February 16, 2009: "This government is working with First Nations to develop a *Recognition and Reconciliation Act* that will establish a new statutory framework to further the implementation of the New Relationship."[8] Although substantive issues remained unresolved, Campbell may have believed that including the act within the Throne Speech would offer protection from any accusations of secrecy – the initiative was out in plain sight!

Negotiations were successfully concluded on February 19, 2009, with joint sign-off on a confidential six-page discussion paper that circulated among some government officials and First Nations but not, remarkably, cabinet. As

Vaughn Palmer wryly noted, "Business leaders who wondered why they'd been kept in the dark to that point found they were not alone. Most Liberal ministers and backbenchers learned of their government's intentions at about the same time as the information appeared in the newspapers."[9]

The discussion paper and the New Relationship agreement had common elements, which is not surprising given the paper's title, "Discussion Paper on Instructions for Implementing the New Relationship." Among the key commitments were shared decision making on land and resource issues, revenue and benefit sharing, and dispute-resolution processes. Both documents offered recognition of Indigenous rights and title, a commitment that had been broadly acknowledged by the province since the 1992 Throne Speech.

The discussion paper also included a few notable additions to the New Relationship, including the potential transformation of Indigenous political and governmental structures. It promised that the Recognition and Reconciliation Act would "set out a vision of re-building Indigenous Nations and establish a new institution," the Indigenous Nation Commission, "to support and facilitate the process." The discussion paper also anticipated the creation of a Council of Indigenous Nations, composed "of leaders of reconstituted Indigenous Nations" and supplemented by representatives of the First Nations Leadership Council. Appended to the paper was a coloured map setting out the boundaries of twenty-three "sovereign Indigenous Nations in British Columbia."[10]

Those additions, while consistent with the Royal Commission on Aboriginal Peoples' recommendation that "Aboriginal nations have to be reconstituted," proved highly controversial.[11] First Nations across the province would air their concerns over the summer of 2009, but some business organizations were immediately critical of the paper.

The Mining Association of BC led the way, engaging lawyers Tom Isaac and Keith Clark to review, in the absence of draft legislation, the discussion paper.[12] "Discussions with senior officials regarding the paper," Isaac and Clark argued, "appear to confirm that there is a fundamental lack of understanding by the persons who drafted this paper for BC concerning the significance of recognizing aboriginal title throughout BC." They suggested that "shared decision making" would likely be interpreted plainly by the courts as meaning "either both parties agree on a particular action or decision or no decision is made." Recognition of Aboriginal title across British Columbia would, they argued, give First Nations a veto over land use and management decisions. In a swipe at Campbell's long-time call for certainty regarding the land base, they submitted a withering conclusion: "The only certainty arising from this legislation may be certainty that resource development will be dramatically reduced in BC as potential investors look elsewhere, including to other Canadian provinces."[13]

The discussion paper's recommendations on shared decision making and recognition of Aboriginal title mirrored provisions that had been set out in the New Relationship agreement four years earlier. So what accounts for the business sector's concern? Some undoubtedly hoped the New Relationship's commitment to establishing "processes and institutions for shared decision-making" would not be elevated into law.

But I think far more was at play. Part of the problem lay in the fact the paper was created without public consultation. As columnist Gary Mason noted, "The whole matter seemed to come out of the blue and, for policy that is potentially so groundbreaking, you would have thought there would have been some type of public discussion beforehand."[14] Not everyone, whether Indigenous or non-Indigenous, appreciated that the report largely reflected the New Relationship agreement. Further, as former attorney general Geoff Plant suggested in his assessment of business angst:

> Part of the challenge here is that the discussion paper is a political document, not a legal document. We don't yet have a draft act so the commentators are forced to do the best they can with the words in the discussion paper. But it is a mistake to read a political document as if it were a legal structure.[15]

In the absence of clarity and certainty about what, precisely, might be included within the act, observers were inclined to fill any gaps with the worst (or best) assumptions about what the government intended.

Political rhetoric elevated and amplified hopes and fears. Minister de Jong was loath to understate the significance of his pending legislation. He challenged the notion that the as-yet-unwritten act might be mainly symbolic: "This is not a one-off. This is not symbolism." As he told the First Nations Summit on March 5, 2009, "The time is now ... If we do this together, it will represent change on a seismic scale."[16] His words resonated with one audience, Indigenous leaders, but alarmed another, industry and business.

The promise of a Recognition and Reconciliation Act also caught the federal government by surprise. Canada's Indian and northern affairs deputy minister, Michael Wernick, dispatched a letter in March 2009 to his provincial counterpart that was diplomatic but pointed. "We have recently learned through media reports that British Columbia is considering landmark legislation dealing with questions that are at the core of many initiatives, such as treaty negotiations, litigation and policy development," he wrote, and he suggested that "having a better understanding of and appreciation for this initiative by means of a briefing will allow the federal government to provide answers that avoid unnecessary misunderstandings and wrong impressions." Wernick was also aggrieved by British Columbia's "unprecedented, unexpected and last-minute decision" to suspend its participation in the *Ahousaht Indian Band and Nation v Canada* case, which left the federal co-plaintiffs in an awkward position: "Canada has received no explanation or briefing to help us understand better your intentions or the implications that this decision may have on many other critical files before us."[17] That decision, he stated, had been founded explicitly on the recognition and reconciliation legislative initiative.

Ahousaht was argued in the BC Supreme Court in 2009 and involved five Nuu-chah-nulth Nations defending their inherent Indigenous right to fish in their Traditional Territories and to sell those fish into the commercial marketplace, beyond what may or may not be contained in future treaties. The Nations also asserted that Canada's regulatory regime for fisheries infringed on that right.[18]

British Columbia's decision to withdraw from *Ahousaht* had been announced by Mike de Jong at a gathering of the First Nations Summit in early March 2009, arguing that the case "contradicts everything the BC government has been working toward at a political level on the question of aboriginal title." The pending Recognition and Reconciliation legislation, he said, will be "unprecedented ... I think the whole country is watching."[19]

Ottawa was certainly watching, but with obvious puzzlement and vexation. Isaac and Clark's review of the discussion paper reinforced doubts within the business community and also unnerved some MLAs in the BC Liberal caucus. The official launch of the 2009 campaign was only weeks away. Minister de Jong remained confident that the Recognition and Reconciliation Act could be drafted, and a bill potentially introduced, before the adjournment of the legislature on April 2.

The looming deadline – in combination with the controversial character of the bill – prompted a long and spirited caucus debate. Did the caucus really want to hitch its re-election wagon to an undrafted piece of legislation that was already hugely controversial among core supporters? With a world recession wreaking havoc, why not emphasize that the BC Liberals were sound and dependable economic managers?

On March 11, the premier pulled the plug on passing the still unseen Recognition and Reconciliation Act before the election, arguing, "we need to take the time to get this right."[20]

Campbell had plenty of reasons to retreat in the face of caucus sentiment. Only a few legislative sitting days remained before he'd be obliged, by the fixed election date, to visit the lieutenant-governor to request dissolution and launch his re-election campaign. Campbell could extend the sitting hours and debate through Friday and the weekend. But to what purpose? His approach would be characterized as heavy-handed and dictatorial. The bill would be deemed a rush job, potentially fraught with errors and demands for amendment. Even if the NDP supported the bill, could Campbell risk a potential schism within his own ranks on the eve of an election? The answer was no.

Canada and the world experienced a serious recession in the fall of 2008, which would create economic challenges for years to come. In British Columbia, the recession coincided with the provincial election set for May 12, 2009. The government was suddenly saddled with an unwelcome and unexpected budgetary deficit. Despite the challenge, Campbell extolled his government as capable economic managers, a safe choice for voters in perilous times. His party's 2009 platform, titled "Keep BC Strong: Proven Leadership for BC's Economy," reflected that strategy. The platform also highlighted his government's record of achievement in Indigenous relations, notwithstanding the intense controversy provoked by the proposed Recognition and Reconciliation Act.

"Keep BC Strong" reminded voters of the New Relationship, an agreement that, the platform claimed, had "already led to more progress in the last four years than in the previous 150 years combined." According to the platform, the premier's bold leadership had, "for the first time in our province's history," British Columbia "poised to repair the damage caused by so many years of mistrust and misguided policies." Any lingering memories of "one law for all," or of the referendum on treaty principles, were buried in a flurry of superlatives that ran in the opposite direction; the platform eclipsed all previous uses of "new" as an adjective, with thirteen on page 37 alone.[21]

BC Liberal MLAs (like me) who believed that economic management was a far safer electoral battleground than a Recognition and Reconciliation Act had good reason to be pleased with Campbell's election campaign and its outcome. Despite the precampaign controversy surrounding the Act, journalist Gary Mason observed, "There wasn't a protester to confront or an uncomfortable question to field about his plan. Even his political opponents refrained from asking him to explain himself."[22] Indigenous relations was not a chosen battleground for either the NDP or the Greens. The controversial BC Liberal carbon tax and a faltering economy offered more fertile ground for political debate.

The Recognition and Reconciliation Discussion Paper Gets a Rough Ride

As Gordon Campbell hit the election trail, the First Nations Leadership Council launched Indigenous community consultations focused on the Recognition and Reconciliation discussion paper. Initial consultations in Prince George were critical of the package, particularly its proposal to reconstitute 203 First Nations into 30 Indigenous Nations. According to de Jong, reconstitution was included because the First Nations Leadership Council had "indicated a strong desire and preference for moving back to traditional alignments of approximately 30 indigenous nations that existed before contact."[23] An attached map purporting to represent precontact Indigenous boundaries was the object of particular suspicion and derision.

Louise Mandell, for many years legal counsel to the Union of British Columbia Indian Chiefs, claims (contrary to de Jong) that the province insisted on attaching the map to the discussion paper: "In many ways a map is dangerous because it displaces the reality of the geography and the people within it. In this situation, the boundaries of the map were inaccurate ... But, in spite of its inaccuracies, and over the objections of the First Nations Leadership Council, the Province insisted on using it and attaching it to the Paper."[24]

The discussion paper was likely destined to encounter serious opposition with or without the attached map. The paper's written words sparked steep resistance from a range of perspectives and well beyond concerns surrounding the reconstitution of Indigenous governance.[25] Grand Chief Ed John argued that a "lack of trust in this government forced people to say no."[26] However, based on the wide-ranging critiques advanced at community consultations, that lack of trust also extended to the full contents of the paper that the First Nations Leadership Council had negotiated with the government.[27]

After consultations concluded, more than two hundred Chiefs and band representatives met for three days in late August 2009 to discuss the fate of the initiative. Their conclusion was unambiguous. "This is the demise of the 'New Relationship' and the death of the legislation," Stewart Phillip declared. Lest anyone misunderstand his words, he reiterated, "The legislation is dead, dead, dead."[28] A potential "seismic shift" thus became one more lost opportunity.

Louise Mandell offered a retrospective assessment of how and why the initiative ultimately failed: "The Paper was silent about what actually would change on the ground. I came to realize this was a fatal flaw. The Paper was a proposal for a framework with no details." But could British Columbia's long-standing and lingering tight-fistedness have also contributed to its demise?

Mandell noted: "Matters were not helped by the province's refusal to discuss even a modest proposal for sharing gaming revenues in the interim, notwithstanding such agreements are in place with First Nations in many other provinces."[29] British Columbia had long shared gaming revenues with municipalities, but extending revenues to First Nations was deemed out of the question, given the premier's preoccupation with deficit containment during a global recession.

Former attorney general Geoff Plant suggests that, despite its unceremonious demise, the initiative has had a continuing impact on the conduct of Indigenous relations: "The key elements of that initiative are alive and well today, and you can see them in the deals that government makes with First Nations about shared decision-making on a number of fronts, including under the UNDRIP legislation." He defends the main framework of the Recognition and Reconciliation Act as "a good approach, albeit a victim of bad timing": even though it did not take hold, "its principles have informed discussions between government, the business community and First Nations ever since."[30]

I was appointed minister of Aboriginal relations and reconciliation on June 10, 2009, shortly after the provincial election and had an opportunity to review a draft copy of the Recognition and Reconciliation Act, furnished by the Ministry of the Attorney General. Sundry gaps in the document suggested important issues had yet to be addressed. Rejection of the act as "dead, dead, dead" brought further drafting work to a halt.[31]

Gary Mason noted that with the collapse of the act, the "task of mopping up this mess lies with George Abbott. This is Mr. Abbott's reward, apparently, for doing such a stellar job the past four years in the hardest ministry in government, Health. Few want the Aboriginal Relations Ministry because so many of the issues are complex and intractable. Nothing is black and white."[32] Mason was accurate in his assessment, certainly about Indigenous relations being complex, perhaps less so about them being intractable. More than anything, I was surprised by the goodwill, patience, and understanding I encountered in my time as minister.

One notable development saw British Columbia sign a land-use and economic-development agreement in December 2009 with the Haida Nation, titled Kunst'aa Guu. The agreement created a joint management council to determine resource decisions. Ratified by the BC legislature as the Haida Gwaii Reconciliation Act, the agreement embodied elements that had been secured through negotiation since the Supreme Court of Canada's landmark *Haida* decision in 2004. The Supreme Court's direction had again prompted governmental action. Of equal (but greater emotional) note, under section 2 of the

Reconciliation Act, the islands known as the Queen Charlotte Islands were returned to their precolonial name, Haida Gwaii.[33] Several months later, in an Indigenous-led initiative, coastal waters off British Columbia's south coast were officially named the Salish Sea.[34]

The vital work of the BC Treaty Commission also continued, with some notable successes. A comprehensive treaty agreement was initialled by the Yale First Nation, British Columbia, and Canada in February 2010. A year later, the Maa-nulth First Nations Treaty came into effect, breaking new ground as the first multi–First Nation treaty in British Columbia and the first modern treaty on Vancouver Island. Soon after, the Tla'amin Final Agreement was initialled by all parties, paving the way for successful ratification. Progress was slow but steady and punctuated by periodic controversies and setbacks. Frustration with the pace of negotiation has led some First Nations to consider alternative paths, including litigation.[35]

The demise of the Recognition and Reconciliation Act quickly became old news amid the "worst recession since the great depression." Confronted by a rapidly growing deficit, Campbell sought retrenchment. Any program not buttressed by a written legal contract was subject to cuts, but some were averted by the infusion of $1.6 billion in federal support of a harmonized sales tax.[36] In turn, intense public controversy over the tax led to Campbell's resignation in November 2010 and the election of Christy Clark as BC Liberal leader and premier.

Premier Clark did not share her predecessor's fascination with public policy as an instrument of reform. There would be no big and bold Indigenous relations initiatives during her tenure. Clark's focus was on economic expansion, specifically on making the province a major player in the development of liquefied natural gas. Indigenous relations was of interest only when it facilitated economic development. I received a first-hand lesson in Clark's approach to treaty making in 2014–15.

Premier Clark Surprises with a Sudden and Unilateral Shift on Treaty Making

I enjoyed the honour of serving as Clark's education minister in 2011–12, before retiring from politics before the 2013 provincial election. During the summer of 2014, I received an unexpected phone call from John Rustad, then British Columbia's minister of Aboriginal relations and reconciliation. To my surprise, he advised me that all three partners in the treaty process – the First

Nations Summit, British Columbia, and Canada – had identified me as the leading candidate for the role of chief commissioner at the BC Treaty Commission. At that time, I was pursuing a doctorate in political science at the University of Victoria and engaged in some private consulting projects, but I was genuinely honoured to enjoy his support and promised to give the exciting opportunity serious consideration.

A few days later, I called Rustad back, intent on accepting what I thought was a remarkably important role. But I nursed lingering doubts about my acceptability among some former colleagues, so I asked him to reconfirm the provincial government's support for my appointment. His answer was "yes."

The first step in the process came on October 17, 2014, when the First Nations Summit Chiefs passed Resolution 1014.02, which formally appointed me as chief commissioner.[37] The next step would be the ratification of my appointment by the BC government.

But nothing happened. In early December, I called Rustad, who assured me cabinet was working through policy issues. I had no reason to be concerned. He assured me again in early 2015 as the clock ticked down to the current chief commissioner's, Sophie Pierre's, scheduled retirement on April 1.

The Treaty Commission organized transition meetings in Kelowna, which I attended, beginning on March 18. A few minutes before the first meeting was called to order, I received a phone call from Rustad advising me that he had been "unable to secure cabinet approval" for my appointment. My initial reaction to the news was that "some knives came out in cabinet" and that political animosity stemming from past battles had come into play.[38]

Why this shift occurred, several months after I'd been invited to enter the process, was far from clear. Rustad said "cabinet confidentiality" prevented him from offering any details. I was surprised (perhaps more than I should have been, given the long wait) and disappointed, but mostly, I was saddened, as I later told Vaughn Palmer, to be "denied the opportunity to be a critical part of repairing the damage a century of bad public policy has inflicted on First Nations."[39]

Within the next hour, as I waited at Kelowna airport for a flight home to Victoria, Chief Commissioner Pierre issued a blistering press release: "This retraction of the chief commissioner selection after months of agreement, expectation and reliance by the other parties raises questions about British Columbia's commitment to the treaty negotiations process. To pull this away at the 11th hour questions the commitment of BC – this is not how to effect reconciliation."[40] The First Nations Summit, in a letter to Premier Clark, said it was "taken aback and extremely disappointed in this unexpected and late arriving decision ... inconsistent with the joint agreement we made as Principals to appoint Mr. Abbott as Chief Commissioner."[41]

Clark faced tough questions from the media. She told Justine Hunter of the *Globe and Mail* that she would "not appoint anyone to the position of chief commissioner because she doesn't think the treaty process is working." She denied that political animosity had played any role in the government's decision: "We made a principled policy decision. The decision is not to continue with the status quo ... In terms of next steps – whether or not the treaty commission will change or whether it will continue to exist – is going to be something we decide together with First Nations."[42] In other words, despite – or perhaps consistent with – British Columbia's long and tortured history of opposing treaty negotiations, Clark was unilaterally calling the continued existence of the Treaty Commission into question.

Is it possible that political animosity played a role, despite Clark's denials? Perhaps. But Pierre may have offered the best explanation when she stated, "BC, we can see you want to pull away from negotiations because you have been removing negotiators from treaty tables – of course that makes those tables less effective."[43] Pierre's assertion was consistent with Hunter's report that the "province has already subtly pulled back by giving all of its senior negotiators at the treaty table additional responsibilities for liquefied natural gas negotiations."

I don't expect to ever know the full story. My main concern today, as during the controversy, is that any delay in the treaty process prolongs the primacy of the Indian Act, which I described to Hunter at the time as "one of those reprehensible relics of the past that has marginalized First Nations and that we need to move beyond." I paused, then added after a moment of reflection, "Maybe I am explaining why I got offed as chief commissioner."[44]

Clark's promise to rethink and renew the treaty process was apparently embodied in "Proposals for the Principals' Consideration: Multilateral Engagement Process to Improve and Expedite Treaty Negotiations in British Columbia."[45] The proposals, characterized by Vaughn Palmer as "a 38-page statement of good intentions," were endorsed by the principals but did not alter the trajectory of treaty completion in British Columbia.[46] The biggest news in Indigenous relations would once again come from the Supreme Court of Canada.

14

New Ideas, Long-Standing Injustices

In British Columbia, reforms to Indigenous relations typically proceed at a frustratingly slow pace, punctuated by court decisions and political initiatives that promise substantial shifts. The Supreme Court of Canada has been the prime source for punctuation points through key decisions from *Calder* and *Sparrow* to *Delgamuukw* and *Haida*. Even as the provincial government pulled back from treaty making in 2014, a landmark case for Indigenous rights and title in Canada was reaching a dramatic conclusion in the nation's highest court.

Back in 1983, the Tŝilhqot'in had challenged British Columbia's right to grant a commercial logging licence on lands the Nation regarded as its Traditional Territory. In 2014, the Supreme Court of Canada finally resolved the dispute, breaking new ground in *Tsilhqot'in Nation v British Columbia*, the first appellate decision in Canadian history upholding a finding of Aboriginal title. The Supreme Court granted the Tŝilhqot'in a declaration of title to 1,750 square kilometres of land, an amount that surely would have had Joseph Trutch rolling in his grave.

Significantly, the Supreme Court utilized a "territorial basis for determining Aboriginal title, rather than a site-specific basis."[1] It overturned the BC Court of Appeal's prior ruling that Aboriginal title required proof of intensive use on defined tracts of land such as village sites. Much of the Tŝilhqot'in title area was sparsely populated but had been used for hunting, fishing, trapping, foraging, and other cultural uses; hence, in the Supreme Court's view, it merited inclusion. The Supreme Court rejected "the impoverished view of

Aboriginal title advanced by Canada and British Columbia, characterized by the plaintiff as a 'postage stamp' approach to title," which, the Court said, "cannot be allowed to pervade and inhibit genuine negotiations."[2]

The *Tsilhqot'in* decision was widely viewed as a dramatic victory not only for the Tŝilhqot'in but also for other First Nations. Grand Chief Stewart Phillip claimed, "For me it's simple. BC land is Indian land."[3] Comments from other Indigenous leaders were more circumspect, but all shared the view of one major law firm – that the "judgement today is an enormous victory for First Nations. It represents a key milestone on the road to reconciliation and will likely be a game-changer for First Nations–Crown relations."[4] Even under the most favourable governmental construction of the decision's import and implications, *Tsilhqot'in* represented a major setback for the BC government after earlier winning at the BC Court of Appeal. The Supreme Court quashed elements of the colonial narrative that had underpinned the province's approach to Indigenous rights and title for 150 years.

Premier Christy Clark attempted to put the best face on a ringing defeat. She described the *Tsilhqot'in* judgment as "a fork in the road" and "our chance to be on the right side of history." Grand Chief Ed John was quick to rework Clark's metaphor. Indigenous people, he quipped, were "historically accustomed to forked tongues and we can't have that."[5]

Sadly, the history of British Columbia's Indigenous relations as a colony and a province reveals far more examples of forked tongues than of adherence to the right side of history. However, British Columbia's path forward is far clearer with the Supreme Court's emphatic rebuttal of the long-running narrative, launched 150 years earlier by Joseph Trutch, that First Nations have no right to the lands they claim.

Governments may sometimes deplore, but can never ignore, the legal direction provided by the Supreme Court of Canada, and governmental inaction sometimes produces its own perils. Canada recently received a first-hand lesson on the cost of inaction in a case rooted in early BC history. When the threat of Indigenous insurgency mounted in 1874, Father Grandidier had reminded the BC government that its aggressive promotion of settler pre-emptions was causing First Nations to be "corralled on a small piece of ground, as at Canoe Creek and elsewhere, or even have not an inch of ground, as at Williams Lake." Over a century later, the Williams Lake First Nation submitted a claim to the Specific Claims Tribunal based on Canada's failure to protect it from dispossession. After years in the courts, the claim proved successful, resulting in a 2022 settlement between Canada and the Williams Lake First Nation for $135 million.[6]

Two years later, the Esk'etemc First Nation (formerly the Alkali Lake Indian band, located fifty-two kilometres south of Williams Lake) reached a $147.6 million settlement with Canada over another perennial issue: Canada's failure to obtain and safeguard water rights. In the 1890s, the Esk'etemc had attempted to construct an irrigation ditch from Vert Lake to their Wycott's Flat Reserve. As noted in the *Quesnel Cariboo Observer*, "They dug with picks and shovels for 5.5 kilometres but then were told to stop by the federal government when they only had one kilometre left to go."[7] The settlement reflected the value of crops that could have been grown with irrigation over 130 years as well as the economic deprivation stemming from lost opportunity. As Esk'etemc Kukpi7 (Chief) Fred Robbins stated, "The settlement amount for the loss of water rights is substantial, but the impacts on generations of Esk'etemc who lived in poverty because of the loss of water rights is also substantial."[8]

Many claims await resolution elsewhere in the province, some linked to Joseph Trutch's reserve reductions in the 1860s, others to the McKenna-McBride Commission's decisions fifty years later. In 1990, the Tk'emlúps Nation launched a six-year legal battle over a 130-hectare (320-acre) parcel lost to settler pre-emption in the 1860s, resulting in a $2.2 million judgment against the province.[9] Multiple specific claims by the Tk'emlúps and other First Nations await resolutions, whether through the courts or alternative processes.

An Apparent Step Forward Confronts a Potential Step Back

When the BC legislature unanimously adopted the Declaration on the Rights of Indigenous Peoples Act (DRIPA) in 2019, Premier Horgan described it as "only one step on our journey to advance reconciliation and undo 150 years of colonial harms that we see very clearly continue to be felt today."[10] Indigenous leader and author Jody Wilson-Raybould agreed with that assessment, noting that the United Nations Declaration of the Rights of Indigenous Peoples (UNDRIP, the inspiration for DRIPA) "is the start, not the finishing line."[11] British Columbia may have been the first jurisdiction in Canada to pass such legislation, but its long and vigorous resistance to Indigenous land reform leaves many challenges to be addressed.

Both the start and the finishing lines have been blurred by the sudden rise of the Conservative Party of BC. John Rustad, the former minister of Aboriginal relations who supported my ill-fated nomination as chief commissioner of the BC Treaty Commission in 2014, is now that party's leader.[12] During the 2024 provincial election campaign, Rustad promised to return Traditional

Territories and resources to First Nations while at the same time promising to repeal DRIPA, or at least portions of it, despite his support for the act in 2019.[13]

The Conservative party platform, released late in the campaign, pointedly emphasized an ostensible distinction between DRIPA and UNDRIP. It promised to honour UNDRIP as it was intended, as a "central set of guiding principles," but argued that the NDP's implementation and interpretation of DRIPA had "stalled Indigenous-led development in industries like mining, forestry, natural gas, and other sectors." The platform promised to "return 20% of British Columbia's forests to First Nations Indigenous groups to manage these resources sustainably and in line with their traditions and values."[14] One press report cited Rustad as claiming First Nations "would be 'landlords of that land' and reap the benefits rather than governments getting stumpage fees with only a fraction going to First Nations."[15]

The Conservative platform was greeted with skepticism by most First Nations leaders. A joint press release from the British Columbia Assembly of First Nations, the First Nations Summit, and the Union of British Columbia Indian Chiefs argued that the platform fell "drastically short of what is needed to advance meaningful reconciliation efforts with First Nations" and that it failed to recognize the need for "free, prior and informed consent of rights and title holders – rights that are deeply rooted in our unceded territories."[16] Grand Chief Stewart Phillip of the Union of British Columbia Indian Chiefs claimed that overturning DRIPA would lead to renewed "conflict and confrontation" over industrial development projects. "The acceleration of industrialized destruction of our homelands, our territories, is nothing to cheer about," he said. "It's not economic reconciliation. It's economic exploitation."[17]

The Conservatives came close to forming a government in the 2024 election and – given the possibility of nonconfidence motions, defections, and by-elections – may win power in coming years. Given such a scenario, how would a Conservative government achieve its promise to strategically and collaboratively return land to First Nations?

One existing model for reconciliation outside of conventional treaty processes is the Lake Babine Nation Foundation Agreement of September 2020. The agreement engaged substantial commitments from both the province and Canada, consistent with the principles of UNDRIP.[18] In its preamble, the agreement makes direct reference to the Supreme Court's *Tsilhqot'in* decision, noting that it "motivates the Parties to move beyond the denial of Indigenous rights that led to disempowerment and assimilationist policies and practices into a new nation-to-nation relationship based on reconciliation, and the recognition and implementation of rights and title."[19] The Lake Babine Nation, located 230 kilometres west of Prince George, is one of British Columbia's largest First Nations by population (2,535 as of July 2024). But the Nation has only 3,093.90 hectares of reserve land, only 1.22 hectares per person, which sorely limits opportunities.[20]

Under the agreement, the province will transfer 20,000 hectares (200 square kilometres) of Crown land to the Nation in fee simple; in addition, Canada is providing $50 million to support Lake Babine's infrastructure and economic development.[21] "What this means to our people is opportunity," said Chief Murphy Abraham. He saw it as "Lake Babine's roadmap to independence from the devastating impacts of colonialism."[22] Chief Abraham's words offer a stark reminder of how and why so many BC First Nations continue to be fettered by the tight-fisted reserve allocations of Joseph Trutch and his successors.

Does Haida Gwaii Offer Yet Another Path Forward?

In 1913, when the McKenna-McBride Commission visited Haida Gwaii (the Queen Charlotte Islands), Skidegate councillor Amos Russ alluded to a pending title case at the Court of the Privy Council. The chair of the McKenna-McBride Commission, Edward Wetmore, dismissed the title question with customary arrogance, stating: "Somebody is misleading you or you have misunderstood something."[23]

More than a century later, the BC government and the Council of the Haida Nation jointly announced a draft agreement recognizing Aboriginal title throughout Haida Gwaii. "When the Royal Commission came here to Haida Gwaii, our people were very clear they didn't want to discuss reserves and accept what the government was trying to lay down," said Gaagwiis Jason Alsop, president of the Haida Nation. "It's all Haida land, the whole territory – the land and the sea. It's been a consistent position, and a consistent effort for the Haida Nation now for well over 100 years, and 50 years since we formed our own government to deal with it."[24]

British Columbia's minister of Indigenous relations and reconciliation, Murray Rankin, also recognized the historic character of the draft agreement: "This is the first time that governments will have negotiated, rather than being told by a court, after litigation, to recognize the existence of Aboriginal title," an indirect reference to the Supreme Court of Canada's finding of Aboriginal title in its 2014 *Tsilhqot'in* decision. Critics predictably panned the draft agreement, declaring that it would "deter investment and destabilize the land base across our province."[25]

Rankin anticipated that critique and aimed to assure non-Indigenous British Columbians: "We've managed to secure some important recognitions, like that private property is protected, that local government jurisdiction remains, and there's no impact on infrastructure services, roads, and ferries and highways and medical services." Rankin sought to discourage the notion that the agreement would set a broader precedent: "We had the ideal conditions to lead to the agreement we hope to enter into on Haida Gwaii. But I wouldn't want to say that those conditions are the same in other parts of the province." Douglas White Kwul'a'sul'tun, a Coast Salish lawyer and special counsel to the premier, David Eby, emphasized the "unique position" of the Haida, noting "they have no overlaps with other nations, as in, no other nation claims the islands."[26] Even with such caveats, the Haida agreement would have been far beyond the wildest dreams – or perhaps the most terrifying nightmares – of the McKenna-McBride Commission in 1913.

Does the BC Treaty Commission Remain Active and Relevant?

The BC Treaty Commission argues that a "modern treaty, fairly negotiated and honourably implemented, is the greatest expression of reconciliation."[27] Governments throughout history have made that expression of reconciliation infinitely more difficult by taking 120 years to launch tripartite negotiations. Assembling treaty settlement lands in British Columbia is exponentially more challenging today than it would have been in 1871, given the province now has a population of over 5 million and Indigenous lands bounded by a mix of cities and towns, parks and protected areas, and resource tenures. But challenging or not, assembling the lands or alternative resources (such as cash to enable land purchases) must proceed, or reconciliation will never be achieved.

The BC Treaty Commission is now over thirty years into its labours. The treaty-making process is long and complex. After extensive negotiations with federal and provincial governments, a First Nation defines – after consultations with neighbouring Nations – its treaty settlement lands and crucial elements of its future political structure and operations. Under the commission's leadership, seven First Nations have successfully concluded treaty negotiations, described as Stage 6, "implementation," which follows tripartite ratification. Another eighteen First Nations are at Stage 5, "negotiations to finalize a treaty," and thirty are at Stage 4, "negotiation of an agreement in principle."[28] The commission enjoyed considerable success in 2024 when three coastal Nations at Kitselas, Kitsumkalum, and K'ómoks initialled treaties.[29]

Of vital importance is the ability of treaty partners to initiate reconciliation measures during treaty negotiation and after ratification. The federal and provincial governments acquire future treaty lands that are sometimes deployed as "interim measures" on the road to comprehensive treaty agreements, measures that can make a big difference to individual First Nations. Readers may recall Indian commissioner Peter O'Reilly's refusal in 1881 to offer the Xatśūll First Nation (the Soda Creek Band) anything more than a reserve composed of "a steep hill side ... containing barely 45 acres for agricultural purposes." Almost 140 years later, the 4,170-acre (1,688-hectare) Carpenter Mountain Ranch near 150 Mile House was purchased for $8 million as part of "an innovative treaty solution" for the Xatśūll. In the words of Kukpi7 (Chief) Sheri Sellars, "The opportunity this creates puts tools for economic development into the hands of a community whose life has always been centred around the land."[30]

The intensive and painstaking work of treaty negotiation should be important to all British Columbians. Treaties, as anthropologist Michael Asch observes, offer non-Indigenous settlers "the means to reconcile the fact that we are 'here to stay' with the fact that there were people already here when we first arrived." Asch believes that – with the consent of Indigenous peoples – "this path still offers us a way forward notwithstanding the negative way in which we have dealt with our obligations in the past."[31]

Huu-ay-aht Hereditary Chief and former BC treaty commissioner Tom Happynook reminds us of the critical importance of continued treaty negotiation: "The Huu-ay-aht treaty has woven us into the fabric of Canada. Being constitutionally self-governing and shedding the shackles of the Indian Act makes it possible to flourish by investing in our own territory. The treaty is slowly pulling us out of 150 years of poverty."[32]

I'm heartened by these successes at the BC Treaty Commission's tables and by those achieved through alternative nontreaty processes such as the Lake Babine Nation Foundation Agreement. Future treaty and nontreaty agreements can and should reflect the diversity of the province and its First Nations. Both paths offer choices and opportunities that have too long been denied to First Nations by British Columbia's punitive and tight-fisted reserve policies and by the shackles of Canada's Indian Act. Far too many First Nations are still caught in the grip of our colonialist past.

Epilogue

The Long and Rocky Road to Reconciliation

Milestone anniversaries are typically a time of celebration, but British Columbia's 150th year of provincehood on July 20, 2021, provided little opportunity for festivities. Premier John Horgan suggested that the province's sesquicentennial was "something we'd normally like to celebrate, but we're not making any plans right now, and British Columbians should not make any plans right now."[1] The persistence of COVID-19 discouraged festivities, as did the grim discovery of unmarked graves at the Kamloops Indian Residential School in 2021, the latter suggesting that British Columbia's sesquicentennial might be as much a cause for regret as for celebration.[2]

Anniversaries are also a time for reflection, and British Columbia's 150 years of provincehood offer plenty to think about. British Columbia is today a very different province than it was in 1871, with a population that is much larger and far more diverse. The province's economy has also diversified, although resource development – in the form of sawmills, mines, oil and gas, and agriculture – remains vital to provincial coffers and local economies outside the Lower Mainland and southern Vancouver Island.

When it comes to Indigenous relations, full and proper reconciliation is closer than ever before, but we still have a long way to go. Many of the small and scattered reserves transferred to Canada in 1871 remain small and scattered. Early federal-provincial commissions launched to resolve the land question – from the Joint Indian Reserve Commission to the McKenna-McBride Commission – only exacerbated injustices and anger. Reforming colonial policies, and the inequalities that continue to flow from them, has been painfully slow. All too often, initiatives launched with good intentions – from Israel Powell's attempt to expand reserves in 1874 to the Kelowna Accord in 2005 – have failed to produce much-needed reforms.

The cascading harms that have flowed from destructive policies will not be easily undone, nor will the stain of prejudice and injustice be removed from British Columbia's history by words alone. Indeed, as this book was in production, the ghosts of the colonial past were still haunting BC politics. In the early days of the 2025 spring session of the legislature, John Rustad's prescription for reconciliation was challenged by one of his own newly elected MLAs. Dallas Brodie (Vancouver–Quilchena) called into question the truth of the stories residential school Survivors told about their experiences in those institutions, disputed whether there really were any human remains at the graves identified by ground-penetrating radar at the Kamloops residential school, and then tried to use the doubt sown by residential school denialism to undermine modern treaty-making initiatives. Her arguments were remarkably similar to those wielded by Joseph Trutch in 1871, Amor De Cosmos in 1880, and (among others) the Canadian parliament in 1927. "The truth is a threat to powerful vested interests in the multi-billion-dollar reconciliation industry," wrote Brodie on X. "Politicians like David Eby and John Rustad are willing to sell off British Columbia's wealth and power, transferring it from the public to an elite racial minority – enriching opportunistic lawyers, consultants, and chiefs along the way."[3]

Brodie's ejection from the Conservative caucus, Rustad said, was "a result of her decision to publicly mock and belittle testimony from former residential school students, including by mimicking individuals recounting stories of abuses – including child sex abuse." Brodie told the media that close to twenty of her colleagues agreed with her.[4] At the time of writing, two agreed with her enough to quit the party in protest and are considering starting a new political party of their own.[5]

In stark contrast, back in 2015, the Truth and Reconciliation Commission of Canada set out our shared goal plainly and powerfully: "Together, Canadians must do more than just *talk* about reconciliation; we must learn how to *practise* reconciliation in our everyday lives – within ourselves and our families, and in our communities, governments, places of worship, schools and workplaces."[6] As settlers striving to reach a better understanding of our destructive and often shameful history of Indigenous relations, we are all on a long and challenging learning journey. Perhaps one day – in keeping with the Truth and Reconciliation Commission's laudable goal – we will practise reconciliation in our everyday lives.

Steven Point, British Columbia's first Indigenous lieutenant-governor, offers a compelling vision for the journey ahead, particularly given our shared challenge of climate change: "I've had this belief for some time that if people see our world like a canoe – like we're together – we're not individuals in separate canoes. We're in the same canoe and it's called the Earth, the world. We have to try and work together, paddle in the same direction. Maybe we can accomplish something."[7] Despite the prejudices and injustices that stain our history, British Columbians and Canadians can learn from our painful history and offer renewed hopes for reconciliation in a troubled world. The lives of our grandchildren may depend on it.

Acknowledgments

I would first like to thank the Honourable Steven Point for providing the foreword to *Unceded.* Steven has enjoyed a remarkable career as (among other roles) a lawyer, judge, chief commissioner of the BC Treaty Commission, chancellor of the University of British Columbia, and Grand Chief of the Stó:lō Nation.

I had the good fortune to serve in the Legislative Assembly during Steven's tenure as lieutenant-governor. He invariably brought good humour and a balanced perspective to an assembly where partisan animosity all too often prevailed. Steven is a great and insightful leader who has improved British Columbia in many ways. I'm deeply honoured to have his foreword be a part of my book.

A book such as *Unceded* is largely built on documents derived from archival sources. I particularly want to thank all those who assisted me at the Royal BC Museum and Archives, the Legislative Library of British Columbia, Library and Archives Canada, the BC Hydro and Power Authority Archives, University of Victoria Libraries Special Collections, and the University of British Columbia Library Special Collections Division. I thank *BC Studies* for its ongoing support for scholarship in British Columbia. Chapters 8 and 9 of this book contain portions of an article titled "Persistence of Colonial Prejudice and Policy in British Columbia's Indigenous Relations: Did the Spirit of Joseph Trutch Haunt Twentieth-Century Resource Development?," *BC Studies* 194 (Summer 2017): 39–64.

I was fortunate to enjoy outstanding editorial support from Nadine Pedersen throughout my writing journey for *Unceded.* Nadine and the editorial teams from Purich Books and UBC Press – including Megan Brand, Randy Schmidt, and Andrea Routley – invariably provided sound advice and direction to me, along with consulting editor Lesley Erickson. I'm also appreciative of the keen eyes and valuable insights of the anonymous manuscript readers engaged by UBC Press and Purich Books.

Unceded also draws on the remarkable body of research and insights of a broad range of scholars, authors, and researchers in the field of Indigenous studies. I include "suggestions for further reading" to guide readers to those fascinating works.

Finally, I want to thank friends and colleagues who contributed to the construction of the *Unceded* narrative: James Tully, Jamie Lawson, Colin Bennett, and Evert Lindquist from the University of Victoria; Brant Abbott from Queen's University; and Mary Koyl, Angela Wesley, Eric Denhoff, Wade Abbott, Harry Swain, Bob de Faye, Anna Nyarady, Jim Reynolds, Geoff Plant, Robert Abbott, Gordon Hogg, and Megan Fuller. Special thanks to my wife, Lesley, for her advice and patient answers to my periodic questions about Word and word processing.

Notes

Prologue: Ghosts from the Colonial Past

1 British Columbia, *Sessional Papers,* 1887, 257, quoted in Paul Tennant, *Aboriginal Peoples and Politics: The Indian Land Question in British Columbia, 1840–1989* (Vancouver: UBC Press, 1990), 58.

2 Alex Rose, "The Fisher from Nass River: Chief Joseph Gosnell Brought Home a Treaty to the Nisga'a People," *Vancouver Sun,* August 20, 2020. Ts'msyen (Tsimshian) leaders joined the Nisga'a delegation, likely at a stop in Lax Kw'alaams (Port Simpson).

3 British Columbia, *Debates of the Legislative Assembly,* December 2, 1998, 10860. The journey by cedar canoe is noted in Kevin Griffin, "Canada 150: Joseph Gosnell Helped Negotiate Historic Treaty for the Nisga'a," *Vancouver Sun,* May 12, 2017.

4 Joseph Trutch to the Acting Colonial Secretary, August 28, 1867, in British Columbia, *Papers Connected with the Indian Land Question, 1850–1875* (Victoria: Richard Wolfenden, Government Printer, 1875) (hereafter *PCILQ*), with enclosure titled "Lower Fraser River Indian Reserves," 42. "Indians" in this case meant "Lower Fraser River Indians," but Trutch held the same view regardless of geographic location.

5 Quoted in Hamar Foster, Heather Raven, and Jeremy Webber, *Let Right Be Done: Aboriginal Title, the* Calder *Case, and the Future of Indigenous Rights* (Vancouver: UBC Press, 2007), 217. Campagnolo offered her critique of Joseph Trutch at a 2003 event that celebrated the thirtieth anniversary of the Supreme Court of Canada's landmark decision in *Calder et al v Attorney-General of British Columbia,* as well as the distinguished career of Frank Calder, president of the Nisga'a Tribal Council throughout the extensive litigation process. Calder blazed trails in many ways, perhaps most notably with his election as British Columbia's first Indigenous member of the Legislative Assembly in 1949, the same year that Indigenous suffrage was restored in the province and seventy-seven years after British Columbia's first Legislative Assembly had abolished those voting rights.

6 Steve Zhang, "Richmond Renames Street after BC's First Indigenous Lieutenant-Governor," CBC News, May 7, 2022, https://www.cbc.ca/news/canada/british-columbia/richmond-renames-street-after-indigenous-lieutenant-governor-1.6443411.

7 First Nations Health Authority, "FNHA Overview," https://www.fnha.ca/.

8 George M. Abbott, "Persistence of Colonial Prejudice and Policy in British Columbia's Indigenous Relations: Did the Spirit of Joseph Trutch Haunt Twentieth-Century Resource Development?," *BC Studies* 194 (Summer 2017): 39–64.

9 According to Robert and Jane Cowan, in *Enderby: An Illustrated History* (Vernon, BC: Wayside Press, 2005), Splatsin reserves were formalized by Peter O'Reilly and John Trutch in 1871 based on Trutch's formula of ten acres per family, yielding a reserve of two hundred acres. The Splatsin reserves were among those expanded because of the peacemaking efforts of the Joint Indian Reserve Commission during Indigenous upheavals in 1877 (discussed in Chapter 4).

10 Royal Commission on Indian Affairs in the Province of British Columbia (more commonly known as the McKenna-McBride Commission), "Meeting at Port Essington: Meeting with Aiyansh Band," October 9, 1915, transcript, 163–64. The transcript also describes Chief Naas as Chief John N. Ksidinul.

11 Alan Hanna, "Going Circular: Indigenous Legal Research Methodology as Legal Practice," *McGill Law Journal* 65, 4 (2020): 671.

12 "Report of the Government of British Columbia on the Subject of Indian Reserves," Order in Council, August 18, 1875, in British Columbia, *PCILQ*, 2.

13 Alternatively expressed as *Hisuk ma cawak*. I am grateful to my friend and colleague Angela Wesley for offering this important insight.

14 BC Treaty Commission, "Why Treaties?," https://www.bctreaty.ca/.

15 Angela Wesley, "Ancient Spirit, Modern Mind: The Huu-ay-aht Journey Back to Self-Determination and Self-Reliance," in *Reclaiming Indigenous Governance: Reflections and Insights from Australia, Canada, New Zealand, and the United States*, ed. William Nikolakis, Stephen Cornell, and Harry Nelson (Tucson: University of Arizona Press, 2019), 112.

16 Carolyn Bennett, minister of Crown-Indigenous relations and northern affairs in 2019, is quoted in "Revamped BC Treaty Negotiation Process Drawing Mixed Reaction from First Nations," CBC News, September 5, 2019, https://www.cbc.ca/news/indigenous/bc-treaty-process-new-policy-1.5272531. The reforms noted include automatic recognition of the Indigenous right to self-government and Aboriginal title. The article notes that Stewart Phillip, Grand Chief of the Union of British Columbia Indian Chiefs and long-time critic of the Treaty Commission, welcomed the reforms.

17 British Columbia, *Declaration on the Rights of Indigenous Peoples Act, 2020/2021 Annual Report*, https://www2.gov.bc.ca/assets/gov/government/ministries-organizations/ministries/indigenous-relations-reconciliation/declaration_act_annual_report_2021.pdf, and British Columbia, Legislative Assembly, "Historical Timeline, 1874," https://www.leg.bc.ca/dyl/Pages/1872-Indigenous-and-Chinese-Peoples-Excluded-from-the-Vote.aspx.

18 British Columbia Assembly of First Nations, "FNLC Condemns BC Conservative Platform Budget," press release, October 16, 2024, https://www.bcafn.ca/news/fnlc-condemns-bc-conservatives-party-platform-budget.

19 A BC government news release characterized the agreement as "an innovative new model for future agreements in BC" and "a concrete example of how the Province and Canada are working with First Nations to put the principles of the United Nations Declaration on the Rights of Indigenous Peoples into practice": British Columbia, BC Gov News, January 27, 2023, https://news.gov.bc.ca/releases/2023IRR0001-000099.

20 What we heard was reflective of a broader issue noted by political philosopher James Tully: "Western sciences often dismiss Indigenous knowledges and life ways as primitive,

superstitious, soon to die off, lower, or less-developed relative to the superior knowledge and processes of civilization, modernization, and globalization spread around the globe by Western peoples." See James Tully, "Reconciliation Here on Earth," in *Resurgence and Reconciliation: Indigenous-Settler Relations and Earth Teachings,* ed. Michael Asch, John Borrows, and James Tully (Toronto: University of Toronto Press, 2018), 85.

21 George Abbott and Maureen Chapman, *Addressing the New Normal: 21st-Century Disaster Management in British Columbia,* a report for government and British Columbians, April 30, 2018, https://www2.gov.bc.ca/assets/gov/public-safety-and-emergency-services/emergency-preparedness-response-recovery. Chief Chapman has been Hereditary Chief of Sq'ewá:lxw (Skawahlook) First Nation in the Fraser Valley region of British Columbia since 1999.

22 John Borrows, "Earth-Bound: Indigenous Resurgence," in Asch, Borrows, and Tully, *Resurgence and Reconciliation,* 69.

23 Gary Mason, "Rejection of Aboriginal Rights Act Shatters Campbell's Dream of Leaving a Legacy," *Globe and Mail,* September 5, 2009.

Chapter 1: A Bold Vision Meets Resistance

1 Colony of Vancouver Island, *Journals of the Legislative Council of Vancouver Island,* July 12, 1854, 14 (hereafter *Journals of the Legislative Council*).

2 Cole Harris, review of *To Share, Not Surrender: Indigenous and Settler Visions of Treaty Making in the Colonies of Vancouver Island and British Columbia,* ed. Peter Cook, Neil Vallance, John Lutz, Graham Brazier, and Hamar Foster, *Canadian Historical Review* 103, 2 (June 2022): 319.

3 Laura Spitz, "Colonialism, Law, and the Social Construction of Humanity on Vancouver Island, 1849–64," in Cook et al., *To Share, Not Surrender* (Vancouver: UBC Press, 2021), 220–45. For a summary of Blanshard's brief, unhappy tenure, see James E. Hendrickson, "Blanshard, Richard," in *Dictionary of Canadian Biography,* vol. 12, University of Toronto/Université Laval, 2003–, http://www.biographi.ca/en/bio/blanshard_richard_12E.html.

4 Keith Thor Carlson, "'The Last Potlatch' and James Douglas's Vision of an Alternative Settler Colonialism," in Cook et al., *To Share, Not Surrender,* 295.

5 Richard Mackie, "The Colonization of Vancouver Island," *BC Studies* 96 (Winter 1992): 33.

6 James Douglas to Edward Bulwer Lytton, March 14, 1859, in British Columbia, *Papers Connected with the Indian Land Question, 1850–1875* (Victoria: Richard Wolfenden, Government Printer, 1875) (hereafter *PCILQ*), 16.

7 Cole Harris, "The Native Land Policies of Governor James Douglas," *BC Studies* 174 (Summer 2012): 103.

8 Hamar Foster, "Letting Go the Bone: The Idea of Indian Title in British Columbia, 1849–1927," in *Essays in the History of Canadian Law,* vol. 6, *British Columbia and the Yukon,* ed. Hamar Foster and John McLaren (Toronto: University of Toronto Press/Osgoode Society for Canadian Legal History, 1995), 56.

9 Douglas quoted in Carlson, "Last Potlatch," 209. Douglas is similarly quoted in Alexander Globe, *Gold, Grit, Guns: Miners on BC's Fraser River in 1858* (Vancouver: Rondale Press, 2022), 91, 228.

10 Wendy Wickwire, *At the Bridge: James Teit and an Anthropology of Belonging* (Vancouver: UBC Press, 2019), 38–39.

11 Conflict during the Fraser River Gold Rush is fascinating in its own right. Douglas was not alone in attempting to quell violent conflict and a potential war. See Globe, *Gold, Grit,*

Guns, 92–104, and Wickwire, *At the Bridge,* 38–40. See also Marianne Ignace and Ronald E. Ignace, *Secwépemc People, Land, and Laws* (Montreal/Kingston: McGill-Queen's University Press, 2017), 438–40, which offers a Secwépemc perspective on gold rush conflicts.

12 All quotes from Douglas to Lytton, March 14, 1859, *PCILQ,* 16–17. The two colonies were not formally united until 1866, but they had a common governor until Douglas's retirement in 1864.

13 Lytton to Douglas, May 20, 1859, *PCILQ,* 18.

14 Douglas to Lytton, March 25, 1861, *PCILQ,* 19. The Douglas Treaties were simple documents when compared with modern treaties in British Columbia, but they nevertheless signified a recognition of continuous occupation and possessory rights by the HBC (through Chief Factor Douglas) and Great Britain (through Douglas as governor of Vancouver Island). The Douglas Treaties are recognized by the Supreme Court of Canada.

15 John Sutton Lutz, "The Rutters' Impasse and the End of Treaty Making on Vancouver Island," in Cook et al., *To Share, Not Surrender,* 223.

16 Cole Harris, *Making Native Space: Colonialism, Resistance, and Reserves in British Columbia* (Vancouver: UBC Press, 2002), 25. John Lutz offers an excellent analysis of the Douglas Treaties in "Rutters' Impasse," 220–45.

17 Douglas to Lytton, March 25, 1861, *PCILQ,* 19.

18 Lord Carnarvon (on behalf of Secretary of State E.B. Lytton) to Douglas, April 11, 1859, *PCILQ,* 18.

19 See Colony of Vancouver Island, *Journals of the Legislative Council of Vancouver Island,* June 9, 1856, 18, where the model is summarized, including the property qualifications for membership. Colonial political institutions evolved quickly during the 1860s. At different points, they were referred to as the "Legislative Council," "Legislative Assembly," and "House of Assembly." See also J.I. Little, "The Foundations of Government," in *The Pacific Province: A History of British Columbia,* ed. Hugh J.M. Johnston (Vancouver: Douglas and McIntyre, 1996), 68–74.

20 J.S. Helmcken (as Speaker of the House of Assembly) to the Lord Newcastle, February 6, 1861, petition enclosed in Douglas to the Lord Newcastle, March 25, 1861, CO 305:17, no. 4779, 126, *The Colonial Despatches of Vancouver Island and British Columbia, 1846–1871,* 2.4 ed., ed. James Hendrickson and the Colonial Despatches project, Victoria, British Columbia, https://bcgenesis.uvic.ca/V61024.html.

21 Lutz, "Rutters' Impasse," 226. Lutz notes that "virtually every settler" in the Cowichan and Chemainus regions signed a petition supporting the treaty submitted to Governor Douglas in 1861.

22 Quoted in Sarah Pike, "The Colony of British Columbia's Unsurveyed Land System," in Cook et al., *To Share, Not Surrender,* 268.

23 Douglas to Lord Newcastle, March 25, 1861, *PCILQ,* 19.

24 Lord Newcastle to Douglas, October 19, 1861, *PCILQ,* 20. John Lutz, in "Rutters' Impasse," 234–39, provides an excellent and comprehensive account of tensions surrounding treaty funding and the players involved.

25 Douglas to Lord Carnarvon (in the absence of Lytton), March 25, 1861, *PCILQ,* 19.

26 Hamar Foster, "'We Want a Strong Promise': The Opposition to Indian Treaties in British Columbia, 1850–1990," *Native Studies Review* 18, 1 (2009): 117–18.

27 Douglas to Lytton, March 14, 1859, *PCILQ,* 17. Douglas's views on Indigenous ownership were perhaps less widely understood than he might have liked. In 1862, R.C. Moody asked

William Young whether "an Indian" could purchase a suburban lot in New Westminster "just as a white man would?" Young responded, "I am directed by the Governor to inform you that there can be no objection to your selling lands to the Natives on the same terms as they are disposed of to any purchasers in the Colony whether British subjects or aliens": Moody to Young, May 27, 1862, *PCILQ*, 23, and Young to Moody, June 18, 1862, *PCILQ*, 24.

28 Douglas to Israel Powell, October 14, 1874, BC Archives (BCA), Sir James Douglas Correspondence Outward 1874, F/52/D74, also cited as item 4 in appendices, Robert E. Cail, *Land, Man, and the Law: The Disposal of Crown Lands in British Columbia* (Vancouver: UBC Press, 1974), 302–3.

29 Douglas to Moody, October 7, 1859, quoted in Harris, *Making Native Space*, 34. The 1859 circular from Douglas to "Gold Commissioners and Magistrates" on the Mainland is quoted in Pike, "Colony of British Columbia's Unsurveyed Land System," 259. Colonel Moody led the Royal Engineers in conducting much of the early survey and engineering work. Tensions between Douglas and Moody are discussed ably in Jean Barman, *British Columbia in the Balance, 1846–1871* (Madeira Park, BC: Harbour, 2022), 83–137.

30 Young (on behalf of Douglas) to the Chief Commissioner of Lands and Works, R.C. Moody, March 5, 1861, *PCILQ*, 21.

31 Moody to R.M. Parsons, April 13, 1861, and Moody to Parsons and Turner, April 13, 1861, and April 15, 1861, are quoted in Dorothy I.D. Kennedy, *A Reference Guide to the Establishment of Indian Reserves in British Columbia, 1849–1911* (Ottawa: Indian and Northern Affairs Canada, Claims Research and Assessment Directorate, 1994), 33–34. Emphasis in original.

32 Douglas to Moody, April 27, 1863, *PCILQ*, 27.

33 William Cox to Moody, February 12, 1861, and Moody to Cox, March 6, 1861, *PCILQ*, 20, 21.

34 Moody to Douglas, April 28, 1863, *PCILQ*, 27. Emphasis in original.

35 Douglas to Moody, April 27, 1863, and Young to Moody, May 11, 1863, *PCILQ*, 26, 28.

36 Parsons to Sapper Turnbull, May 1, 1861, *PCILQ*, 22. One consequence of such qualification was, as historical geographer Cole Harris points out, "Turnbull's [Fraser] Canyon reserves were tiny, out of all proportion to Douglas's instructions": Harris, "Native Land Policies," 111.

37 Moody to Cox, March 6, 1861, *PCILQ*, 21, wherein Moody notes that under the Aliens Act, 1859, and the Pre-emption Act, 1860, "every alien shall have the same capacity to take, hold, enjoy, recover, convey and transmit title to lands and real estate of every description" as would a "natural born British subject," subject only to the swearing of an oath of allegiance.

38 Paul Tennant, *Aboriginal Peoples and Politics: The Indian Land Question in British Columbia, 1840–1989* (Vancouver: UBC Press, 1990), 29–30. The opportunity for pre-emption by Indigenous people was unique to British Columbia under Douglas. British Columbia's Legislative Council effectively eliminated these opportunities after Douglas retired.

39 Begbie was responding to a question from Louis-Joseph d'Herbomez, a priest who would become a senior Roman Catholic official. Quoted in Kennedy, *Reference Guide*, 23.

40 Moody to the Colonial Secretary, William Young, June 11, 1862, *PCILQ*, 25.

41 Moody to Douglas, April 28, 1863, *PCILQ*, 27. D'Herbomez was likely among the Roman Catholic priests dispensing advice to First Nations.

42 Quoted in Little, "Foundations," 78, quoting Margaret McDonald, "New Westminster, 1859–1871" (master's thesis, University of British Columbia, 1947).

43 Moody to Young, June 2, 1862, *PCILQ*, 24.
44 Young to Moody, June 18, 1862, *PCILQ*, 24. Emphasis in original.
45 Joseph Trutch to Young, January 17, 1866, *PCILQ*, 32, and A.R. Howse, Lands and Works Department, Report to Trutch, May 29, 1867, *PCILQ*, 40.
46 Colony of British Columbia, *Journals of the Legislative Council of British Columbia* (hereafter *JLCBC*), January 21, 1864, 2.
47 "Douglas to Dr. I.W. Powell, Indian Commissioner, re Colonial Indian Lands, October 14, 1874," item 4 in appendices, in Cail, *Land, Man, and the Law*, 302–3.
48 Douglas cited in *JLCBC*, January 21, 1864, 2.
49 *JLCBC*, May 3, 1864, 41.
50 Robin Fisher, "Joseph Trutch and Indian Land Policy," *BC Studies* 12 (Winter 1971–72): 17; and Harris, *Making Native Space*, 43.

Chapter 2: Joseph Trutch and the Road to Dispossession

1 John Helmcken, *The Reminiscences of Doctor John Sebastian Helmcken*, ed. Dorothy Blakey Smith (Vancouver: UBC Press, 1975), 259.
2 Joseph Trutch to Charlotte Trutch, June 23, 1850, UBC Library Special Collections, Joseph Trutch Papers, 5. This dehumanizing view of Indigenous people was hardly uncommon in Oregon. In the 1850s, settlers engaged in horrific violence toward Indigenous people, leading to their forcible displacement.
3 Hills is quoted in Jean Barman, *British Columbia in the Balance, 1846–1871* (Madeira Park, BC: Harbour, 2022), 175.
4 John Trutch was a surveyor sometimes employed in reserve creation. Dorothy Kennedy notes his employment on surveys on the Saanich Peninsula in 1858: see Dorothy I.D. Kennedy, *A Reference Guide to the Establishment of Indian Reserves in British Columbia, 1849–1911* (Ottawa: Indian and Northern Affairs Canada, Claims Research and Assessment Directorate), 16.
5 Joseph Trutch to the Colonial Secretary, September 20, 1865, in British Columbia, *Papers Connected with the Indian Land Question, 1850–1875* (Victoria: Richard Wolfenden, Government Printer, 1875), 30 (hereafter *PCILQ*).
6 Joseph Trutch to the Colonial Secretary, August 28, 1867, *PCILQ*, 42.
7 Joseph Trutch to Walter Moberly, October 10, 1865, *PCILQ*, 31.
8 Lieutenant-Governor Joseph Trutch to Sir John A. Macdonald, October 14, 1872, Library and Archives Canada, Sir John A. Macdonald Papers, vol. 278. The letter is presented in full as item 2 of the appendices to Robert E. Cail, *Land, Man, and the Law: The Disposal of Crown Lands in British Columbia* (Vancouver: UBC Press, 1974), 297–99.
9 Lieutenant-Governor Joseph Trutch to the Secretary of State for the Provinces, September 26, 1871, *PCILQ*, 101.
10 *PCILQ*, 99.
11 Laura Ishiguro, *Nothing to Write Home About: British Family Correspondence and the Settler Colonial Everyday in British Columbia* (Vancouver: UBC Press, 2019), 178–79.
12 See, for example, Tina Loo, "The Road from Bute Inlet: Crime and Colonial Identity in British Columbia," in *Essays in the History of Canadian Law*, vol. 5, *Crime and Criminal Justice*, ed. Jim Phillips, Tina Loo, and Susan Lewthwaite (Toronto: Osgoode Society for Canadian Legal History, 1994), 112–42; and Edward S. Hewlett, "The Chilcotin Uprising of 1864," *BC Studies* 19 (Autumn 1973): 50–73.

13 Governor Seymour's Speech to the Legislative Council, December 13, 1864, in Colony of British Columbia, *Journals of the Legislative Council of British Columbia,* December 13, 1864, 249–50 (hereafter *JLCBC*).
14 William Young, on behalf of Governor Seymour, to Joseph Trutch, November 6, 1867, *PCILQ*, 45.
15 Philip Nind to Young, July 17, 1865, *PCILQ*, 29–30.
16 Joseph Trutch to Young, September 20, 1865, *PCILQ*, 30.
17 Young, on behalf of Governor Seymour, to Joseph Trutch, September 25, 1865, *PCILQ*, 30–31.
18 Joseph Trutch to Walter Moberly, October 10, 1865, *PCILQ*, 31.
19 Moberly to Joseph Trutch, December 22, 1865, *PCILQ*, 33–34.
20 Joseph Trutch to Young, January 17, 1866, *PCILQ*, 32.
21 J.I. Little, "The Foundations of Government," in *The Pacific Province: A History of British Columbia,* ed. Hugh J.M. Johnston (Vancouver: Douglas and McIntyre, 1996), 80.
22 Joseph Trutch to the Colonial Secretary, January 17, 1866, *PCILQ*, 32–33.
23 Barman, *British Columbia in the Balance,* 229.
24 Report from J. Turnbull to Joseph Trutch, January 17, 1866, 35–36, enclosure in Trutch to Young, January 17, 1866, *PCILQ*, 32–33.
25 Joseph Trutch to Young, February 5, 1866, *PCILQ*, 34.
26 Joseph Trutch to Young, September 20, 1865, *PCILQ*, 30.
27 Colony of British Columbia, *Minutes of the Legislative Council,* February 8, 1867, 24.
28 Colony of British Columbia, *Minutes of the Legislative Council,* February 11, 1867, 25.
29 Joseph Trutch, "Lower Fraser Indian Reserves," report enclosed in Trutch to the Acting Colonial Secretary, August 28, 1867, *PCILQ*, 41.
30 "Mr. William McColl's Report," May 16, 1864, included as an enclosure in Joseph Trutch to the Acting Colonial Secretary, August 28, 1867, *PCILQ*, 43.
31 Joseph Trutch, "Lower Fraser River Indian Reserves," included in letter to the Acting Colonial Secretary, August 28, 1867, *PCILQ*, 41–43. Emphasis in original.
32 Estimates are from Little, "Foundations," 78.
33 The Colonial Secretary, on behalf of Governor Seymour, to Joseph Trutch, November 6, 1867, *PCILQ*, 45. Emphasis added.
34 The petition and Seymour's response are quoted in Kennedy, *Reference Guide to the Establishment of Indian Reserves*, 47.
35 Joseph Trutch to Young, November 19, 1867, *PCILQ*, 46.
36 Paul Tennant, *Aboriginal Peoples and Politics: The Indian Land Question in British Columbia, 1840–1989* (Vancouver: UBC Press, 1990), 42.
37 Bruce Granville Miller, "A Short Commentary on Land Claims in BC," 11th Annual National Land Claims Workshop, October 2003, 5, Union of British Columbia Indian Chiefs website, https://www.ubcic.bc.ca/a_short_commentary_on_land_claims_in_bc.
38 H.M. Ball to Governor Seymour, October 17, 1868, *PCILQ*, 52.
39 Quoted in Nancy J. Turner and Pamela Spalding, "Learning from the Earth, Learning from Each Other: Ethnoecology, Responsibility, and Reciprocity," in *Resurgence and Reconciliation: Indigenous-Settler Relations and Earth Teachings,* ed. Michael Asch, John Borrows, and James Tully (Toronto: University of Toronto Press, 2018), 270.
40 Governor Seymour's Speech to the Legislative Council, in Colony of British Columbia, *Minutes of the Legislative Council,* May 1, 1868, 164.

41 Joseph Trutch to Peter O'Reilly, August 5, 1868, *PCILQ*, 50. O'Reilly was Trutch's colleague on the Legislative Council and a county court judge. O'Reilly also played a prominent role in post-Confederation Indigenous relations as Indian reserve commissioner from 1880 to 1898.
42 B.W. Pearse to Joseph Trutch, October 21, 1868, *PCILQ*, 53.
43 Peter O'Reilly, diary, September 27 and 28 and October 1 and 4, 1870, BC Archives, O'Reilly Family Fonds, MS-2894, box 1, file 14.
44 Teit is quoted in Wendy Wickwire, *At the Bridge: James Teit and an Anthropology of Belonging* (Vancouver: UBC Press, 2019), 176. Teit can also be described as an amateur anthropologist. He did extensive fieldwork for anthropologist Franz Boas but lacked his professional credentials. Teit was also a tenacious supporter of Indigenous rights. Wickwire offers a fascinating account of his life and times.
45 Cole Harris, *Making Native Space: Colonialism, Resistance, and Reserves in British Columbia* (Vancouver: UBC Press, 2002), 64.
46 Notably, the deputy superintendent-general of Indian affairs, Duncan Campbell Scott, would cite Joseph Trutch's words in his 1927 presentation to the Special Joint Committee of Parliament on Claims of Allied Tribes of BC, 16th Parl., 1st Sess., vol. 1, March 20, 1927, 39.
47 Quoted in Dennis F.K. Madill, *British Columbia Indian Treaties in Historical Perspective,* prepared for the Research Branch, Corporate Policy, Department of Indian and Northern Affairs, 1981, 31; and a memorandum from Joseph Trutch titled "Memorandum on a Letter Treating of Conditions in Vancouver Island, Addressed to the Secretary of the Aborigines' Protection Society, by Mr. William Sebright Green," enclosed in Anthony Musgrave to Lord Granville, January 29, 1870, *PCILQ*, App. B, 11.
48 "An Ordinance Further to Define the Law Regulating Acquisition of Land in British Columbia" is quoted in Tennant, *Aboriginal Peoples,* 41. Section 3 of the Land Ordinance Act of 1870 specified that the "right of pre-emption shall not be held to extend to any of the Aborigines of this Continent, except to such as shall have obtained the Governor's special permission in writing to that effect." See "Report of the Government of British Columbia on the Subject of Indian Reserves," approved by the lieutenant-governor, August 18, 1875, *PCILQ*, 3–4.
49 Helmcken, *Reminiscences,* 252. For a broader account of events leading to British Columbia's union with Canada, see Barman, *British Columbia in the Balance,* 253–92. On his marriage to Cecelia Douglas in December 1852, Helmcken became James Douglas's son-in-law. See Dorothy Blakey Smith's introduction to *Reminiscences,* xvi–xvii.
50 Helmcken, *Reminiscences,* App. 3, 341–42. Helmcken cites the *Victoria Daily British Colonist,* February 16, 1870, as his source for the Musgrave quote.
51 See, for example, Patricia E. Roy, "'The Interests of Confederation Demanded It': British Columbia and Confederation," in *Reconsidering Confederation: Canada's Founding Debates, 1864–1999,* ed. Daniel Heidt (Calgary: University of Calgary Press, 2017), 179. Given the importance of union with British Columbia, Musgrave undoubtedly received generous amounts of advice from both Ottawa and the Colonial Office in London.
52 Musgrave to Lord Lisgar, February 20, 1870, as quoted by Scott in his report to the Special Joint Committee, 38–39.
53 Helmcken, *Reminiscences,* 256.
54 Jean Barman, *The West beyond the West: A History of British Columbia,* rev. ed. (Toronto: University of Toronto Press, 2004), 379.

55 Colony of British Columbia, Legislative Council, *Debate on the Subject of Confederation with Canada,* March 25, 1870, https://primarydocuments.ca/british-columbia-legislative-council-debate-on-the-subject-of-confederation-with-canada-whole-collection-1870/ (hereafter *Debate on the Subject of Confederation*).

56 Nicolas Claxton and John Price, "Nothing 'Liberal' about Colonial Policy Prior to Confederation," *Victoria Times-Colonist,* April 2, 2021. Keith Thor Carlson quotes John Robson from his newspaper, *The British Columbian,* criticizing Douglas's purported gift of "seven or eight miles square, including their ranches" to First Nations. Carlson, "'The Last Potlatch' and James Douglas's Vision of an Alternative Settler Colonialism," in *To Share, Not Surrender: Indigenous and Settler Visions of Treaty Making in the Colonies of Vancouver Island and British Columbia,* ed. Peter Cook, Neil Vallance, John Lutz, Graham Brazier, and Hamar Foster (Vancouver: UBC Press, 2021), 288.

57 *Debate on the Subject of Confederation,* March 25, 1870.

58 All quotes from *Debate on the Subject of Confederation,* March 25, 1870.

59 Colony of British Columbia, *Minutes of the Legislative Council,* April 23, 1870, 353. On that date, Governor Musgrave announced his intent to dispatch a delegation to Ottawa "to explain our views and wants" and to "learn how far the expectations of the people of this Colony can be fulfilled in any arrangement for Union."

60 Helmcken, *Reminiscences,* 258.

61 Joseph Trutch to George-Étienne Cartier, February 20, 1872, BCA, Trutch Fonds, Correspondence Outward, MS-2897, box 4, file 2.

62 Helmcken, *Reminiscences,* 259.

63 Helmcken, *Reminiscences,* App. 3, "Helmcken's Diary of the Confederation Negotiations, 1870," 357. Some scholars suggest that Joseph Trutch was the author of Article 13. He was certainly a leading participant in the Dominion-provincial negotiations that produced it. See, for example, Robin Fisher, *Contact and Conflict: Indian-European Relations in British Columbia, 1774–1890* (Vancouver: UBC Press, 1992), 176. Cole Harris suggests that Trutch was "almost certainly the principal author of article 13": *Making Native Space,* 73. Musgrave's letter to Lord Lisgar of February 20, 1870, discussed earlier in this chapter, strongly suggests that the governor might have had a hand in constructing a draft term for Indigenous relations. Trutch's role, if any, in finalizing the content of Article 13 is unclear. Nevertheless, we can be certain that Article 13 would not have proceeded without Trutch's approval, given his leadership of the BC delegation.

64 Harris, *Making Native Space,* 91.

65 Early treaties in Upper Canada, which became Ontario, were generally based on 160 acres per family. The quantum expanded to 640 acres in the Numbered Treaties in the Prairie provinces and the northeast corner of British Columbia, as I discuss in Chapter 5.

66 See Crown-Indigenous Relations and Northern Affairs Canada, "The Numbered Treaties (1871–1921)," https://www.rcaanc-cirnac.gc.ca/eng/1360948213124/1544620003549.

67 J.R. Miller, *Compact, Contract, Covenant: Aboriginal Treaty-Making in Canada* (Toronto: University of Toronto Press, 2009), 146.

68 Article 13's provision for reference of disputes to the secretary of state for the colonies was never used by the provincial or federal government, despite the federal government's deep dissatisfaction with British Columbia's resistance to reserve expansion in the early years after union. I discuss one opportunity for reference in Chapter 4. For the full terms of union, see Canada, "The Province of British Columbia: Enactment No. 4," https://www.justice.gc.ca/eng/rp-pr/csj-sjc/constitution/lawreg-loireg/p1t41.html.

69 Helmcken laid out his concerns about union with Canada early in the Confederation debates. See *Debate on the Subject of Confederation with Canada,* March 9, 1870, 8–13. However, a transcontinental railway was of huge appeal, as he notes in Helmcken, *Reminiscences,* 255. Joseph Trutch's note on Helmcken's shifting views is recorded in his letter to H.P.P. Crease, August 1, 1870, BCA, Crease Correspondence Inward, GR-1372, quoted in H. Keith Ralston, "British Columbia's Entry into Confederation: Documents," author's private collection.

70 J.D. Helmcken, "Woodstock Speech," *The Globe,* June 10, 1870.

71 Helmcken, *Reminiscences,* 264.

72 Joseph Trutch to Cartier, October 27, 1870, BCA, Trutch Fonds, MS 2897, box 4, file 2.

73 Joseph Trutch to Helmcken, April 17, 1871, BCA, Helmcken Papers, quoted in Margaret A. Ormsby, *British Columbia: A History,* student ed. (Vancouver: Macmillan, 1971), 249–50.

74 W.J. Macdonald to H.P.P. Crease, June 5, 1870, BCA, Crease Papers Inward, quoted in Ralston, "British Columbia's Entry."

Chapter 3: Confederation Brings Conflict

1 My thanks to an anonymous reviewer for pointing out that Canada was technically a colony until the Statute of Westminster in 1931.

2 E.G. Alston to H.P.P. Crease, July 19, 1871, BC Archives (BCA), Crease Papers Inward, quoted in Margaret A. Ormsby, *British Columbia: A History,* student ed. (Vancouver: Macmillan, 1971), 250. Crease was a Confederation skeptic who remained in British Columbia as a prominent jurist.

3 Robert A.J. McDonald, *A Long Way to Paradise: A New History of British Columbia Politics* (Vancouver: UBC Press, 2021), 17. British Columbia's second premier, Amor De Cosmos, was an advocate for responsible government and brought a quick end to Joseph Trutch's participation in cabinet.

4 Joseph Trutch to the Secretary of State for the Provinces, September 26, 1871, in British Columbia, *Papers Connected with the Indian Land Question, 1850–1875* (Victoria: Richard Wolfenden, Government Printer, 1875), 30 (hereafter *PCILQ*), 99–101.

5 Nicholas Xemtoltw Claxton and John Price, "Whose Land Is It? Rethinking Sovereignty in British Columbia," *BC Studies* 204 (Winter 2019–20): 135–36. See also John Lutz, *Makúk: A New History of Aboriginal-White Relations* (Vancouver: UBC Press, 2009), 236.

6 Robson represented Nanaimo in the legislature after union with Canada. British Columbia, *Debates of the Legislative Assembly,* March 11, 1872, 34, and April 5, 1872, 65. The amendment to the Qualification and Registration of Voters Act was passed on April 5, 1872.

7 Joseph Trutch to Sir John A. Macdonald, July 16, 1872, BCA, Trutch Correspondence Outward, MS-2897, box 4, file 6.

8 Macdonald to Joseph Trutch, September 25, 1872, BCA, Trutch Correspondence Inward, MS-2897, Roll 02, AO 1948.

9 Joseph Trutch to Macdonald, October 14, 1872, quoted in its entirety as Appendix, item 2, by Robert E. Cail, *Land, Man, and the Law: The Disposal of Crown Lands in British Columbia* (Vancouver: UBC Press, 1974), 297–99; the full letter is included on 397–99.

10 Joseph Trutch to Macdonald, October 14, 1872, quoted by Duncan Campbell Scott in his report to the Special Joint Committee of Parliament on Claims of Allied Indian Tribes of BC, 16th Parl., 1st Sess., vol. 1, March 20, 1927, 40.

11 Macdonald to Joseph Trutch, October 30, 1872, BCA, Trutch Correspondence Inward, MS-2897, Roll 02, AO 1948.

12 Macdonald to Joseph Trutch, December 27, 1872, Trutch Correspondence Inward, MS-2897, Roll 02, AO 1948.

13 Dorothy I.D. Kennedy, *A Reference Guide to the Establishment of Indian Reserves in British Columbia, 1849–1911* (Ottawa: Indian and Northern Affairs Canada, Claims Research and Assessment Directorate), 69, identifies the date of the board's establishment as February 9, 1874, approximately three months after Macdonald's defeat. Joseph Trutch's note to Laird of May 11 most likely reflected his dissatisfaction with the absence of a detailed (and amenable) description of the commission's roles and responsibilities.

14 Joseph Trutch to David Laird, June 18, 1874, BCA, MS-2897, box 4, file 15.

15 Joseph Trutch to Laird, June 30, 1874, quoted in Kennedy, *Reference Guide,* 70.

16 Laird to Joseph Trutch, July 8, 1874, BCA, MS-2897, box 4, file 15.

17 The request is noted in Joseph Trutch to the Secretary of State for the Provinces, October 5, 1871, *PCILQ,* 101.

18 Enclosure from Pearse to the Colonial Secretary, October 16, 1871, 102, in correspondence from Joseph Trutch (as lieutenant-governor) to the Secretary of State for the Provinces, November 3, 1871, *PCILQ,* 101–3.

19 Pearse to the Colonial Secretary, October 16, 1871, 102.

20 Pearse to the Colonial Secretary, October 16, 1871, 103.

21 George Walkem to Israel Powell, December 5, 1872, *PCILQ,* 110–11.

22 Robert Beaven to Powell, January 15, 1873, *PCILQ,* 111.

23 Powell to Beaven, January 15, 1873, *PCILQ,* 112. Emphasis in original.

24 Beaven to Powell, April 16, 1873, *PCILQ,* 113. Emphasis added.

25 Walkem to Powell, December 26, 1873, and Powell to Walkem, December 29, 1873, *PCILQ,* 123.

26 J.R. Miller discusses the long presence of assimilationism within the Department of Indian Affairs in *Compact, Contract, Covenant: Aboriginal Treaty-Making in Canada* (Toronto: University of Toronto Press, 2009), 231–36. Powell's role in advocating for residential schools and other assimilationist policies (such as banning the Potlatch, a ceremonial feast featuring gift giving) is discussed in Know History Historical Services, "Israel Wood Powell's Legacy," a report submitted to the Tla'amin Nation, 2021, https://www.tlaaminnation.com/wp-content/uploads/2022/05/Israel-Wood-Powell-Legacy.pdf.

27 John Sutton Lutz, "Powell, Israel Wood," in *Dictionary of Canadian Biography,* vol. 14, University of Toronto/Université Laval, 2003–, http://www.biographi.ca/en/bio/powell_israel_wood_14E.html.

28 See, for example, the *Victoria Daily Standard,* November 29, 1873, 6. McCreight was defeated in a nonconfidence motion following the 1872 Speech from the Throne.

29 *British Daily Colonist,* "Indian War Threatened!!," January 11, 1874, 3, and "Indian Affairs," January 19, 1874, 3.

30 *Victoria Daily Standard,* December 29, 1873; January 1, 1874; and January 28, 1874.

31 Powell noted on February 4, 1875, that "no general census has yet been taken of the Indians of British Columbia." His 1872 initial estimate of 28,500 was based on "the average given by various gentlemen acquainted with the Tribes." Based on his experience, Powell believed the population was "five or six thousand in excess of the first estimate": Canada, *Annual Report of the Department of the Interior for the Year Ended 30th June, 1874* (Ottawa: Maclean, Roger, 1875), 125. A deadly and devastating smallpox epidemic had hit Indigenous communities hard in the previous decade.

32 Powell to Walkem, January 9, 1874, telegram dispatched from Clinton during Powell's visit, citing Grandidier's concerns, *PCILQ,* 126.

33 Walkem to Powell, December 26, 1873, *PCILQ*, 123.
34 Powell to Walkem, December 29, 1873, *PCILQ*, 123.
35 Walkem to Powell, February 26, 1874, *PCILQ*, 128.
36 Powell to Beaven, April 17, 1873, *PCILQ*, 114, with an enclosure titled "Excerpts from Copy of a Report of the Honorable the Privy Council Approved by His Excellency the Governor-General in Council, on the 21st of March 1873."
37 Beaven to Powell, April 18, 1873, *PCILQ*, 114.
38 Powell to Beaven, April 19, 1873, *PCILQ*, 115.
39 Beaven to Powell, April 30, 1873, *PCILQ*, 115. In the absence of a full and credible census, officials used estimates of British Columbia's Indigenous population to buttress their arguments. As noted above, the lieutenant-governor, Joseph Trutch, quoted "30 to 40,000 Indians along our Coast" as a rationale for granting extraordinary powers. Similarly, Beaven was happy to use a different population estimate to support his estimate of the average reserve size in British Columbia before Confederation.
40 Powell to Joseph Trutch, June 21, 1873, *PCILQ*, 116.
41 Copy of "A Report of a Committee of the Honourable the Executive Council, Approved by His Excellency the Lieutenant-Governor, on the 25th day of July 1873," sent by W.J. Armstrong, Clerk of Executive Council, to Powell, July 25, 1873, *PCILQ*, 118–19.
42 John Ash to Powell, July 28, 1873, *PCILQ*, 119.
43 Powell to Ash, December 27, 1873, *PCILQ*, 124, and Ash to Powell, December 29, 1873, *PCILQ*, 124.
44 Walkem to Powell, December 29, 1873, *PCILQ*, 124.
45 Peter Ayessik to Powell, July 14, 1874, *PCILQ*, 137–38.
46 Powell to Beaven, July 31, 1874, *PCILQ*, 134.
47 Beaven to Powell, August 6, 1874; and Powell to Beaven, August 7, 1874, *PCILQ*, 134–35.
48 Beaven to Powell, August 10, 1874, *PCILQ*, 135.
49 Powell to Beaven, July 31, 1874, *PCILQ*, 135; Beaven to Powell, August 6, 1874, *PCILQ*, 136; and Powell to Beaven, August 7, 1874, *PCILQ*, 136.
50 Beaven to Powell, August 10, 1874, *PCILQ*, 135.
51 Powell to Ash, August 15, 1874, *PCILQ*, 139–40. Emphasis in original. A telegram was attached to the letter of August 15, 1874, from Walkem to Powell, dated June 12, 1874. The province was always reluctant to state a clear position on existing pre-Confederation reserves. In his telegram to Powell, Walkem proposed adjusting pre-Confederation reserves based on an allocation of twenty acres per family but with the condition that existing reserves exceeding twenty acres per family would be reduced. To test Walkem's commitment, Powell sent survey teams to begin the work.
52 Ash to Powell, September 2, 1874, *PCILQ*, 140. The reference to the lieutenant-governor likely reflects Joseph Trutch's continuing role as chief commissioner of the Indian Board. De Cosmos excluded Trutch from cabinet deliberations.
53 Powell to Ash, September 2, 1874, *PCILQ*, 141.
54 Joseph Trutch is quoted in Kennedy, *Reference Guide*, 68.
55 Ash to Powell, September 28, 1874, *PCILQ*, 143.
56 Powell to Ash, September 28, 1874, *PCILQ*, 140, 142–43.
57 Ash to Powell, September 28, 1874, *PCILQ*, 143.

Chapter 4: Intransigence Breeds Discord

1 Professor James Tully describes the Indian Act as "a vast administrative dictatorship that governs every detail of Indigenous life ... imposed over Indigenous people and their lands

without their consent": James Tully, "Reconciliation Here on Earth," in *Resurgence and Reconciliation: Indigenous-Settler Relations and Earth Teachings,* ed. Michael Asch, John Borrows, and James Tully (Toronto: University of Toronto Press, 2018), 105.

2 Canada, *Annual Report of the Department of the Interior for the Year Ended 30th June, 1874* (Ottawa: Maclean, Roger, 1874), 15.

3 Laird knew of Douglas's more generous approach to reserve creation via Powell's 1874 correspondence with Douglas, if not from elsewhere. Laird set out his case in detail in Enclosure no. 2, Memo from the Minister of the Interior, in E.J. Langevin (Undersecretary of State) to the Lieutenant-Governor, October 14, 1874, in British Columbia, *Papers Connected with the Indian Land Question, 1850–1875* (Victoria: Richard Wolfenden, Government Printer, 1875), 151–55 (hereafter *PCILQ*).

4 Laird, Memorandum to the Honorable Privy Council, November 2, 1874, in Canada, *Annual Report of the Department of the Interior for the Year Ended 30th June, 1875* (Ottawa: Maclean, Roger, 1876), 57.

5 Canada, *Annual Report,* 1875, 125–26.

6 Superintendent Powell's report, Canada, *Annual Report,* 1875, 126.

7 Quoted in Dorothy I.D. Kennedy, *A Reference Guide to the Establishment of Indian Reserves in British Columbia, 1849–1911* (Ottawa: Indian and Northern Affairs Canada, Claims Research and Assessment Directorate), 72.

8 Father Grandidier, letter to the editor, *Victoria Standard,* August 28, 1874, in *PCILQ*, 145–48.

9 Bishop Louis-Joseph d'Herbomez to James Lenihan (Powell's deputy), September 24, 1874, *PCILQ*, 145.

10 Lenihan to John Ash, October 8, 1874, *PCILQ*, 144.

11 Ash to Lenihan, October 12, 1874, *PCILQ*, 148.

12 Israel Powell to Laird, October 1, 1875, Canada, *Annual Report,* 1875, 168.

13 British Columbia, "Report of the Government of British Columbia on the Subject of Indian Reserves," Order in Council, August 18, 1875, *PCILQ*, 2. Walkem framed Laird's "little short of a mockery" comment as a criticism of British Columbia's colonial government when it was clearly directed at the provincial cabinet.

14 British Columbia, "Report of the Government," 2–8.

15 British Columbia, "Report of the Government," 7–8.

16 British Columbia, "Report of the Government," 3.

17 John Lutz, *Makúk: A New History of Aboriginal-White Relations* (Vancouver: UBC Press, 2009), 176–78, 235. With the rise of race-based employment, small reserves moved from boon for Indigenous people's progress to a recipe for Indigenous people's poverty. Economic despair was further exacerbated by restrictions on hunting, trapping, and hand logging, as well as Canada's imposition of "white preference" regulations in coastal fisheries.

18 British Columbia, "Report of the Government," 9.

19 Canada, *Annual Report,* 1875, 20.

20 Hamar Foster, "'We Want a Strong Promise': The Opposition to Indian Treaties in British Columbia, 1850–1990," *Native Studies Review* 18, 1 (2009): 122.

21 Edward Blake, Report to Cabinet, April 28, 1876, quoted by Duncan Campbell Scott in his report to the Special Joint Committee of Parliament on Claims of Allied Indian Tribes of BC, 16th Parl., 1st Sess., vol. 1, March 20, 1927, 41.

22 Memorandum of Instructions to Archibald McKinlay, October 23, 1876, BC Archives (BCA), RG 494/1/2, quoted in Dennis F.K. Madill, *British Columbia Indian Treaties in*

Historical Perspective, prepared for the Research Branch, Corporate Policy, Department of Indian and Northern Affairs, 1981, 26.

23 Robert E. Cail, *Land, Man, and the Law: The Disposal of Crown Lands in British Columbia* (Vancouver: UBC Press, 1974), 215.

24 Robin Fisher, "An Exercise in Futility: The Joint Commission on Indian Land in British Columbia, 1875–1880," *Historical Papers/Communications historiques* 10, 1 (1975): 81.

25 Joseph Trutch to the Secretary of State for the Colonies, January 8, 1876, *PCILQ,* 170.

26 Gilbert Sproat to the Superintendent-General, June 30, 1877, Library and Archives Canada, RG 10 (Department of Indian Affairs), vol. 3650, file 8497, quoted in Sarah P. Pike, "Gilbert Malcolm Sproat, British Columbia Indian Reserve Commissioner (1876–1880), and the "'Humanitarian Civilizing' of Indigenous Peoples" (master's thesis, University of British Columbia, 2018), 100.

27 Quoted in D. Duane Thomson, "A History of the Okanagan: Indians and Whites in the Settlement Era, 1860–1920" (PhD diss., University of British Columbia, 1985), 131.

28 R.W. Scott (Secretary of State for Canada) to Sproat and Alexander Anderson, July 19, 1877, quoted in Pike, "Gilbert Malcolm Sproat," 108.

29 David Mills to Sproat, August 3, 1877, quoted in Pike, "Gilbert Malcolm Sproat," 140. Mills's claim of even-handed consistency in Canada's pursuit of treaties east of the Rockies was overstated but nevertheless deliberate. He wanted to underline British Columbia's resistance to treaties and the results in terms of reserve creation.

30 Quoted in Wilson Duff, *The Indian History of British Columbia,* vol. 1 (Victoria: Queen's Printer, 1992), 67.

31 Mills to Sproat, August 3, 1877, quoted in Pike, "Gilbert Malcolm Sproat," 139–40.

32 A.C. Elliott to Sproat, September 27, 1877, quoted in Pike, "Gilbert Malcolm Sproat," 142. Elliott likely heard of Mills's opinion via Sproat.

33 Quoted in Michael Asch, *On Being Here to Stay: Treaties and Aboriginal Rights in Canada* (Toronto: University of Toronto Press, 2014), 158–59.

34 Elliott to Sproat, September 27, 1877, quoted in Pike, "Gilbert Malcolm Sproat," 143.

35 Pike, "Gilbert Malcolm Sproat," 99.

36 Sproat to Mills, July 16, 1877, quoted in Pike, "Gilbert Malcolm Sproat," 105. David Mills offered his retrospective assessment to the House of Commons in 1880: "Before this Commission got to work, the country was on the brink of an Indian war ... a Confederation was organized between the Indians of Washington Territory and British Columbia, and it was only the failure of Chief Joseph in his contest [the Nez Perce War] with the United States troops that saved us from that calamity": Canada, *Debates of the House of Commons,* April 21, 1880, 1633.

37 Elliott to Mills, January 27, 1877, *PCILQ,* 433–44.

Chapter 5: Colonial Prejudice Meets Purposeful Ignorance

1 Clement Cornwall to Joseph Trutch, June 22, 1880, Library and Archives Canada (LAC), RG 10 (Department of Indian Affairs), Williams Lake Agency, vol. 3716, file 22, 209.

2 Joseph Trutch to Sir John A. Macdonald, July 4, 1880, LAC, RG 10, Williams Lake Agency, vol. 3716, file 22, 209.

3 Joseph Trutch to Sir John A. Macdonald, May 19, 1880, quoted in D. Duane Thomson, "A History of the Okanagan: Indians and Whites in the Settlement Era, 1860–1920" (PhD diss., University of British Columbia, 1985), 139.

4 Cole Harris, "The Native Land Policies of Governor James Douglas," *BC Studies* 174 (Summer 2012): 101.

5 Sproat's concerns are thoroughly documented in Cole Harris, *Making Native Space: Colonialism, Resistance, and Reserves in British Columbia* (Vancouver: UBC Press, 2002), 141.

6 Dorothy I.D. Kennedy, *A Reference Guide to the Establishment of Indian Reserves in British Columbia, 1849–1911* (Ottawa: Indian and Northern Affairs Canada, Claims Research and Assessment Directorate), 105–6.

7 All quotes in this section are drawn from Canada, *Debates of the House of Commons,* April 21, 1880, 1633–36. The Legislative Council resolution is discussed in Chapter 1.

8 De Cosmos provided no description of Alexander Munro beyond "settler." One Victoria resident of the period was Alexander Munro, chief factor of the Hudson's Bay Company, but no confirmation can be drawn from De Cosmos's comments in the House of Commons. See St. Andrew's Church, "Alexander Munro, 1824–1911," https://web.uvic.ca/vv/student/st_andrews/munro.php.

9 All quotes in this section are drawn from Canada, *Debates of the House of Commons,* February 28, 1881, 1158–60.

10 Recall Joseph Trutch's reaction to the suggestion that De Cosmos be asked to join him in the Confederation negotiations with Ottawa, noted in Chapter 2. De Cosmos, Trutch suggested, was burdened by a vanity so ludicrous and a disposition so cantankerous he was ill-suited for the task.

11 In the federal election of 1878, the Liberal government of Alexander Mackenzie was defeated, and the Conservative government of Macdonald returned to power. Macdonald's government was less inclined to challenge provincial policy. Historical geographer Cole Harris notes that even Israel Powell, Indian superintendent and a determined advocate for larger reserves in the early post-Confederation years, turned against Sproat: Harris, *Making Native Space,* 163–64. George Walkem returned to the premiership from 1878 to 1882.

12 For example, his diary for August 1881 notes several reserves created around Lillooet, four in the Fountain Valley alone: BC Archives (BCA), O'Reilly Family Fonds, diary, August 25, 1881. See also Harris, *Making Native Space,* 171–80, for details on O'Reilly's travels and approach to reserve creation and adjustment. According to Harris, O'Reilly was responsible for creating more than half (654) of the approximately 1,000 reserves created by the JIRC/IRC processes. See Harris, *Making Native Space,* 207.

13 Chief Commosaltz and O'Reilly are quoted in Union of British Columbia Indian Chiefs, *The Lands We Lost: A History of Cut-Off Lands and Land Losses from Indian Reserves in British Columbia* (UBCIC, 1974), 10.

14 Robert E. Cail, *Land, Man, and the Law: The Disposal of Crown Lands in British Columbia* (Vancouver: UBC Press, 1974), 218.

15 Quoted in Cail, *Land, Man, and the Law,* 218–19.

16 Dorothy Kennedy, *A Reference Guide to the Establishment of Indian Reserves in British Columbia, 1849–1911* (Ottawa: Indian and Northern Affairs Canada, Claims Research and Assessment Directorate), 118. The "one instance" noted by Kennedy does not specify the location, but the shortage of lands for reserve creation was an issue in at least a few corners of the Cariboo. Cail notes in *Land, Man, and the Law,* 219, that in the Cariboo case, "Rather than attempt to force the issue, Powell purchased for the Indians a tract of 1,464 acres from the estate of A.S. Bates."

17 O'Reilly to Chief Commissioner of Lands and Works, April 26, 1890, BCA, GR-2982, box 4, file 41.1, quoted in Nicholas Xemtoltw Claxton and John Price, "Whose Land Is It? Rethinking Sovereignty in British Columbia," *BC Studies* 204 (Winter 2019–20): 125.

18 The annual report references "Provincial Governments," but the claim of "no outstanding questions" is found at the start of the British Columbia section of the report: Canada,

Annual Report of the Department of Indian Affairs for the Year Ended 31st December, 1887 (Ottawa: Maclean, 1888), 68.

19 The government was perhaps mindful of the North-West Rebellion, of only two years before. For an excellent brief summary of events in the Saskatchewan District, see Stewart Mein, "North-West Resistance," *Indigenous Saskatchewan Encyclopedia*, https://teaching.usask.ca/indigenoussk/import/north-west_resistance.php.

20 Canada, *Annual Report*, 1887, 11–12.

21 O'Reilly to White, October 15, 1887, "Special Appendix No. 1," *Annual Report*, 1887, 91.

22 O'Reilly to White, October 15, 1887, "Special Appendix No. 1," *Annual Report*, 1887, 97.

23 Canada, *Annual Report*, 1887, 286.

24 The tax might have been of local or regional origin. Legislative records show no statutory link to such a tax, but the confusion was understandable. The 1885 and 1886 sessions of the BC legislature featured over a dozen statutes prohibiting use of Chinese labour in various settings. Those sessions also led to prohibitions on Indigenous and Chinese participation in municipal and school district elections. See British Columbia, "Discriminatory Legislation in British Columbia 1872–1948," https://www2.gov.bc.ca/assets/gov/british-columbians-our-governments/our-history/historic-places/documents/heritage/chinese-legacy/discriminatory_legislation_in_bc_1872_1948.pdf.

25 Canada, *Annual Report of the Department of Indian Affairs for the Year Ended 31st December, 1886* (Ottawa: Maclean, Roger, 1887), 195; and *Annual Report*, 1887, 283.

26 See, for example, *Annual Report*, 1887, 12, 13, 74, 112, 281, 283, 286, 288–89, and 296.

27 Canada, *Annual Report*, 1887, 296.

28 Dennis F.K. Madill, *British Columbia Indian Treaties in Historical Perspective*, prepared for the Research Branch, Corporate Policy, Department of Indian and Northern Affairs, 1981, Preface.

29 Madill, *British Columbia Indian Treaties*, 42–45.

30 Paraphrased in Privy Council Order in Council no. 2749 and quoted in Arthur J. Ray, "Treaty 8: A British Columbian Anomaly," *BC Studies* 123 (Autumn 1999): 31.

31 Privy Council, Memorandum, December 6, 1898, quoted in Ray, "Treaty 8," 43.

32 Madill, *British Columbia Indian Treaties*, 43, 63.

33 "Treaty Eight and Expert Witnesses: A Reply to Dr. Robert Irwin," *BC Studies* 127 (Autumn 2000): 103.

34 Ray, "Treaty 8," 37–38.

35 The Dominion government became aware of potential petroleum resources in the North-West Territories as early as 1891; Ray, "Treaty 8," 12. British Columbia looked at the potential for oil and gas in several corners of the province early in the twentieth century, but test drilling in the Peace River region did not begin until the 1920s. See British Columbia, "A Brief History of Oil and Gas Exploration in British Columbia," https://www2.gov.bc.ca/assets/gov/farming-natural-resources-and-industry/natural-gas-oil/petroleum-geoscience/brief_hi.

36 Quoted in Ray, "Treaty 8," 57. The provincial legal argument was advanced in 1996.

37 The Band, mindful of the stark discrepancy, engaged in a long political and legal battle, securing the McLeod Lake Indian Band Treaty no. 8 Adhesion and Settlement Agreement Act in 2000. Today, the band holds thirty-nine reserves that cover 49,420 acres of land. They enjoy an economic base that, more than 150 years after Confederation, stands in stark contrast to the small and scattered reserves of many BC First Nations.

38 Chris Kelly, *The Creation of Indian Reserves in British Columbia (A Research Guide)*, prepared for the Litigation Support Directorate, Department of Indian Affairs and Northern Development, June 15, 1995, 10.

39 Fulton is quoted in Kelly, *Creation of Indian Reserves,* 26.

40 Kelly, *Creation of Indian Reserves,* 26.

41 Foster, quoted in Wendy Wickwire, *At the Bridge: James Teit and an Anthropology of Belonging* (Vancouver: UBC Press, 2019), 192. Recall Beavan's note to Powell of August 6, 1874, regarding Tsawwassen Reserve lands and stating that the province knew nothing about land being returned to the Dominion government as an Indian reserve and as part of the Act of Union. The note suggests that Beavan, as chief commissioner of lands and works, believed reserve lands had been transferred to Canada as of 1871. Reserves not yet conveyed to Canada in 1938 would be those created by the Joint Indian Reserve Commission and its successor, the Indian Reserve Commission.

42 Kelly, *Creation of Indian Reserves,* 27. A related case study is offered by David Vogt and David Alexander Gamble, "'You Don't Suppose the Dominion Government Wants to Cheat the Indians?': The Grand Trunk Pacific Railway and the Fort George Reserve, 1908–12," *BC Studies* 166 (Summer 2010): 55–72.

43 Quoted in Wickwire, *At the Bridge,* 196.

44 Hamar Foster, "'We Want a Strong Promise': The Opposition to Indian Treaties in British Columbia, 1850–1990," *Native Studies Review* 18, 1 (2009): 127.

45 See Hamar Foster, "The Imperial Law of Aboriginal Title at the Time of the Douglas Treaties," in *To Share, Not Surrender: Indigenous and Settler Visions of Treaty Making in the Colonies of Vancouver Island and British Columbia,* ed. Peter Cook, Neil Vallance, John Lutz, Graham Brazier, and Hamar Foster (Vancouver: UBC Press, 2021), 107.

46 Deputy Minister Newcombe, Laurier, and McBride are all quoted in Foster, "Imperial Law," 107. Laurier appeared sincere in his hope of getting the province into court to settle the title issue and said as much in a letter to the Chiefs, quoted in Kelly, *Creation of Indian Reserves,* 40.

47 "Memorial to Sir Wilfrid Laurier, Premier of the Dominion of Canada from the Chiefs of the Shuswap, Okanagan and Couteau Tribes of British Columbia," August 25, 1910, https://www.tru.ca/__shared/assets/memorial-to-sir-wilfrid-laurier58605.pdf.

48 Acreage drawn from Wickwire, *At the Bridge,* 205.

49 Wetmore's comments are from RCIA, Queen Charlotte Agency, "Skidegate," September 13, 1913, 35, OHAB. "Memorial to Sir Wilfrid Laurier," 1–7. Wendy Wickwire details the work of anthropologist James Teit in drafting the memorial for the Chiefs in *At the Bridge,* 202–4.

50 Laurier's remarks are quoted by Duncan Campbell Scott in his report to the Special Joint Committee of Parliament on Claims of Allied Tribes of BC, 16th Parl., 1st Sess., vol. 1, March 20, 1927, 45.

51 The Indigenous submission or memorial was presented by the Reverend Peter Kelly, a Haida then residing in Hartley Bay. Both Kelly and McBride are quoted in Patricia E. Roy, "McBride of McKenna-McBride: Premier Richard McBride and the Indian Question in British Columbia," *BC Studies* 172 (Winter 2011–12): 65.

52 The letter to Oliver was signed by the sixty-eight Chiefs who had met with McBride: "Letter Addendum: Memorial to the Hon. Frank Oliver," *Kamloops This Week,* February 12, 2013, https://www.kanakabarband.ca/files/letter-addendum-memorial-to-the-hon-frank-oliver.pdf.

Chapter 6: A Royal Commission Frustrates Hopes

1 Numbers are drawn from Jean Barman, *The West beyond the West: A History of British Columbia,* rev. ed. (Toronto: University of Toronto Press, 2004), Table 5, 379. By 1911,

Indigenous people made up only 5 percent of British Columbia's population (compared with 70 percent in 1871). The Asian portion of the province's non-Indigenous population grew from 1,548 at Confederation to 30,864 in 1911. As noted in Chapter 3, prior to a comprehensive census, government estimates of the Indigenous population varied widely depending on the purpose of the estimates.

2 Royal Commission on Indian Affairs for the Province of British Columbia (RCIA), *Report of the Royal Commission on Indian Affairs for the Province of British Columbia* (Victoria: Acme Press, 1916), 24, 1912, 1:10, https://publications.gc.ca/site/eng/9.828361/publication.html (hereafter *Report*).

3 Duncan Campbell Scott, in his report to the Special Joint Committee of Parliament on Claims of Allied Tribes of BC, 16th Parl., 1st Sess., vol. 1, March 20, 1927, 48. Scott shared McBride's aversion to judicial review, suggesting, "if the Indians win, there will be a cloud on all land titles issued by the province."

4 Scott to Special Joint Committee, 42.

5 RCIA, "Memorandum of Agreement," September 24, 1912.

6 RCIA, "Memorandum of Agreement," September 24, 1912.

7 RCIA, "Interim Report, No. 91," in *Report,* 1:126–27.

8 RCIA, Okanagan Agency, "Meeting with the Spulmacheen [Spallumcheen] or Enderby Band," Enderby, October 2, 1913, 10, Union of British Columbia Indian Chiefs, Library and Archives, Our Homes are Bleeding Collection, https://collections.ubcic.bc.ca/s/ourhomesarebleeding/page/welcome (hereafter OHAB).

9 RCIA, "Examination of Agent Brown," Victoria, November 7, 1913, 143–49, OHAB.

10 RCIA, "Examination of Agent Brown."

11 RCIA, "Examination of Inspector of Agencies T.J. Cumisky," Victoria, November 11, 1913, 221, OHAB. "Cummiskey" is consistently misspelled as "Cumisky" in RCIA documents. Although Cummiskey appears supportive of First Nations under the commission's questioning, Wendy Wickwire, in *At the Bridge: James Teit and an Anthropology of Belonging* (Vancouver: UBC Press, 2019), 213–14, notes his determination to criminalize the act of advocating for Indigenous rights and title.

12 RCIA, *Report,* Okanagan Agency, Table A, vol. 3, 9. The Splatsin (Spallumcheen) Band did not accept the replacement reserve and never occupied it, making it easy pickings as unused land for the commission. Some reductions were later reversed at Canada's insistence, including the Splatsin reserve near Sicamous.

13 RCIA, "Examination of Agent Brown," Victoria, November 10, 1913, 179, OHAB.

14 RCIA, "Examination of Inspector of Agencies T.J. Cumisky," Victoria, November 11, 1913, 222, OHAB.

15 In cases where the Dominion commissioners were supported by Chair Wetmore, their wishes prevailed. As Cole Harris reports in *Making Native Space: Colonialism, Resistance, and Reserves in British Columbia* (Vancouver: UBC Press, 2002), 244, in the first year of the commission's operations, the Dominion commissioners commonly voted against the reductions proposed by their provincial colleagues, but in subsequent years, almost all decisions were unanimous.

16 Ian Pooley and Patricia E. Roy, "A Tale of Three Towns: Transportation, Fruit-Growing, and Regional Growth in the Okanagan Valley, c. 1891–c. 1941," *BC Studies* 219 (Autumn 2023): 50; and RCIA, *Report,* Okanagan Agency, "Summary and Minutes of Decision," 3:698.

17 Wickwire, *At the Bridge,* 189.

18 RCIA, *Report,* Okanagan Agency, "Summary and Minutes of Decision," 3:716–22.

19 Thompson Rivers University Library, "Kamloops and Region Census Statistics: 1870–1971," https://libguides.tru.ca/KamloopsRegionalCensus.
20 Kamloops Museum and Archives, "Fulton Family Fonds," https://www.kamloops.ca/sites/default/files/docs/parks-recreation/fultonfamily.pdf; and RCIA, Kamloops Agency, "Kamloops Board of Trade Meeting," October 30, 1913, 2–3, OHAB, https://ourhomesarebleeding.ubcic.bc.ca/Testimonies2/index.html.
21 RCIA, Kamloops Agency, "Kamloops Board of Trade Meeting," 3.
22 RCIA, "Examination of Indian Agent J.F. Smith at Victoria," November 19 and 20, 1913, 145–48, OHAB.
23 For more on Smith's story, see Jessica Klymchuk, "Spirit of a True Pioneer," *Kamloops This Week,* February 16, 2017.
24 RCIA, Kamloops Agency, "Kamloops Tribe (Kamloops Indian Reserve No. 1)," October 28, 1913, 63–64, OHAB.
25 RCIA, *Report,* Kamloops Agency, Introduction, 1:306.
26 RCIA, "Salmon Arm Meeting at Montebello Hotel," October 22, 1913, 11, OHAB. The cut-off lands were incorporated into the City of Salmon Arm and today are home to a major shopping centre and other amenities.
27 RCIA, "North Thompson Reserve No. 1," October 27, 1913, 56, OHAB.
28 RCIA, "Adams Lake Reserve No. 4," October 14, 1913, 30, OHAB.
29 Like governments in British Columbia in previous decades, the commission did not recognize the value of activities associated with seasonal rounds such as hunting, fishing, trapping, and gathering. RCIA, *Report,* Kamloops Agency, Introduction, 1:306.
30 RCIA, *Report,* Kamloops Agency, "Additional Lands Applications 1," 1:333.
31 RCIA, "Meeting with North Vancouver Board of Trade," June 25, 1913, 74, OHAB.
32 The 130-acre reduction of Reserve no. 5 was among the commission recommendations approved by the Dominion and BC governments in 1930. The cut-off left 293 acres in Reserve no. 5. See Union of British Columbia Indian Chiefs, "What Are Cut-Off Lands?," April 19, 2015, https://www.yumpu.com/en/document/view/38327552/what-are-cut-off-lands-union-of-british-columbia-indian-.
33 RCIA, *Report,* New Westminster Agency, 3:626, and table titled "Reductions and Cut-Offs of Reserves: New Westminster Agency," 3:674.
34 See Jim Reynolds, *Canada and Colonialism: An Unfinished History* (Vancouver: Purich Books, 2024), 185.
35 Quoted in Reynolds, *Canada and Colonialism,* 185.
36 Laurier typically sounded sympathetic to Indigenous appeals for justice, as noted earlier in this chapter. Oliver was a powerful figure in the Laurier government, and his views tended to reflect those of Alberta and western Canada. His views on Indigenous and immigration issues were controversial even in his own time, far more so today, where they would be seen as anti-Indigenous and anti-immigrant. See, for example, David J. Hall, "Oliver, Frank," in *Dictionary of Canadian Biography,* vol. 16, University of Toronto/Université Laval, 2003–, http://www.biographi.ca/en/bio/oliver_frank_16E.html.
37 Adele Perry, *On the Edge of the Empire: Gender, Race, and the Making of British Columbia, 1849–1871* (Toronto: University of Toronto Press, 2001), 111. The expropriation powers conferred by Oliver were soon used elsewhere on the Lower Mainland. See Angela Sterritt, "The Little-Known History of Squamish Nation Land in Vancouver," CBC News, April 21, 2019, https://www.cbc.ca/news/canada/british-columbia/little-known-history-of-squamish-nation-land-in-vancouver-1.5104584.

38 Oliver is quoted in Canada, *Report of the Royal Commission on Aboriginal Peoples,* vol. 1, *Looking Forward, Looking Back* (Ottawa: Indian and Northern Affairs Canada, 1996), 450.
39 Sterritt, "Little-Known History," quoting Rudy Reimer, a member of the Squamish Nation.
40 RCIA, *Report,* New Westminster Agency, 3:626, and table titled "Additional Lands Applications," 3: 33–41.
41 RCIA, Cowichan Agency, "Meeting with Duncan Board of Trade," May 26, 1913, 3–7, OHAB. Other notable discussions of reserve removal can be found in RCIA, Stikine Agency, "Meeting with Atlin Board of Trade," June 16, 1915, 13–16, OHAB; "Statement Made by Mr. Clarke at Hope," Hope, BC, November 20, 1914, 338–39, OHAB; Lytton Agency, "Meeting with the Agassiz Board of Trade," November 23, 1914, 393, OHAB; and "Second Examination of Agent H. Graham," Victoria, February 3, 1915, 452–55, OHAB.
42 RCIA, Cowichan Agency, "Examination of W.E. Ditchburn, Inspector of Indian Affairs," July 3, 1913, 287, OHAB.
43 RCIA, Cowichan Agency, "Argument by Ditchburn," July 11, 1913, 314–15, OHAB.
44 RCIA, *Report,* Cowichan Agency, 3:275.
45 Harris, *Making Native Space,* 243.
46 RCIA, *Report,* Cowichan Agency, table titled "Cowichan Agency: Additional Lands Applications," 3:292.
47 RCIA, Cowichan Agency, "Meeting at the Nanaimo City Reserve," June 2, 2013, 101, OHAB.
48 RCIA, Bella Coola Agency, "Hartley Bay," September 3, 1913, 117–18, OHAB.
49 Hamar Foster, "'We Want a Strong Promise': The Opposition to Indian Treaties in British Columbia, 1850–1990," *Native Studies Review* 18, 1 (2009): 131. See also Jim Aldridge, "Legal Counsel, Nisga'a Nation," discussion paper posted by the Land Claims Agreements Coalition, undated, 3–4, https://www.landclaimscoalition.ca/assets/Jim-Aldridge-Overview-of-Modern-Treaties.pdf.
50 RCIA, *Report,* Queen Charlotte Agency, "Agency Summary," 3:726–28.
51 As early as the 1880s, the Dominion government had purchased land for Indigenous people after the province had alienated other potential reserve sites. RCIA, *Report,* Williams Lake Agency, 4:916, notes "1464 acres purchased from the Bates Estate." Cole Harris also describes a purchase at Williams Lake in *Making Native Space,* 180, 209, and near Pemberton, 222.
52 Mark Abley, "The Tarnished Legacy of Duncan Campbell Scott," *The Walrus,* August 29, 2022, https://thewalrus.ca/the-tarnished-legacy-of-duncan-campbell-scott/.
53 Scott is quoted in Reynolds, *Canada and Colonialism,* 162–63. Scott is also quoted in Canada, *Report of the Royal Commission on Aboriginal Peoples,* 1:577.
54 Enfranchisement was enabled by 1920 amendments to the Indian Act (sections 107 and 122a). Scott reported in 1926 that thirty-four Indigenous males had been enfranchised during the past fiscal year under section 122a and another four under section 107. See Canada, *Annual Report of the Department of Indian Affairs for the Year Ended March 31, 1926* (Ottawa: King's Printer, 1926), 21.

Chapter 7: Composition Changes, Disposition Does Not

1 Royal Commission on Indian Affairs for the Province of British Columbia (RCIA), Babine Agency, "Meeting with Getanmax Band or Tribe, April 21, 1915, 39–40, Union of British Columbia Indian Chiefs, Library and Archives, Our Homes Are Bleeding Collection, https://collections.ubcic.bc.ca/s/ourhomesarebleeding/page/welcome (hereafter OHAB).
2 RCIA, Naas Agency, "Meeting at Port Simpson," September 29, 1915, 38, 49, OHAB.

3 RCIA, *Report of the Royal Commission on Indian Affairs for the Province of British Columbia* (Victoria: Acme Press, 1916), https://publications.gc.ca/site/eng/9.828361/publication.html (hereafter *Report*), Naas Agency, 3:550, and table titled "Reductions and Cut-Offs of Reserves: Naas Agency," 3:574.

4 RCIA, Kwawkewlth Agency, "Meeting with the Turner Island Band," Alert Bay, June 2, 1914, 160–62, OHAB.

5 RCIA, *Report,* Kwawkewlth Agency, 2:380.

6 RCIA, *Report,* Kwawkewlth Agency, table titled "Additional Lands Applications," 2:414–15.

7 RCIA, Kwawkewlth Agency, "Meeting with the Principle Tribes of the Kwawkewlth Nation," June 1, 1914, 87, OHAB.

8 RCIA, Kwawkewlth Agency, "Meeting with the Mahmahlillikullah Band," Alert Bay, June 2, 1914, 132, OHAB.

9 RCIA, Nass Agency, "Meeting at Kincolith," October 2, 1915, 69–70, OHAB. The exchange was between the chair and the Reverend Archdeacon Collison, who suggested that old "Indian" settlements had been overlooked in survey work. Collison is misspelled "Collinson" in the transcripts.

10 RCIA, Nass Agency, "Meeting at Grease Harbour," October 10, 1915, 181–82, OHAB.

11 Enclosure from B.W. Pearse to the Colonial Secretary, October 16, 1871, in British Columbia, *Papers Connected with the Indian Land Question, 1850–1875* (Victoria: Richard Wolfenden, Government Printer, 1875), 102 (hereafter *PCILQ*), in correspondence from Lieutenant-Governor Joseph Trutch to the Secretary of State for the Provinces, November 3, 1871, *PCILQ,* 101–3. The full quote and additional commentary appear in Chapter 3 of this book.

12 Marianne Ignace and Ronald E. Ignace, *Secwépemc People, Land, and Laws* (Montreal/Kingston: McGill-Queen's University Press, 2017), 153.

13 RCIA, *Report,* West Coast Agency, 4:851.

14 RCIA, *Report,* Kwawkewlth Agency, 2:380.

15 RCIA, *Report,* Kwawkewlth Agency, table titled "Additional Lands Applications," 2:409.

16 RCIA, Bella Coola Agency, "Iver Fougner (Further Examination)," Victoria, December 9, 1915, 166, OHAB. The commission records also note a conflict between a provisional new reserve in the Kootenay Agency and a newly established timber licence. The latter prevailed. See RCIA, Kootenay Agency, "Meeting with the Lower Kootenay Band," September 11, 1914, 7, OHAB.

17 R.E. Gosnell, *The Year Book of British Columbia and Manual of Provincial Information,* Coronation ed. (Victoria: King's Printer, 1911), 247.

18 Wendy Wickwire, *At the Bridge: James Teit and an Anthropology of Belonging* (Vancouver: UBC Press, 2019), 189.

19 RCIA, Bella Coola Agency, "Iver Fougner (Further Examination)," 183, OHAB.

20 RCIA, "Meeting at Port Essington," October 9, 1915, 6, OHAB. Chief Wise was from the Kitselas First Nation.

21 RCIA, "Meeting with C.A. Cox, Indian Agent," Kyuquot, May 23, 1914, 196, OHAB.

22 RCIA, Nass Agency, "Examination of Indian Agent Perry in Victoria," December 15, 1915, 191–92, OHAB. For more on the suppression of Indigenous fisheries, see Cole Harris, *Making Native Space: Colonialism, Resistance, and Reserves in British Columbia* (Vancouver: UBC Press, 2002), 201–3; and John Lutz, *Makúk: A New History of Aboriginal-White Relations* (Vancouver: UBC Press, 2009), 241.

23 RCIA, *Report,* Lytton Agency, 2:445.

24 RCIA, Lytton Agency, "Meeting with Fountain Band," November 9, 1914, 83, OHAB. Agent Graham attended the Fountain (Xaxli'p) First Nation meeting and offered his comments. Cole Harris also notes cases where the limited agricultural land around Lytton was taken up by whites, contrary to directions from Governor Douglas: *Making Native Space,* 141.

25 Robert E. Cail, *Land, Man, and the Law: The Disposal of Crown Lands in British Columbia* (Vancouver: UBC Press, 1974), 216.

26 RCIA, *Report,* Lytton Agency, table titled "Lytton Agency: Additional Lands Applications," 2:485–97. Near Lytton, the Skuppah Band's application for 160 acres to connect Reserve no. 1 and Reserve no. 4 and to provide additional farmland was "not entertained, in view of other allowances to the applicant tribe." Among others, an application by the Lytton First Nation to expand Reserve no. 15 for pasturage on "vacant and available" land was rejected as "not reasonably required" (RCIA, *Report,* Lytton Agency, 2:489) as was a Siska band's request for 160 acres of vacant and available land to connect Reserve no. 1 and Reserve no. 4 and for farming, pasturage, and wood supply (RCIA, *Report,* Lytton Agency, 2:494).

27 RCIA, Bella Coola Agency, "Ulkatcho Band, Meeting at Fort Fraser," June 7, 1915, 128, OHAB.

28 Harris, *Making Native Space,* 220.

29 RCIA, *Report,* Stikine Agency, 4:745.

30 RCIA, *Report,* Williams Lake Agency, table titled "Analysis of Evidence: Table C – Population, Social Conditions," 4:922.

31 RCIA, *Report,* Stuart Lake Agency, 4:767. The Blackwater amalgamated with the Nazko First Nation in 1957.

32 RCIA, *Report,* Stuart Lake Agency, table titled "Stuart Lake Agency: Additional Lands Applications," 4:789.

33 RCIA, *Report,* Kwawkewlth Agency," 2:380.

34 RCIA, Babine Agency, "Meeting with the Kuldoe Band or Tribe," Old Hazelton, July 13, 1915, 74–77, OHAB.

35 The value assigned for reductions was expressed as a range ($1,247,912 to $1,522,704) from which I drew the average of $1,385,308. The value assigned to the additions was the single figure of $444,838. See RCIA, *Report,* graph titled "Indian Reserves in British Columbia," Final Report: 177.

36 Harris, *Making Native Space,* 249.

37 Chris Kelly, *The Creation of Indian Reserves in British Columbia (A Research Guide),* prepared for the Litigation Support Directorate, Department of Indian Affairs and Northern Development, June 15, 1995, 14. In 1920, a joint review initiated under W.E. Ditchburn and Major J.W. Clark, representing the Dominion and the province, respectively, produced mixed results: five of the recommended cut-offs were reversed, but twenty of the recommended new reserves were refused.

38 Hamar Foster, "'We Want a Strong Promise': The Opposition to Indian Treaties in British Columbia, 1850–1990," *Native Studies Review* 18, 1 (2009): 133; and Harris, *Making Native Space,* 251–59.

39 Historian Sarah A. Nickel in *Assembling Unity: Indigenous Politics, Gender, and the Union of BC Indian Chiefs* (Vancouver: UBC Press, 2019), 40–41, suggests that one of the few good things to come of the commission process was "encouraging First Nations to unite under the new banner of Allied Tribes of British Columbia in pursuit of overall land claims."

40 Canada, Report to the Special Joint Committee of Parliament on Claims of Allied Tribes of BC, 16th Parl., 1st Sess., vol. 1, March 20, 1927, 14–15.

41 Scott would cite Joseph Trutch's words in his 1927 presentation to the Special Joint Committee of Parliament on Claims of Allied Tribes of BC, 16th Parl., 1st Sess., vol. 1, March 20, 1927, 39, and in his report to the Special Joint Committee of Parliament on Claims of Allied Indian Tribes of BC, 16th Parl., 1st Sess., vol. 1, March 20, 1927, 40. Trutch is quoted in Chapters 2 (in quote and endnote 46) and 3 (in quote and endnote 10) above.

42 Canada, Report to the Special Joint Committee, 24.

43 For the precise wording of the amendment and useful commentary, see Bob Joseph, *21 Things You May Not Know about the Indian Act: Helping Canadians Make Reconciliation with Indigenous Peoples a Reality* (Port Coquitlam, BC: Indigenous Relations Press, 2018), 73–74.

44 J.R. Miller, *Compact, Contract, Covenant: Aboriginal Treaty-Making in Canada* (Toronto: University of Toronto Press, 2009), 238.

45 British Columbia, "A Brief History of Oil and Gas Exploration in British Columbia," https://www2.gov.bc.ca/assets/gov/farming-natural-resources-and-industry/natural-gas-oil/petroleum-geoscience/brief_history_of_oil_and_gas_exploration_in_bc.pdf.

46 Union of British Columbia Indian Chiefs, "What Are Cut-Off Lands?," May 19, 2015, 7, https://www.yumpu.com/en/document/view/38327552/what-are-cut-off-lands-union-of-british-columbia-indian-. Emphasis in original. See also Union of British Columbia Indian Chiefs and Reuben Ware, "The Lands We Lost: A History of Cut-off Lands and Land Losses from Indian Reserves in British Columbia," 1974, 48–49, https://epub.sub.uni-hamburg.de/epub/volltexte/2012/13608/pdf/LandsWeLost1974.pdf, which describes the genesis of the BC-Canada Agreement. See also D. Duane Thomson, "A History of the Okanagan: Indians and Whites in the Settlement Era, 1860–1920" (PhD diss., University of British Columbia, 1985), 158–59; and Harris, *Making Native Space,* 248–59.

47 Kelly, *Creation,* 114–15, 173.

Chapter 8: Dispossession and Despair

1 For more on the enfranchisement provisions within the Indian Act, see Chapter 6 and footnote 54. I thank one of the anonymous peer reviewers for reminding me that the opportunity to vote had, at points in our history, been offered up by governments as an inducement for assimilation. See, for example, Jim Reynolds, *Canada and Colonialism: An Unfinished History* (Vancouver: Purich Books, 2024), 183.

2 See J.R. Miller, *Compact, Contract, Covenant: Aboriginal Treaty-Making in Canada* (Toronto: University of Toronto Press, 2009), 247. In another notable amendment, Parliament also repealed the ban on Potlatch ceremonies.

3 George M. Abbott, "Persistence of Colonial Prejudice and Policy in British Columbia's Indigenous Relations: Did the Spirit of Joseph Trutch Haunt Twentieth-Century Resource Development?," *BC Studies* 194 (Summer 2017): 39–64.

4 Hanna Petersen, "A Life of Service: Remembering Indigenous WWII Veteran Abel Peters," *Prince George Citizen,* November 11, 2021.

5 Cheslatta Carrier Nation, "Remembering Abel Peters, Rifleman," https://www.cheslatta.com/.

6 Internal Alcan correspondence, November 4, 1941, quoted in *Thomas and Saik'uz v Rio Tinto Alcan Inc,* 2022 BCSC 15 (*CanLii*), para. 65, https://www.canlii.org/en/bc/bcsc/doc/2022/2022bcsc15/2022bcsc15.html. My thanks to James Tully for advising me of these important documents.

7 On November 3, 1941, Duff Pattullo was the recently re-elected premier of British Columbia. The timing of his outreach to Alcan is interesting. Pattullo's Liberal government

had been reduced to a minority in the election of October 21, 1941, and he was beset by demands to form a Liberal-Conservative coalition government. See George M. Abbott, "Duff Pattullo and the Coalition Controversy of 1941," *BC Studies* 102 (Summer 1994): 30–53.

8 Cited in Susan Klassen, "The Heart of Ingenika," a three-part series in the *Mackenzie Times,* March 7, 1989.

9 E.T. Kenney to President of Alcan, June 16, 1948, in *Thomas v Rio Tinto,* para. 68. Kenney was a coalition minster and (after the coalition's breakup) a Liberal minister.

10 The act provided some hefty incentives for Alcan, as noted in Bev Christensen, *Too Good to Be True: Alcan's Kemano Completion Project* (Vancouver: Talonbooks, 1995), 64, 74–75.

11 Kenney, undated speech linked to the December 29, 1950, announcement, British Columbia Archives (BCA), Kenney Papers, 5, 10, 12, 21.

12 Kenney to E.T. Applewhaite, February 8, 1951, BCA, Kenney Papers. Kenney also expressed "a great deal of confidence" in C.D. Howe and felt sure he would overcome Fisheries' objections. The stipulation to refer project plans to agencies was noted in a speech on December 29, 1950.

13 W.S. Arneil to Indian Affairs Branch (IAB), July 30, 1951, Library and Archives Canada (LAC), RG 10 (Department of Indian Affairs), acc. PV13515, vol. 1, file 985/34A. Arneil was the senior IAB official in British Columbia. During the 1950s, the IAB was part of the Department of Citizenship and Immigration.

14 The management of salmon within the overall Alcan project, including the more recent Kemano Completion Project, remained a controversial issue decades after the dispossession of the Cheslatta. See, for example, Mark Hume, "Who's Looking Out for Salmon in Alcan Project?," *Globe and Mail,* September 18, 2006.

15 Alcan to Arneil, March 28, 1952, LAC, RG 10, vol. 11074, file 161/341A, pt. 2. See also C.E. Webb of Alcan to Arneil, October 12, 1951, LAC, RG 10, vol. 11074, file 161/341A, pt. 2, and a report titled "Flooding of Indian Reserves on Cheslatta Lake Due to Spillway from Tweedsmuir Park Reservoir." The two graveyards were submerged in 1952, but the scouring effect of periodic high water at high velocity eroded the soil that covered the graves. An IAB superintendent at the Burns Lake Agency reported that seventeen graves had washed away in 1957: W.J. Desmarais to Arneil, May 7, 1957, LAC, RG 10, acc. PV 13485, file 985/30–3; and more recently, "Band Proposes Relief Facility after Dam Floods Graveyards, Bodies Wash Away," *Globe and Mail,* May 31, 2012.

16 Amanda Follett Hosgood, "A 'Significant' Archeological Dig Resumes after 70 Years," *The Tyee,* August 31, 2022, https://thetyee.ca/News/2022/08/31/70-Year-Hiatus-Cheslatta-Resumes-Archeological-Dig/.

17 W.J. MacGregor, Regional Supervisor of Indian Agencies, "Memorandum of Preliminary Meeting Held April 3rd and Surrender Meetings Held April 20th and 21st re Acquisition of Cheslatta Indian Reserves by the Aluminum Company of Canada," Cheslatta Lake, LAC, RG 10, vol. 11074, file 161/341A, pt. 2.

18 D.J. Allan to Arneil, December 1, 1951, LAC, RG 10, acc. PV13515, vol. 1, file 985/34A.

19 Harry Swain, former federal deputy minister, correspondence with the author, April 4, 2020.

20 Arneil to R.H. Tredcroft, April 29, 1952, LAC, RG 10, vol. 11074, file 161/341A, pt. 2.

21 Webb to Arneil, October 12, 1951, LAC, RG 10, acc. PV13515, vol. 1, file 985/34A. On September 7, 1951, Arneil advised Superintendent Howe of the Stuart Lake Agency "to value the land and improvements to avoid any last-minute rush and the possibility that

some flooding might occur before the valuations are made": LAC, RG 10, acc. PV13515, vol. 1, file 985/34A.

22 Arneil to Howe, October 26, 1951, LAC, RG 10, acc. PV13515, vol. 1, file 985/34A.

23 Howe to Arneil, October 31, 1951, LAC, RG 10, acc. PV13515, vol. 1, file 985/34A.

24 Webb to Arneil, November 23, 1951, LAC, RG 10, acc. PV13515, vol. 1, file 985/34A. The adjustment moved the Alcan appraisal from $113,900 (on the area where occupation would be prohibited) to $107,830 (the area to be flooded).

25 Arneil to IAB, December 5, 1951, LAC, RG 10, acc. PV13515, vol. 1, file 985/34A.

26 MacGregor, "Memorandum."

27 MacGregor, "Memorandum."

28 Howe to Arneil, April 28, 1952, LAC, RG 10, vol. 11074, file 161/341A, pt. 2.

29 MacGregor, "Memorandum." IAB and Alcan travelled in and out in a helicopter furnished by Alcan.

30 Unidentified official (L.B.) to Arneil, April 9, 1952, LAC, RG 10, vol. 11074, file 161/341A, pt. 2. The letter is signed by the director, but the signature itself is indecipherable.

31 MacGregor, "Memorandum."

32 Howe to Arneil, May 1, 1952, LAC, RG 10, vol. 11074, file 161/341A, pt. 2.

33 MacGregor, "Memorandum."

34 Howe to Arneil, May 1, 1952, LAC, RG 10, vol. 11074, file 161/341A, pt. 2. The margin between individual compensation of $109,450 and a total compensation of $129,000 was intended to go to the First Nation, but the margin was ultimately much smaller.

35 MacGregor, "Memorandum."

36 E.A. Clark to Howe, May 19, 1952, LAC, RG 10, vol. 11074, file 161/341A, pt. 2.

37 Allan to Arneil, December 1, 1951, LAC, RG 10, acc. PV13515, vol. 1, file 985/34A.

38 Arneil to Allan, December 5, 1951, LAC, RG 10, acc. PV13515, vol. 1, file 985/34A.

39 The First Nation suffered physically, socially, and economically following relocation. See J.E. Windsor and J.A. McVey, "Annihilation of Both Place and Sense of Place: The Experience of the Cheslatta T'En Canadian First Nation within the Context of Large-Scale Environmental Projects," *Geographical Journal* 171 (2005): 156–58.

40 For an excellent account of Indigenous and non-Indigenous resettlement in postwar Canada, see Tina Loo, *Moved by the State: Forced Relocation and Making a Good Life in Postwar Canada* (Vancouver: UBC Press, 2019).

41 Canada, *Report of the Royal Commission on Aboriginal Peoples,* vol. 1, *Looking Forward, Looking Back* (Ottawa: Indian and Northern Affairs Canada, 1996), 395–429. According to the Gwa'sala-'Nakwaxda'xw Nation's website, "Our History," the Tsulquate Reserve was unoccupied (because of poor conditions for building) and used only periodically for shellfish harvesting. The challenges associated with viable building sites and safe harbour for fishing boats are detailed in Canada, *Report of the Royal Commission,* and on the Nation's website.

42 Canada, *Report of the Royal Commission,* 426. The poisonous ongoing and multigenerational legacies of public policy were evident in the daily challenges faced by the Gwa'sala-'Nakwaxda'xw and are tragically reflected in contemporary headlines such as Michael John Lo's "Port Hardy-Area First Nations Declare State of Emergency after 11 Deaths in Two Months," *Victoria Times Colonist,* March 3, 2024.

43 Howe to Arneil, May 30, 1952, LAC, RG 10, vol. 11074, file 161/341A, pt. 2.

44 Canada, *Report of the Royal Commission,* 456–57.

45 Howe to Arneil, May 30, 1952, LAC, RG 10, vol. 11074, file 161/341A, pt. 2.

46 Howe to Arneil, July 21, 1952, LAC, RG 10, vol. 11074, file 161/341A, pt. 2.

47 Christensen, *Too Good to Be True,* 90–91; and Windsor and McVey, "Annihilation of Both Place and Sense of Place," 156–58.

48 Canada, *Report of the Royal Commission,* 456. Marvin Charlie was a Chief of the Cheslatta Nation when he presented his testimony.

49 Cheslatta Carrier Nation, "Cheslatta Carrier Nation Backgrounder," 4–5, https://www.cheslatta.com/ccn-backgrounder-lightbox.

50 Given W.A.C. Bennett's long tenure in government, a host of books and articles look at various aspects of his story. Among them, a good starting point is David Mitchell's *W.A.C. Bennett and the Rise of British Columbia* (Vancouver: Douglas and McIntyre, 1983).

51 Cyril Shelford, "Maiden Speech in the Legislature," February 26, 1953, LAC, RG 10, vol. 11074, file 161/341A, pt. 2.

52 *Vancouver New-Herald,* March 17, 1953, LAC, RG 10, vol. 11074, file 161/341A, pt. 2. According to Windsor and McVey, "Annihilation of Both Place and Sense of Place," 152, the Kemano project enjoyed 94 percent public support in May 1949.

53 Unlabelled and undated newspaper article, "Agreement with Alcan 'Disastrous,'" LAC, RG 10, vol. 11074, file 161/341A, pt. 2. A 1990s BC government report estimated that 32,000 hectares of unharvested forest land had been flooded. Quoted in Christensen, *Too Good to Be True,* 56. The Liberal-Conservative coalition formally ended in 1951 and was succeeded by a Liberal government led by Byron Johnson.

Chapter 9: Refugees on Their Own Lands

1 British Thomson-Houston Co., "British Columbia Development of Hydro-Electric Power," 1958, BC Hydro and Power Authority Archives (BCHPAA), Z0812, vol. 1. The document references the first memorandum of intent between Wenner-Gren Development Company and British Columbia in November 1956.

2 W.A. Dow to W.C. Mearns, "Inter-Office Memo," February 3, 1959, author's private collection.

3 "BC Starts Peace River Project," *Construction World,* September 1961, 10, BCHPAA.

4 All of the names and titles in this paragraph are drawn from an extensive chronology of events set out in District Supervisor, A.C. Roach, to Regional Director, January 5, 1971, Library and Archives Canada (LAC), RG 10 (Department of Indian Affairs), vol. 1, box 75549, file 985/19–4. Total trapline compensation (and all compensation until 1989) was $33,900. The department's "Fleury" document offers a similar chronology: LAC, RG 10, vol. 1, 4507–609, box 1, pt. 2.

5 Undated notes from Two River Fonds, BCHPAA. His objections related to "property and compensation for property" and "loss of an age-old pursuit of trapping and hunting."

6 Mary Koyl, "Cultural Chasm: A 1960s Hydro Development and the Tsay Keh Dene Native Community of Northern British Columbia" (master's thesis, University of Victoria, 1992), 48.

7 Roach, chronology to regional supervisor, LAC, RG 10, vol. 1, box 75549, file 985/19–4. For over a century, the province had claimed ownership of the subsurface resources under reserves. See Cole Harris, *Making Native Space: Colonialism, Resistance, and Reserves in British Columbia* (Vancouver: UBC Press, 2002), 217.

8 Failure to harvest forest land in advance of the Bennett dam created long-term issues in the area. See *British Columbia Lumberman,* December 1978, 8.

9 All quotes in this paragraph are from Susan Klassen, "The Heart of Ingenika," a three-part series in *The Mackenzie Times,* March 7, 1989. Other portions of this series appeared in the February 7 and April 18, 1989, editions.

10 Quoted in Zoe Yunker, "Their Land Was Drowned by a Flood of Hydropower," *The Tyee,* April 19, 2022, https://thetyee.ca/News/2022/04/19/Their-Land-Was-Drowned-By-A-Flood-Of-Hydropower/.

11 Emil McCook and Susan McCook, quoted in Jonny Wakefield, "For Kwadacha First Nation, Healing from W.A.C. Bennett Dam a Work in Progress," *Alaska Highway News,* June 13, 2016.

12 Quoted in Yunker, "Their Land Was Drowned," from an audiotape in BC Archives.

13 Canadian Press, "Life of Squalor Described as Band Seeks Aid," *Vancouver Sun,* April 16, 1987.

14 A.M. Cunningham to W.I. Coplick, April 8, 1971, LAC, RG 10, vol. 1, box 75549, file 985/19–4. The dwellings were still in use in 1989.

15 DIAND, "Fleury" document.

16 Quoted in the minutes of a meeting between Presloski and First Nation members on February 19, 1965, LAC, RG 10, vol. 1, box 75549, file 985/19–4.

17 The new reserves at Tutu Creek and Parsnip River were located, respectively, thirteen kilometres northwest and seventeen kilometres south of the municipality of Mackenzie.

18 Suzanne Veit, "Draft Report," on the Ingenika predicament, March 22, 1977, 5, LAC, RG 10, vol. 1994–95/559, vol. 1, box 1, file 985/19–4–609.

19 Quoted in Klassen, "Heart of Ingenika."

20 Veit, "Draft Report," 4.

21 The $35,000 figure came from BC Hydro and was quoted in Terry Glavin, "Officials Rediscover Remote Indian Band," *Vancouver Sun,* June 12, 1987.

22 Edward John to Bill McKnight, Minister of Indian and Northern Affairs, June 19, 1987, author's private collection.

23 Roach, quoted in a letter from Cunningham to Coplick, April 8, 1971, LAC, RG 10, vol. 1, box 75549, file 985/19–4.

24 DIAND, "Fleury" document.

25 Dennis F.K. Madill, *British Columbia Indian Treaties in Historical Perspective,* prepared for the Research Branch, Corporate Policy, Department of Indian and Northern Affairs, 1981, 49–61. Original documents refer to "Fort Grahame," but "Fort Graham" is a more common spelling in later documents. The reference to "Sekanis in the Fort Grahame-Finlay River area" is on page 50. Laird was Indian commissioner from his appointment in 1898 until his death in 1914.

26 G.S. Brown to W.T. Vergette, October 23, 1973, and J.W. Evans to L.E. Wright, November 13, 1973, LAC, RG 10, 4507–609, box 1, pt. 2. The question of whether the Ingenika First Nation could or should enjoy the potential benefits of adhesion to Treaty 8 is both important and largely unanswered. The question was considered by the 1912–16 Royal Commission on Indian Affairs and then by senior DIAND officials in 1960, but interest dissipated. See also Madill, *British Columbia Indian Treaties,* 53–59.

27 L.E. Wright to D. Borthwick, December 18, 1973, LAC, RG 10, 4507–609, box 1, pt. 2.

28 Roach to W.J. Faryna, December 5, 1973, LAC, RG 10, 4507–609, box 1, pt. 2.

29 G.A. Rhoades to committee members, "Report on Ingenika Band of Indians in Occupation of Crown Lands at Ingenika River," February 19, 1974, 4, LAC, RG 10, vol. 1, box 75549, file 985/19–4–604.

30 Rhoades, "Report on Ingenika Band," 5–7.

31 V. Rhymer to L. Wright, January 14, 1975, LAC, RG 10, vol. 1, box 75549, file 985/19–4–604. Oberle was a Progressive Conservative, Buchanan a Liberal. The James Bay and Northern Quebec Agreement was signed on November 11, 1975, by Cree and Inuit representatives as well as the governments of Quebec and Canada.

32 Memo to file, R.M. McIntyre to J. Wilkins, December 5, 1975, LAC, RG 10, vol. 1, box 75549, File 985/19-4-604.
33 McIntyre to Wilkins, July 7, 1976, LAC, RG 10, vol. 1, box 75549, File 985/19-4-604.
34 McIntyre to Edward John, November 18, 1981, LAC, RG 10, vol. 1, box 75549, File 985/19-4-604.
35 BC Hydro, briefing note, 1987, author's private collection.
36 Eric Denhoff, "Jack Was Ground-Breaking 'Minister of Native Affairs,'" *Orders of the Day: The Publication of the Association of Former MLAs of British Columbia* 28, 6 (2022): 6. The minister, Jack Weisgerber, died on June 3, 2022.
37 In Ontario, Ian Scott served concurrently as attorney general and minister responsible for Native affairs. In British Columbia, Jack Weisgerber served as minister of state for Nechako and the northeast as well as minister of Native affairs.
38 Denhoff, correspondence with the author, March 26, 2020.
39 Chief Gordon Pierre, quoted in Canadian Press, "Life of Squalor Described."
40 Terry Glavin, "Officials Rediscover Remote Indian Band," and "Disenchanted Natives Stake Out New Homeland," *Vancouver Sun,* June 12, 1987; Tom Barrett, "Victoria Advocating Reserve for Band," *Vancouver Sun,* June 16, 1987; and Bev Christensen, "Indians Plead for an End to Misery from Bennett Dam," *Victoria Times-Colonist,* June 14, 1987.
41 BC Ministry of Intergovernmental Relations, briefing note, June 9, 1987, 1, author's private collection.
42 British Columbia, *Debates of the Legislative Assembly,* June 15, 1987, 1763. Rogers's comments followed his second visit to Ingenika Point, when he was accompanied by NDP MLAs Lois Boone and John Cashore. Cashore used the expression "shaken and shocked" in his Question Period comments.
43 Denhoff, correspondence with the author, March 26, 2020.
44 Minutes of Edward John's report to the Carrier Sekani Tribal Council and DIAND, June 16, 1987, LAC, RG 10, 1997-98/230, box 3, file 4527-609.
45 Denhoff to Owen Anderson, June 12, 1987, author's private collection.
46 BC Ministry of Intergovernmental Relations, memorandum, July 17, 1987, 1, author's private collection. Marnie Dobell, acting director of social policy for the ministry, was part of the delegation and the author of the note.
47 Memorandum from Marnie Dobell to Eric Denhoff, July 20, 1987, author's private collection. Dobell joined Anderson, Ed John, and others on the trip to Ingenika and detailed DIAND's commitments.
48 Manfred Klein to Denhoff, May 16, 1988, author's private collection. Most correspondence from this period is also available in LAC, RG 10.
49 Denhoff to Anderson, August 15, 1988, 1, author's private collection.
50 Minutes of a meeting between the Carrier Sekani Tribal Council, Ingenika First Nation members, and federal-provincial officials at Ingenika Village (hereafter Minutes of a meeting), August 16, 1988, 2-5, author's private collection.
51 Minutes of a meeting, 3.
52 Minutes of a meeting, 4.
53 Denhoff, correspondence with the author, March 26, 2020.
54 Jack Davis to Weisgerber, September 8, 1988, author's private collection.
55 Harry Swain, correspondence with the author, April 4, 2020.
56 See Government of British Columbia, "Tsay Keh Dene Vote Yes to Williston Settlement Agreement," press release, July 2, 2009. This is the agreement I reference in the book's

introduction. It involved apologies from the province (which I offered) and from BC Hydro (provided by Chris O'Riley, now president and CEO at Hydro).

57 Tsay Key Enterprises Agreement, August 31, 2009, https://www2.gov.bc.ca/assets/gov/environment/natural-resource-stewardship/consulting-with-first-nations/agreements/final_tsay_keh_dene_bchydro_enterprises.pdf; and for links to various agreements, see the BC government's "First Nations A-Z List" for Tsay Keh Dene First Nation, https://www2.gov.bc.ca/gov/content/environment/natural-resource-stewardship/consulting-with-first-nations/first-nations-negotiations/first-nations-a-z-listing/tsay-keh-dene-band.

58 "Cheslatta Carrier Nation Signs Agreement with Company That Forced Them from Their Homes 68 Years Ago," CBC News, February 28, 2020, https://www.cbc.ca/news/canada/british-columbia/cheslatta-carrier-nation-rio-tinto-new-day-agreement-1.5480597.

Chapter 10: A Slow Shift in Indigenous Relations

1 Geoff Meggs and Rod Mickleburgh, *The Art of the Impossible: Dave Barrett and the NDP in Power, 1972–1975* (Madeira Park, BC: Harbour, 2012), 104. The book also details Calder's departure from the NDP.

2 British Columbia, *Response of the Government of British Columbia to the Position Paper of the Nishga Tribal Council* (Victoria: Queen's Printer, 1978), 5. This document, dated January 10, 1978, was Appendix H in a larger document and was perhaps prepared for talks with Canada, as it does not appear to have had broad public circulation despite its Queen's Printer origins. A Government of Canada publication note supports that suggestion:

> On April 27, 1976 the Nishga Tribal Council presented to the BC and Federal negotiating teams a position paper on the claim of the Nishga people. During the following six months, several clarification meetings were held and it was understood in October, 1976, that the two Governments would make a joint formal response. This response has been prepared by the Federal Government on its own behalf without being able to engage in discussions on any of the substantive issues with the Government of British Columbia. It reflects only the Federal view of the claim and the direction negotiations might take and is presented at this time on the understanding that the Government of British Columbia, to whom the claim was also submitted, will be tabling its own response separately.

3 British Columbia, *Response,* 5.

4 British Columbia, *Response,* 5–6.

5 British Columbia, *Response,* 4.

6 British Columbia, *Response,* 2.

7 Paul Tennant, "Aboriginal Peoples and Aboriginal Title in British Columbia Politics," in *Politics, Policy, and Government in British Columbia,* ed. R.K. Carty (Vancouver: UBC Press, 1996), 45.

8 Jim Aldridge, "Legal Counsel, Nisga'a Nation," discussion paper posted by the Land Claims Agreements Coalition, undated, 2, https://www.landclaimscoalition.ca/assets/Jim-Aldridge-Overview-of-Modern-Treaties.pdf.

9 Aldridge, "Legal Counsel," 3.

10 Thomas R. Berger, "One Man's Justice: My Life in the Courts," *McGill Law Journal* 50, 4 (2005): 990.

11 Quoted in Michael Asch, *On Being Here to Stay: Treaties and Aboriginal Rights in Canada* (Toronto: University of Toronto Press, 2014), 12. Berger notes that Chief Justice Davey of the BC Court of Appeal revealed "attitudes that were prevalent in those days, which obscured and obstructed recognition of Aboriginal title and rights: he said that Aboriginal people were, at the time of European settlement, a primitive people with none of notions of private property": Berger, "One Man's Justice," 990.

12 Asch, *On Being Here,* 12–13.

13 In "The Imperial Law of Aboriginal Title at the Time of the Douglas Treaties," in *To Share, Not Surrender: Indigenous and Settler Visions of Treaty Making in the Colonies of Vancouver Island and British Columbia,* ed. Peter Cook, Neil Vallance, John Lutz, Graham Brazier, and Hamar Foster (Vancouver: UBC Press, 2021), 95, Hamar Foster notes:

> Subjects (whether Indigenous or non-Indigenous) were free to sue one another but could not sue the Crown without a fiat from the attorney general, that is, without the Crown's permission ... In the twentieth century, jurisdiction after jurisdiction repealed the doctrine. In Canada, British Columbia was the last to do so, in 1974 – too late for the Nisga'a. Because the province had a long history of opposing any and all attempts to have the courts decide the "BC Indian Land Question," the Nisga'a had not sought a fiat.

Framing their action as pursuit of a declaration allowed the Nisga'a to escape this conundrum.

14 Meggs and Mickleburgh, *Art,* 102.

15 Berger, "One Man's Justice," 990.

16 Foster, "Imperial Law," 94.

17 Asch, *On Being Here,* 14–15.

18 Quoted in Asch, *On Being Here,* 15.

19 Berger, "One Man's Justice," 990. La Forest was himself a justice of the Supreme Court from 1985 to 1997.

20 Asch, *On Being Here,* 16. Similarly, Hamar Foster notes that *Calder* prompted Pierre Trudeau "to concede that 'perhaps' the Nisga'a had more 'legal rights' than he had thought": Foster, "Imperial Law," 94.

21 Hamar Foster, "'We Want a Strong Promise': The Opposition to Indian Treaties in British Columbia, 1850–1990," *Native Studies Review* 18, 1 (2009): 115.

22 Quoted in Foster, "Imperial Law," 112. Calder was speaking in 2003 at a conference at the University of Victoria to mark the thirtieth anniversary of the Supreme Court's decision in *Calder.*

23 The conference produced substantial federal-provincial agreement but at the price of an angry and isolated Quebec. Negotiations involved a range of issues beyond recognition of Aboriginal title and rights. See, for example, Roy Romanow, John Whyte, and Howard Leeson, *Canada ... Notwithstanding* (Toronto: Carswell/Methuen, 1994).

24 Mel Smith offered his perspective in "Some Perspectives on the Origins and Meaning of Section 35 of the Constitution Act, 1982," *Public Policy Sources* 41 (2000): 6, a publication of the Fraser Institute.

25 Smith, "Some Perspectives," 7. Smith adds in a footnote that "Bill Bennett said in an interview later that he might not have signed the accord if the native-rights sections had been left in with the original wording."

26 Barry L. Strayer, *Canada's Constitutional Revolution* (Edmonton: University of Alberta Press, 2013), 166, 179–89. Britain's prime minister, Margaret Thatcher, supported Trudeau's

constitutional initiative, but the broad support of Britain's Parliament was less certain. British parliamentary committee meetings aired issues of public concern in Canada – Indigenous rights and title prominent among them – but set the expectation for sufficient provincial support.

27 Strayer, *Canada's Constitutional Revolution,* 199.

28 Smith, "Some Perspectives," 8–10.

29 Smith, "Some Perspectives," 9, 10–12. Smith's account of the 1983 federal-provincial-territorial conference is particularly illuminating. With section 35 in place, British Columbia and Alberta were anxious to minimize its importance by reflecting on its meaning and origins. Consistent with Smith, Gordon Gibson on page 3 of his foreword to Smith's article states:

> He [Smith] leads us through the fascinating history of section 35 – the slight consideration given, the cosmetic and minimalist intent, the politics involved. This paper will surely be quoted to the court in arguing for a restrained interpretation of section 35 insofar as self-government is concerned, based on the carefully laid-out evidence as to the actual intent of the framers.

30 Berger's comment in the *Globe and Mail* is quoted in Ian Waddell, "The Laboured Birth of Section 35," *The Advocate* 66 (November 2008): 894. Berger believed his intervention had "something to do with Mr. Trudeau and the other premiers deciding to reinstate what is now section 35." See Berger, "One Man's Justice," 991. Speaking out brought an investigation against Berger by a Quebec judge, Chief Justice Jules Deschenes. Berger left the Supreme Court of British Columbia in 1983.

31 Waddell, "Laboured Birth," 894.

32 Strayer, *Canada's Constitutional Revolution,* 203.

33 See Erin Hanson, "Constitution Express," Indigenous Foundations, https://indigenousfoundations.arts.ubc.ca/constitution_express/.

34 Eric Denhoff, quoted in Justine Hunter, "Breaking through the First Nations Wall," *Globe and Mail,* July 14, 2013.

35 Denhoff and Weisgerber, quoted in Hunter, "Breaking through."

36 Terry Glavin, Martin Dunphy, and Justine Hunter, "Broken Promises Led to New Roadblock, Chief Says," *Vancouver Sun,* July 24, 1990.

37 Glavin, Dunphy, and Hunter, "Broken Promises."

38 Glavin, Dunphy, and Hunter, "Broken Promises."

39 Denhoff, correspondence with the author, March 26, 2020.

40 CBC News provides a good summary of the complex events at Oka based on CBC News accounts from a decade earlier. See Loreen Pindera and Laurene Jardin, "78 Days of Unrest and an Unresolved Land Claim Hundreds of Years in the Making," CBC News, July 11, 2020, https://www.cbc.ca/news/canada/montreal/oka-crisis-timeline-summer-1990-1.5631229.

41 The summer of 1995 saw violent conflict at Gustafsen Lake in British Columbia and Ipperwash in Ontario. As described by the Government of Canada, the royal commission was "mandated to investigate and propose solutions to the challenges affecting the relationship between Aboriginal peoples (First Nations, Inuit, Métis Nation), the Canadian government and Canadian society as a whole." It was established in August 1991 and submitted its report in October 1996. See Library and Archives Canada, "Royal Commission on Aboriginal Peoples," https://www.bac-lac.gc.ca/eng/discover/aboriginal-heritage/royal-commission-aboriginal-peoples/Pages/introduction.aspx.

42 The location of those eighteen schools is noted in National Centre for Truth and Reconciliation, "Residential School History," https://nctr.ca/education/teaching-resources/residential-school-history/, and UBC's Indian Residential School History and Dialogue Centre, "Residential Schools," https://irshdc.ubc.ca/learn/indian-residential-schools/.
43 Canada, *Report of the Royal Commission on Aboriginal Peoples,* vol. 1, *Looking Forward, Looking Back* (Ottawa: Indian and Northern Affairs Canada, 1996), 232.
44 Canada, *Report of the Royal Commission on Aboriginal Peoples,* vol. 3, *Gathering Strength* (Ottawa: Indian and Northern Affairs Canada, 1996), 32–33.
45 See Chapter 12, this book, for further discussion of the agreement and the Truth and Reconciliation Commission.
46 *Regina v Sparrow* (1987), 32 CCC (3d) 65 (BCCA), quoted in Foster, "We Want a Strong Promise," 116.
47 Foster, "We Want a Strong Promise," 116.
48 J.R. Miller, *Compact, Contract, Covenant: Aboriginal Treaty-Making in Canada* (Toronto: University of Toronto Press, 2009), 273.
49 Denhoff, correspondence with the author, February 2, 2022.
50 Denhoff, correspondence with the author, July 24, 2024.
51 Denhoff, correspondence with the author, February 2, 2022. See also Hunter, "Breaking through."
52 For example, Keith Baldrey and Gary Mason, *Fantasyland: Inside the Reign of Bill Vander Zalm* (Toronto: McGraw-Hill Ryerson, 1989) ably documents the conflict-of-interest issues that eventually led to his downfall.

Chapter 11: The Nisg̱a'a Canoe Finally Reaches Home

1 British Columbia, *Debates of the Legislative Assembly,* March 17, 1992, 6.
2 The Ministry of Native Affairs became the Ministry of Aboriginal Affairs after the 1991 election. All quotes are from Director, Quantitative Analysis Branch, Ministry of Finance and Corporate Relations, briefing note, May 5, 1992, author's private collection.
3 Deborah Wilson, "Hailed as Keeper of Process 'New Era' Natives Jubilant over Creation of Land-Claims Body," *Globe and Mail,* September 22, 1991.
4 Stewart Bell, "Government Land-Claim Share Pact Should Get Us to Table, Natives Say," *Vancouver Sun,* June 22, 1993.
5 Vaughn Palmer, "This Landmark Stands on Shaky Ground," *Vancouver Sun,* June 22, 1993.
6 Justine Hunter, "Land Talks Expected to Collapse: BC Deal with Nisga'a Torpedoed by Ottawa," *Vancouver Sun,* July 14, 1995.
7 Vaughn Palmer, "Negotiators at Loggerheads over Resource Revenue," *Vancouver Sun,* July 26, 1995.
8 George M. Abbott, *Big Promises, Small Government: Doing Less with Less in the BC Liberal New Era* (Vancouver: UBC Press, 2020), 98–99.
9 Vaughn Palmer, "Remembering Jack Ebbels: A Man Who Got Things Done," *Alaska Highway News,* March 16, 2010.
10 Justine Hunter, "Irwin Vows to Break Impasse with Nisga'a," *Vancouver Sun,* August 16, 1995.
11 Justine Hunter, "End of Secrecy on Nisga'a Talks Urged: Stakeholders in Region 'Scared by Silence,'" *Vancouver Sun,* February 14, 1995.
12 Justine Hunter, "Nisga'a Treaty Faces Threat," *Vancouver Sun,* January 31, 1996.
13 Justine Hunter, "Hostile Reception Cheers Liberals: Heckling of Gordon Campbell by National Caucus Is Seen as a Plus for His BC Campaign," *Vancouver Sun,* February 1, 1996.

14 Stewart Bell and Justine Hunter, "Nisga'a Deal Initialled into History," *Vancouver Sun*, February 16, 1996.

15 Chief Joseph Gosnell, *Globe and Mail*, August 13, 1996, quoted in J.R. Miller, *Compact, Contract, Covenant: Aboriginal Treaty-Making in Canada* (Toronto: University of Toronto Press, 2009), 275.

16 Quotes from Duncan and Campbell are in Bell and Hunter, "Nisga'a Deal."

17 BC Liberal Party, "The Courage to Change," 1996, 10. A more extensive analysis of shifting platform content is provided in Abbott, *Big Promises*, 28–32.

18 British Columbia, Elections BC, *Statement of Votes: 36th Provincial General Election, May 28, 1996*, 3, 10, https://elections.bc.ca/docs/rpt/1996-SOVGeneralElection.pdf. The BC Liberals secured thirty-three seats and 42 percent of the popular vote; the NDP won thirty-nine seats and 39 percent of the vote; and Reform secured two seats with 9 percent of the vote.

19 Justine Hunter, "Clark Cranks Up Effort to Reach Land-Claim Deal," *Vancouver Sun*, March 9, 1998. My thanks to an anonymous peer reviewer for pointing out that the "First Nations did not get a ruling that they had Aboriginal title. The issue was referred back to the lower courts and the implications of the case are still being worked out by the province and the First Nations."

20 Hunter, "Clark Cranks Up."

21 Justine Hunter and Stewart Bell, "Nisga'a Agree to Give Up All Future Claims in Treaty Deal," *Vancouver Sun*, July 22, 1998.

22 Dianne Rinehart and Justine Hunter, "Federal Reform Joins Bid to Force Nisga'a Vote," *Vancouver Sun*, July 24, 1998.

23 Justine Hunter and Dianne Rinehart, "Campbell Vows Referendum for Proposed Nisga'a Treaty," *Vancouver Sun*, July 25, 1996.

24 Justine Hunter, "Campbell Urges Federal Referendum on Treaty: Alternately, at Least Seven Provinces Should Be Required to Approve the Nisga'a Deal, He Declares," *Vancouver Sun*, July 28, 1996.

25 Justine Hunter, "Campbell's Course Takes Another Tack," *Vancouver Sun*, July 31, 1998.

26 Gordon Campbell's quotes from the second reading debate are drawn from British Columbia, *Debates of the Legislative Assembly*, December 7, 1998, 10913–9.

27 Glen Clark and Chief Gosnell, British Columbia, *Debates*, December 2, 1998, 10859–60.

28 British Columbia, *Debates*, December 2, 1998, 10861–63.

29 Quoted in Justine Hunter, "How Campbell Changed His View," *Globe and Mail*, October 13, 2007.

30 Jim Aldridge, "Legal Counsel, Nisga'a Nation," discussion paper posted by the Land Claims Agreements Coalition, undated, 5–6, https://www.landclaimscoalition.ca/assets/Jim-Aldridge-Overview-of-Modern-Treaties.pdf.

31 Quoted in Kevin Griffin, "Canada 150: Joseph Gosnell Helped Negotiate Historic Treaty for the Nisga'a," *Vancouver Sun*, May 12, 2017.

32 Quoted in Vaughn Palmer, "Treaty Mood Turns from One of Self-Congratulation: Native Indian Leaders," *Vancouver Sun*, May 27, 2000. Dosanjh was elected as party leader following Glen Clark's resignation in August 1999. See "Glen Clark Steps Down under Pressure," CBC News, August 28, 1999, https://www.cbc.ca/news/canada/glen-clark-steps-down-under-pressure-1.181192. Dan Miller served as premier during the interim period prior to Dosanjh's election.

33 BC Liberal Party, "A New Era for British Columbia: A Vision for Hope and Prosperity for the Next Decade and Beyond," 2001, 27. Other "New Era" commitments to Indigenous

relations were somewhat less controversial. One promised "to negotiate a delegated, municipal style of self-government" with any First Nation "that wants to move beyond the failed Indian Act," suggesting a path to self-governance outside the tripartite treaty process that was (without explicitly saying so) more compatible with the principle of "one law for all." Other promises – initiatives to protect and promote Indigenous languages, a doubling of the First Citizens' Fund to $72 million, and the creation of a permanent First Citizens Forum – signalled hope for a better relationship between the government and Indigenous peoples.

Chapter 12: A New Era Brings Hope and Vexation

1 George M. Abbott, *Big Promises, Small Government: Doing Less with Less in the BC Liberal New Era* (Vancouver: UBC Press, 2020), 125–77, provides a detailed assessment on the impact of tax cuts (or, more precisely, the loss of tax revenues) on vital social policy areas contained in the Ministries of Human Resources; Children and Family Development; and Community, Aboriginal and Women's Services. Each of these ministries offers supports to vulnerable Indigenous people.

2 Premier Campbell loved to rethink governmental organization, and the Ministry of Community, Aboriginal and Women's Services was a product of that reorganization. The ministry's thirty-one general responsibilities were drawn from, in whole or part, seven former NDP ministries, including a host of socially sensitive policy areas. See Abbott, *Big Promises,* 125–26. I was Opposition critic for Forests and Municipal Affairs prior to the 2001 election, and the latter was within the new ministry.

3 *Campbell v British Columbia (Attorney General)* (2000), BCSC 1123, included Michael G. de Jong and P. Geoffrey Plant as plaintiffs and the attorney general of Canada and the Nisga'a Nation as defendants.

4 "Judge Rejects Challenge to Nisga'a Treaty," CBC News, July 25, 2000. As an anonymous reviewer pointed out, Campbell's challenge "backfired badly," but claiming intent to appeal allowed some face saving as the provincial election approached.

5 "BC Liberals Drop Nisga'a Lawsuit," CBC News, August 30, 2001.

6 Vaughn Palmer, "Liberals Don't Want a Forum for Treaty-Bashing," *Vancouver Sun,* September 8, 2001.

7 Wilson and Sayers are quoted in "BC to Vote on Settling Treaty Claims," CBC Digital Archives, https://www.cbc.ca/player/play/video/1.3334963.

8 For a good sampling of criticism, see Ken MacQueen, "BC Referendum Controversy," *Maclean's,* May 13, 2002, https://www.thecanadianencyclopedia.ca. The article states that the cost was nine million dollars. Abbott, *Big Promises,* offers a detailed analysis of the impact of tax cuts on social ministries, 125–77.

9 Elections BC, "Report of the Chief Electoral Officer on the Treaty Negotiations Referendum," September 9, 2002, 1, 2, and 6.

10 Ian Bailey, "Campbell Says Sorry to Natives," *National Post,* February 12, 2003.

11 British Columbia, *Debates of the Legislative Assembly,* February 11, 2003, 4700.

12 Michael Smyth, "Liberals in Full Retreat from Own Rhetoric on Natives," *Vancouver Province,* February 12, 2003.

13 Vaughn Palmer, "Campbell Looks beyond the Referendum," *Vancouver Sun,* June 13, 2002.

14 Vaughn Palmer, "Liberals Quietly Ponder Dramatic Changes on First Nations Front," *Vancouver Sun,* May 4, 2005. The New Relationship agreement can be accessed at https://

www2.gov.bc.ca/assets/gov/environment/natural-resource-stewardship/consulting-with-first-nations/agreements/other-docs/new_relationship_accord.pdf.

15 Quoted in Les Leyne, "'Intense' Was the Word in Negotiations," *Victoria Times-Colonist*, June 9, 2005.

16 Paul Willcocks, "BC Improves Aboriginal Relationship," *Edmonton Journal*, August 2, 2005.

17 Vaughn Palmer, "Liberals' New Deal with First Nations Still a Secret," *Vancouver Sun*, July 22, 2005.

18 Justine Hunter, "How Campbell Changed His View," *Globe and Mail*, October 13, 2007.

19 In addition to my extensive critique of the 2001 tax cuts, and Campbell's role in them, as set out in my book, *Big Promises*, see "The Precarious Politics of Shifting Direction: The Introduction of a Harmonized Sales Tax in British Columbia and Ontario," *BC Studies* 186 (Summer 2015): 125–48.

20 Quoted in *Prince George Citizen*, June 18, 2005.

21 Quotes and descriptions of the federal process are from Lisa L. Patterson, *Aboriginal Roundtable to Kelowna Accord: Aboriginal Policy Negotiations, 2004–2005*, prepared for Parliamentary Information and Research Services, Library of Parliament, May 4, 2006, 1, 3. The five national leadership organizations were the Assembly of First Nations, the Inuit Tapiriit Kanatami, the Métis National Council, the Congress of Aboriginal Peoples, and the Native Women's Association of Canada.

22 Chief John is quoted in Maclean Kay, "Kelowna, 13 Years Later," *The Orca*, October 29, 2018. John was a representative of the Assembly of First Nations in those discussions. https://www.theorca.ca/residentpod/kelowna-13-years-later-6398856.

23 Gary Mason, "'Third Solitude' Is Not Alone," *Globe and Mail*, October 13, 2005.

24 Patterson, *Aboriginal Roundtable*, 9, 10, 12. The Transformative Change Accord, https://www.fnha.ca/Documents/transformative_change_accord.pdf, introduced annual reporting requirements, thereby offering comparative socioeconomic measures back to 2006 or earlier.

25 Quoted in Kay, "Kelowna."

26 Quoted in Gary Mason, "Liberal Premier of BC Won't Lose Any Sleep over Harper's Triumph," *Globe and Mail*, January 26, 2006.

27 Vaughn Palmer, "Campbell 'Blisters' Federal Conservatives to Applause All Around," *Vancouver Sun*, May 5, 2006.

28 Quoted in Palmer, "Campbell 'Blisters.'"

29 Quoted in Vaughn Palmer, "Kelowna Not Dead," *Regina Leader Post*, May 16, 2006.

30 The Thorne and Baird quotes are from Gerry Bellett, "Delta Treaty Talks Threaten ALR," *Vancouver Sun*, September 20, 1999.

31 Quoted in Vaughn Palmer, "Crafty Liberals Crafted Rules Early to Cover Land Use and Treaty Talks," *Kamloops Daily News*, June 8, 2006.

32 Quoted in Maureen Gulyas, "Council Opposes Bill to Allow ALR Applications," *Delta Optimist*, May 19, 2004.

33 British Columbia, *Debates of the Legislative Assembly*, May 5, 2004, 10875–76.

34 Justine Hunter, "NDP Torn over Tsawwassen Treaty," *Globe and Mail*, August 22, 2007.

35 Hunter, "NDP Torn." For more on the Six Mile Ranch exclusion, by which the NDP government overruled the commission based on the tourism values of the development proposal, see "Battle Brewing over BC Ranch Land," CBC News, April 5, 1999, https://www.cbc.ca/news/canada/battle-brewing-over-b-c-ranch-land-1.162774.

36 British Columbia, *Debates of the Legislative Assembly*, October 17, 2007, 8162.

37 British Columbia, *Debates of the Legislative Assembly,* October 18, 2007, 8653–57. Dan Jarvis, MLA for North Vancouver–Seymour, also voted against the treaty.

38 Miro Cernetig, "Harper Approves Treaty: Tsawwassen Commitment Comes with a Political Price Tag," *Vancouver Sun,* December 9, 2006; and staff author, "Historical Urban Treaty Signing," *Surrey Leader,* December 8, 2006.

39 Quoted in "Historical Urban Treaty."

40 Peter O'Neil, "Cummins Blasts Minister over Tsawwassen Treaty," *Vancouver Sun,* December 12, 2006.

41 Rod Mickleburgh, "Tsawwassen Treaty Goes to Band Vote," *Globe and Mail,* July 24, 2007.

42 Vaughn Palmer, "Liberals Start Skating to Avoid Entanglements over Tsawwassen Treaty," *Vancouver Sun,* September 8, 2006.

43 Tsawwassen First Nation, press release, July 25, 2007, quoted in J.R. Miller, *Compact, Contract, Covenant: Aboriginal Treaty-Making in Canada* (Toronto: University of Toronto Press, 2009), 280.

44 Scott Sutherland, "Agreement with Musqueam Shows Governments Must Consult Aboriginals in Land Deals," Canadian Press, March 11, 2008.

45 Jonathan Fowlie, "Golf Course Deal with Musqueam Finalized," *Vancouver Sun,* March 12, 2008.

46 Rod Mickleburgh, "Region Protests Transfer of Parkland to Musqueam," *Globe and Mail,* November 13, 2007.

47 Kelly Sinoski, "Province within Its Rights in Musqueam Land Expropriation Deal, Court Rules," *Vancouver Sun,* May 2, 2009.

48 Robert Matas, "The 2010 Olympics Legacy," *Globe and Mail,* February 11, 2011.

49 Government of Canada, Crown-Indigenous Relations and Northern Affairs Canada, "Success Stories: Agreements and Land Claims," https://www.rcaanc-cirnac.gc.ca/eng/1307460755710/1536862806124. The properties devolved were related to specific claims advanced by First Nations.

Chapter 13: Recognition, Reconciliation, and Recoil

1 Phillip, quoted in Justine Hunter, "How Campbell Changed His View," *Globe and Mail,* October 13, 2007. Phillip made his comment on November 3, 2006, and the Hunter article underlines how Phillip's views had shifted over a year.

2 Phillip and Kelly, quoted in Hunter, "How Campbell."

3 The Union of British Columbia Indian Chiefs and the First Nations Summit have divergent views on participation in the modern treaty process. The Assembly of First Nations is a national organization that includes First Nations from both organizations. In some circumstances, the three organizations work collectively on issues such as the Recognition and Reconciliation Act.

4 Campbell is quoted in Vaughn Palmer's account of events leading up to the Recognition and Reconciliation discussion paper: "Liberal and Native Leaders Press 'Recognition' Agenda," *Vancouver Sun,* February 26, 2009.

5 Vaughn Palmer, "The 'New Relationship' Looks Good One Day, Not So Fine the Next," *Vancouver Sun,* June 13, 2008.

6 National Centre for Truth and Reconciliation, "Residential School History," https://nctr.ca/education/teaching-resources/residential-school-history/.

7 Canada, "Indian Residential Schools Settlement Agreement," https://www.rcaanc-cirnac.gc.ca/eng/1100100015576/1571581687074.

8 British Columbia, *Debates,* February 16, 2009, 13734.

9 Vaughn Palmer, "Business Leaders Don't Like Liberal Plans for Native 'Recognition Act,'" *Vancouver Sun,* March 11, 2009.

10 All important elements in the act, including the appended map, are thoroughly canvassed in Louise Mandell, "The Ghost Walks the Walk: The Illusive Recognition and Reconciliation Legislation," presented to the Union of British Columbia Indian Chiefs, 2009, https://www.sfu.ca/~palys/Mandell2009-The%20Ghost%20Walks%20the%20Walk.pdf.

11 The quote on reconstitution is drawn from Canada, *Report of the Royal Commission on Aboriginal Peoples,* vol. 5, *Renewal: A Twenty-Year Commitment* (Ottawa: Indian and Northern Affairs Canada, 1996), 52, https://www.bac-lac.gc.ca/eng/discover/aboriginal-heritage/royal-commission-aboriginal-peoples/Pages/introduction.aspx.

12 Mark Hume, "For Industry and First Nations, Shared Wariness in Search for Common Ground," *Globe and Mail,* March 16, 2009.

13 Vaughn Palmer, "Recognizing Rights Could Leave Liberals Vulnerable," *Prince George Citizen,* March 14, 2009.

14 Gary Mason, "It's Time Campbell Talked about Native-Relations Plan," *Globe and Mail,* June 9, 2009.

15 Quoted in Vaughn Palmer, "No Veto in Liberals' Promised Law on Aboriginal Rights, Plant Insists," *Vancouver Sun,* May 1, 2009.

16 Not surprisingly, de Jong's comments were widely quoted: Justine Hunter, "BC Drops Native Fishing Challenge, Gains Support for Sweeping Legislation," *Globe and Mail,* March 6, 2009; and Hume, "For Industry and First Nation."

17 Michael Wernick to Bob de Faye, British Columbia's Deputy Minister of Aboriginal Relations and Reconciliation, March 23, 2009, included as Appendix B in Louise Mandell, "The Ghost Walks the Walk: The Illusive Recognition and Reconciliation Legislation," presented to the Union of British Columbia Indian Chiefs, 2009, https://www.sfu.ca/~palys/Mandell2009-The%20Ghost%20Walks%20the%20Walk.pdf.

18 The Nuu-chah-nulth were successful in the BC Supreme Court and the BC Court of Appeal. Mandell Pinder, "Ahousaht Indian Band and Nation v. Canada, 2013 BCCA 300 – Case Summary," https://www.mandellpinder.com/ahousaht-indian-band-and-nation-v-canada-attorney-general-2021-bcca-155-case-summary/.

19 Vaughn Palmer, "Liberals Get in Great Rush with 'Seismic' Aboriginal Law," *Vancouver Sun,* March 6, 2009.

20 Vaughn Palmer, "Campbell Gets Time to Get It Right," *Vancouver Sun,* March 18, 2009.

21 BC Liberal Party, "Keep BC Strong: Proven Leadership for BC's Economy," 2009.

22 Mason, "It's Time Campbell Talked."

23 Judith Lavoie, "New Bill to Recognize Aboriginal Rights, Title," *Vancouver Sun,* March 6, 2009.

24 Mandell, "Ghost Walks," 18.

25 See, for example, Christine McLaren, "Nadleh Whut'en Protest Recognition Act Process," *The Tyee,* May 28, 2009, https://thetyee.ca/Blogs/TheHook/Aboriginal-Affairs/2009/05/28/ProtestRecognitionProcess/.

26 Justine Hunter, "Aboriginal Law: 'Dead,' New Relationship in Peril," *Globe and Mail,* August 29, 2009.

27 Arthur Manuel provides good examples of concerns in "Beware of BC's Proposed Recognition and Reconciliation," *Georgia Straight,* July 22, 2009, https://www.straight.com/article-241616/beware-reconciliation-act.

28 Hunter, "Aboriginal Law: 'Dead.'"

29 Mandell, "Ghost Walks," 19.

30 Geoff Plant, correspondence with the author, April 4, 2022.
31 The fate of the act was clear in July 2009. To my knowledge, drafting was never completed, nor was a draft ever made public.
32 Gary Mason, "Rejection of Aboriginal Rights Act Shatters Campbell's Dream of Leaving a Legacy," *Globe and Mail*, September 5, 2009.
33 "Queen Charlotte Islands Renamed Haida Gwaii in Historic Deal," CBC News, December 11, 2009, https://www.cbc.ca/news/canada/british-columbia/queen-charlotte-islands-renamed-haida-gwaii-in-historic-deal-1.849161. See also Haida Gwaii Reconciliation Act, SBC 2010, c 17, https://www.bclaws.gov.bc.ca/civix/document/id/complete/statreg/10017_01.
34 The naming of the Salish Sea was strongly supported by the lieutenant-governor, Steven Point: "BC Waters Officially Renamed Salish Sea," CBC News, July 15, 2010, https://www.cbc.ca/news/canada/british-columbia/b-c-waters-officially-renamed-salish-sea-1.909504.
35 The Westbank First Nation withdrew from the treaty process in 2009 based on "no prospect for settlement": Westbank First Nation, "Brief: Westbank First Nation – House of Commons' Standing Committee on Indigenous and Northern Affairs," September 25, 2017, https://www.ourcommons.ca/Content/Committee/421/INAN/Brief/BR9100397/br-external/WestbankFirstNation-e.pdf. In the case of the Yale First Nation, their final agreement has been set back by lingering controversy over the Fraser River fishery between the Yale First Nation and the Stó:lō Nation. In 2018, the Lheidli T'enneh First Nation (near Prince George) rejected an initialled final agreement in a community vote.
36 The story of British Columbia's journey from disparaging to embracing federal-provincial tax harmonization is fascinating. See George Abbott, "The Precarious Politics of Shifting Direction: The Introduction of a Harmonized Sales Tax in British Columbia and Ontario," *BC Studies* 186 (Summer 2015): 125–48.
37 First Nations Summit Political Executive (Grand Chief Edward John, Robert Phillips, and Cheryl Casimer) to Premier Christy Clark, March 20, 2015, author's personal documents.
38 When Vaughn Palmer asked me for my best guess as to what had happened, I replied, "Some knives came out in cabinet. It is the only conclusion I can form": Vaughn Palmer, "Province Pulls a Fast One on George Abbott," *Vancouver Sun*, March 18, 2015. I thought the animosity might be related to the bruising BC Liberal leadership contest of 2010–11, where I finished third to Clark.
39 Palmer, "Province Pulls a Fast One."
40 Palmer, "Province Pulls a Fast One." "Blistering" was Palmer's description of Pierre's news release.
41 First Nations Summit Political Executive to Clark.
42 Justine Hunter, "BC Treaty Process in Limbo after Province Pulls Chief Commissioner," *Globe and Mail*, March 25, 2015.
43 Hunter, "BC Treaty Process in Limbo."
44 Hunter, "BC Treaty Process in Limbo." News coverage of the day, in combination with recent conversations, has led me to conclude that the decision was made by the Agenda and Priorities Committee (effectively "inner cabinet") rather than the full cabinet.
45 "Multilateral Engagement Process to Improve and Expedite Treaty Negotiations in British Columbia: Proposals for the Principals' Consideration," March 17, 2016, https://www2.gov.bc.ca/assets/gov/environment/natural-resource-stewardship/consulting-with-first-nations/agreements/multilateral_engagement_process_for_treaty_-_june_7_2016.pdf.
46 Celeste Haldane served as interim chief commissioner for two years as the reform process unfolded. Vaughn Palmer, "Haldane Gets 'Awkward' Treaty Commission Endorsement,"

Vancouver Sun, March 2, 2017. Treaty completion has been just as painstaking and time-consuming since 2017 as before that date.

Chapter 14: New Ideas, Long-Standing Injustices

1 Indigenous Bar Association, SCC Factum – *Tsilhqot'in* Case, 2. I thank former attorney general Geoff Plant for alerting me to the *Hamlet of Baker Lake* decision, rendered by Federal Court in 1980 regarding Aboriginal title, prompting me to clarify my original suggestion that the Supreme Court had granted, for the first time in Canadian history, a declaration of Aboriginal title.

2 Supreme Court of Canada, *Tsilhqot'in Nation v British Columbia (*2014), SCC 44, 5, https://scc-csc.lexum.com/scc-csc/scc-csc/en/item/14246/index.do.

3 Larry Pynn, "Premier Urges Cooperation, Not More Litigation," *Vancouver Sun,* September 12, 2014.

4 Farris LLP, press release, June 26, 2014, 1.

5 Larry Pynn, "BC Premier Urges Cooperation, Not More Litigation, as Government and Natives Reach 'New Fork in Road,'" *Vancouver Sun,* September 10, 2014.

6 "Williams Lake First Nation Reaches Tentative $135M Settlement, 160 Years after Being Forced off Its Lands," CBC News, April 26, 2022, https://www.cbc.ca/news/canada/british-columbia/williams-lake-135-million-settlement-1.6430335.

7 Monica Lamb-Yorski, "$147.6M Settles BC First Nation's 131-Year-Old Water Rights Claim," *Quesnel Cariboo Observer,* July 24, 2024, https://www.quesnelobserver.com/local-news/bc-interior-first-nation-receives-1476-m-specific-claim-7454845.

8 "Esk'etemc (Alkali Lake Indian Band) Settles with Ottawa for $147 Million after 131 Years of Water Rights Loss," *CFJC Today,* July 24, 2024, https://cfjctoday.com/2024/07/24/esketemc-alkali-lake-indian-band-settles-with-ottawa-for-147-million-after-131-years-of-water-rights-loss/.

9 Author unknown, "BC Natives Win Battle for Reserve Land," *Daily Commercial News and Construction Record,* 69, 7, January 10, 1996.

10 British Columbia, "Declaration on the Rights of Indigenous Peoples Act: 2020/2021 Annual Report," https://www2.gov.bc.ca/assets/gov/government/ministries-organizations/ministries/indigenous-relations-reconciliation/declaration_act_annual_report_2021.pdf.

11 Jody Wilson-Raybould, *From Where I Stand: Rebuilding Indigenous Nations for a Stronger Canada* (Vancouver: Purich Books, 2019), 69.

12 I do not believe John Rustad bears principal responsibility for the BC Liberal government's shift on the Treaty Commission's leadership and processes in 2014–15. Based on his final phone call to me on the matter, I think he was embarrassed and troubled by the shift, or at least by its impact on me.

13 Rustad appeared to reverse course on repeal of DRIPA early in the 2024 provincial election campaign, promising to "continue to use UNDRIP as a guiding principle." Rob Shaw summarizes his position: "So, UNDRIP stays. Until it doesn't. Sometime in the future. Maybe": "BC's Campaign Trail Is Littered with Policy U-Turns, *Business in Vancouver,* October 2, 2024, https://www.biv.com/news/commentary/rob-shaw-policy-u-turns-are-defining-bcs-winding-campaign-trail-9601814.

14 Conservative Party of BC, "Our Platform: Common Sense Change for British Columbians," 2024, https://www.conservativebc.ca/ideas.

15 See Darryl Greer, "BC Conservative Leader Rustad Vows to 'Unleash Potential' for Indigenous Prosperity," Canadian Press, September 30, 2024, https://www.thecanadian

pressnews.ca/prairies_bc/bc/b-c-conservative-leader-rustad-vows-to-unleash-potential-for-indigenous-prosperity/article_c586c82f-5d37-5472-b1dc-7dc8edf353bc.html.

16 See British Columbia Assembly of First Nations, "FNLC Condemns BC Conservative's Party Platform Budget," press release, October 16, 2024, https://www.bcafn.ca/news/fnlc-condemns-bc-conservatives-party-platform-budget.

17 Darryl Greer, "Grand Chief Slams Rustad's Stance on Indigenous Rights and Title," CBC News, October 1, 2024, https://www.cbc.ca/news/canada/british-columbia/bc-conservative-party-indigenous-prosperity-1.7338712. Phillip is the husband of Joan Phillip, an NDP candidate and MLA.

18 A BC government news release characterized the agreement as "an innovative new model for future agreements in BC" and "a concrete example of how the province and Canada are working with First Nations to put the principles of the United Nations Declaration on the Rights of Indigenous Peoples into practice": British Columbia, "BC Transfers Land Back to Lake Babine Nation, Benefits the Region," news release, January 27, 2023, https://news.gov.bc.ca/releases/2023IRR0001-000099.

19 Quoted in section D of the "whereas" preamble of the agreement. Lake Babine Nation, "Foundation Agreement," https://www.lakebabine.com/foundation/.

20 The Nation's population is taken from its website, and the reserve land figure is from British Columbia Assembly of First Nations, "Lake Babine Nation," https://www.bcafn.ca/first-nations-bc/nechako/lake-babine-nation.

21 A BC government news release describes the 20,000 hectares as "waterfront and prime forestry lands." See British Columbia, "BC Transfers Land Back." Details on Canada's contribution are available in Canada, "Lake Babine Nation and Canada Sign Agreement ... " news release, February 21, 2024, https://www.canada.ca/en/crown-indigenous-relations-northern-affairs/news/2024/02/lake-babine-nation-and-canada-sign-agreement-to-support-community-vision-for-governance-capacity-development-and-infrastructure-priorities-for-wita.html.

22 Josh Grant, "BC Returns 200 Square Kilometres of Traditional Territory to Lake Babine Nation," CBC News, January 27, 2023, https://www.cbc.ca/news/canada/british-columbia/lake-babine-nation-land-transfer-1.6729408; and Canada, "Lake Babine Nation and Canada Sign Agreement." In a modest quirk of history, Murphy Abraham ran unsuccessfully against John Rustad in 2024 in the Nechako Lakes riding.

23 Wetmore's assertion was, in fact, incorrect. See the full discussion in Chapter 6, this book.

24 Julie Chadwick, "'It's All Haida Land': Nation's Title to Be Officially Recognized over the Entirety of Haida Gwaii," *Cortes Currents,* March 27, 2024, https://cortescurrents.ca/tag/ministry-of-indigenous-relations/.

25 Chadwick, "It's All Haida Land."

26 Chadwick, "It's All Haida Land."

27 BC Treaty Commission, "Submission to the Standing Committee on Indigenous and Northern Affairs," September 25, 2017, 1, https://www.ourcommons.ca/Content/Committee/421/INAN/Brief/BR9127779/br-external/BritishColumbiaTreatyCommission-e.pdf.

28 The Nisga'a Treaty is not included, because it was not negotiated under the auspices of the commission. See BC Treaty Commission, "Negotiations Update," https://www.bctreaty.ca/.

29 BC Treaty Commission, "Milestones and Innovations Achieved in 2024," media release, November 4, 2024, https://bctreaty.ca/wp-content/uploads/2024/11/2024-Annual-Report-News-Release-Final.pdf. The initialled treaty will be considered by communities and potentially move to ratification.

30 Rebecca Dyck, "Province Purchases Ranch for Interior First Nation as Part of Ongoing Treaty Negotiations," *Williams Lake Tribune,* August 7, 2020, https://www.wltribune.com/news/province-purchases-ranch-for-interior-first-nation-as-part-of-ongoing-treaty-negotiations/.

31 Michael Asch, *On Being Here to Stay: Treaties and Aboriginal Rights in Canada* (Toronto: University of Toronto Press, 2014), 152.

32 BC Treaty Commission, "Submission to the Standing Committee," 6, https://www.ourcommons.ca/Content/Committee/421/INAN/Brief/BR9127779/br-external/BritishColumbiaTreatyCommission-e.pdf.

Epilogue: The Long and Rocky Road to Reconciliation

1 Kenneth Chan, "Without Big Events, British Columbia's 150th Anniversary in 2021 Will Be a Quiet One," *Daily Hive,* January 27, 2021, https://dailyhive.com/vancouver/bc-150-anniversary-events-2021.

2 For example, see "Remains of 215 Children Found Buried at Former BC Residential School, First Nation Says," CBC News, May 27, 2021, https://www.cbc.ca/news/canada/british-columbia/tk-eml%C3%BAps-te-secw%C3%A9pemc-215-children-former-kamloops-indian-residential-school-1.6043778.

3 Dallas Brodie (@Dallas_Brodie) "Politicians like David Eby and John Rustad are willing to sell off British Columbia's wealth and power, transferring it from the public to an elite racial minority—enriching opportunistic lawyers, consultants, and chiefs along the way." X.com, March 7, 2025. 3:04 p.m. https://x.com/Dallas_Brodie/status/1898147773847072880.

4 Andrea Kurjata, Tessa Vikander, and Shaurya Kshatri, "BC Conservative Leader Kicks Dallas Brodie out of Caucus for 'Mocking' Residential School Testimony," CBC News, March 7, 2025, https://www.cbc.ca/news/canada/british-columbia/dallas-brodie-removed-from-b-c-conservative-caucus-1.7478162.

5 Canadian Press, "Three BC Conservative Rebels Will Sit as Independents as They 'Explore' New Party," *Times Colonist,* March 10, 2025, https://www.timescolonist.com/local-news/three-bc-conservatives-will-sit-as-independents-10350609a.

6 Truth and Reconciliation Commission of Canada, *What We Have Learned: Principles of Truth and Reconciliation,* 2015, 126, https://nctr.ca/records/reports/.

7 "Lt.-Gov. Helps to Carve Canoe for People of BC," CBC News, December 29, 2009, https://www.cbc.ca/news/entertainment/lt-gov-helps-to-carve-canoe-for-people-of-b-c-1.785008.

Suggestions for Further Reading

Note: Unceded draws on insights from a broad range of sources. This brief selected bibliography is aimed at readers seeking further information on this important subject.

Abbott, George M. *Big Promises, Small Government: Doing Less with Less in the BC Liberal New Era.* Vancouver: UBC Press, 2020.

Asch, Michael. *On Being Here to Stay: Treaties and Aboriginal Rights in Canada.* Toronto: University of Toronto Press, 2014.

Asch, Michael, John Borrows, and James Tully, eds. *Resurgence and Reconciliation: Indigenous-Settler Relations and Earth Teachings.* Toronto: University of Toronto Press, 2018.

Barman, Jean. *British Columbia in the Balance, 1846–1871.* Madeira Park, BC: Harbour, 2022.

–. *The West beyond the West: A History of British Columbia.* Rev. ed. Toronto: University of Toronto Press, 2004.

Cail, Robert E. *Land, Man, and the Law: The Disposal of Crown Lands in British Columbia.* Vancouver: UBC Press, 1974.

Canada. *Report of the Royal Commission on Aboriginal Peoples.* Vol. 1, *Looking Forward, Looking Back,* and vol. 5, *Renewal: A Twenty-Year Commitment.* Ottawa: Indian and Northern Affairs Canada, 1996.

Cook, Peter, Neil Vallance, John Lutz, Graham Brazier, and Hamar Foster, eds. *To Share, Not Surrender: Indigenous and Settler Visions of Treaty Making in the Colonies of Vancouver Island and British Columbia.* Vancouver: UBC Press, 2021.

Fisher, Robin. *Contact and Conflict: Indian-European Relations in British Columbia, 1774–1890.* Vancouver: UBC Press, 1992.

Foster, Hamar, Heather Raven, and Jeremy Webber, eds. *Let Right Be Done: Aboriginal Title, the* Calder *Case, and the Future of Indigenous Rights.* Vancouver: UBC Press, 2007.

Harris, Cole. *Making Native Space: Colonialism, Resistance, and Reserves in British Columbia.* Vancouver: UBC Press, 2002.

Ignace, Marianne, and Ronald E. Ignace. *Secwépemc People, Land, and Laws*. Montreal/Kingston: McGill-Queen's University Press, 2017.

Ishiguro, Laura. *Nothing to Write Home About: British Family Correspondence and the Settler Colonial Everyday in British Columbia*. Vancouver: UBC Press, 2019.

Loo, Tina. *Moved by the State: Forced Relocation and Making a Good Life in Postwar Canada*. Vancouver: UBC Press, 2019.

Lutz, John Sutton. *Makúk: A New History of Aboriginal-White Relations*. Vancouver: UBC Press, 2009.

McDonald, Robert A.J. *A Long Way to Paradise: A New History of British Columbia Politics*. Vancouver: UBC Press, 2021.

Meggs, Geoff, and Rod Mickleburgh. *The Art of the Impossible: Dave Barrett and the NDP in Power, 1972–1975*. Madeira Park, BC: Harbour, 2012.

Miller, J.R. *Compact, Contract, Covenant: Aboriginal Treaty-Making in Canada*. Toronto: University of Toronto Press, 2009.

Nickel, Sarah A. *Assembling Unity: Indigenous Politics, Gender, and the Union of BC Indian Chiefs*. Vancouver: UBC Press, 2019.

Perry, Adele. *On the Edge of Empire: Gender, Race, and the Making of British Columbia, 1849–1871*. Toronto: University of Toronto Press, 2001.

Reynolds, Jim. *Canada and Colonialism: An Unfinished History*. Vancouver: Purich Books, 2024.

Strayer, Barry L. *Canada's Constitutional Revolution*. Edmonton: University of Alberta Press, 2013.

Tennant, Paul. *Aboriginal Peoples and Politics: The Indian Land Question in British Columbia, 1849–1989*. Vancouver: UBC Press, 1990.

Truth and Reconciliation Commission of Canada. *What We Have Learned: Principles of Truth and Reconciliation*, 2015. https://nctr.ca/records/reports/.

Wesley, Angela. "Ancient Spirit, Modern Mind: The Huu-ay-aht Journey Back to Self-Determination and Self-Reliance." In *Reclaiming Indigenous Governance: Reflections and Insights from Australia, Canada, New Zealand, and the United States*, edited by William Nikolakis, Stephen Cornell, and Harry Nelson, 107–29. Tucson: University of Arizona Press, 2019.

Wickwire, Wendy. *At the Bridge: James Teit and an Anthropology of Belonging*. Vancouver: UBC Press, 2019.

Wilson-Raybould, Jody. *From Where I Stand: Rebuilding Indigenous Nations for a Stronger Canada*. Vancouver: Purich Books, 2019.

Index

Notes: In subheadings, "Trutch" refers to Joseph Trutch. The following abbreviations are used in subentries: "ALR" for Agricultural Land Reserve, "DRIPA" for Declaration on the Rights of Indigenous Peoples Act, and "JIRC" for Joint Indian Reserve Commission.

Printed and bound in Canada

Set in Calibri and Minion by Artegraphica Design Co.

Copy editor: Lesley Erickson

Proofreader: Marnie Lamb

Indexer: Marnie Lamb

Cover designer: David Drummond

Cover images: Shutterstock.com/Shawn.ccf

Authorized Representative: Easy Access System Europe –
Mustamäe tee 50, 10621 Tallinn, Estonia, gpsr.requests@easproject.com